AF328526

Undoing Nothing

Waiting for Asylum, Struggling for Relevance

Paolo Boccagni

UNIVERSITY OF CALIFORNIA PRESS

University of California Press
Oakland, California

© 2025 by Paolo Boccagni

This work is licensed under a Creative Commons (CC BY-NC-ND) license. To view a copy of the license, visit http://creativecommons.org/licenses.

All other rights reserved.

Suggested citation: Boccagni, P. *Undoing Nothing: Waiting for Asylum, Struggling for Relevance*. Oakland: University of California Press, 2025. DOI: https://doi.org/10.1525/luminos.233

Library of Congress Cataloging-in-Publication Data

Names: Boccagni, Paolo, author.
Title: Undoing nothing : waiting for asylum, struggling for relevance / Paolo Boccagni.
Description: Oakland : University of California Press, [2025] | Includes bibliographical references and index.
Identifiers: LCCN 2024047412 (print) | LCCN 2024047413 (ebook) | ISBN 9780520404106 (paperback) | ISBN 9780520404113 (ebook)
Subjects: LCSH: Refugees—Italy—Social conditions. | Male immigrants—Italy—Social conditions. | Refugees—Italy—Psychology. | Refugees—Government policy—Italy. | Asylum, Right of—Italy.
Classification: LCC JV8138 .B64 2025 (print) | LCC JV8138 (ebook) | DDC 305.9/069140945—dc23/eng/20250221

LC record available at https://lccn.loc.gov/2024047412
LC ebook record available at https://lccn.loc.gov/2024047413

GPSR Authorized Representative: Easy Access System Europe, Mustamäe tee 50, 10621 Tallinn, Estonia, gpsr.requests@easproject.com

34 33 32 31 30 29 28 27 26 25
10 9 8 7 6 5 4 3 2 1

Luminos is the Open Access monograph publishing program
from UC Press. Luminos provides a framework for preserving and
reinvigorating monograph publishing for the future and increases
the reach and visibility of important scholarly work. Titles published
in the UC Press Luminos model are published with the same high
standards for selection, peer review, production, and marketing as
those in our traditional program. www.luminosoa.org

Undoing Nothing

to
Karim and Salim,
Sideeq and Obinna,
Mamadou and Assane,
Who most opened the doors of their worlds
From nothing to homing

CONTENTS

ILLUSTRATIONS

Ethnography, whatever the place, is made out of people—protracted interactions; ways of being together; tacit, elusive and generative forms of reciprocity. Ethnography, in a single place, is also a matter of host-guest relationships. I am indebted to hundreds of individuals who, in different ways and degrees, were like hosts over my four-year fieldwork. The first thanks go to those who had an especially meaningful role: Abdou, Abdouramane, Abdul, Abedinago, Aboubacar, Adama D., Adama S., Adnan, Agnese, Aladje, Alberto, Albion, Alessandro, Alfa, Alhassane, Ali, Aliou, Alpha, Amadou B., Amadou C., Amadou M., Andrea, Angelo, Ansou, Arthur, Aruna, Assane, Baboukary, Barim, Beatrice, Biai, Bun, Carlos, Chiara, Christian, Chucks, Claudia, Claudio, Coumakan, Cristina, Demba, Din, Dominic, Douglas, Ednan, Edward, Elena G., Elena P., Elisa, Emeka, Emiliano, Emmanuel, Ermanno, Ezio, Fassambou, Federica A., Federica B., Felix, Fildan, Foulané, Francesco, Franco, Friday, Gibiril, Giovanni, Gory, Hamidou, Hassan, Hassane, Hossin, Husseini, Iaia, Ibrahim, Ibrahima M., Ibrahima S., Idrissa K., Idrissa S., Imad, Imran, Irina, Ismail, Ivan, Kanjoora, Karim, Keita, Kelvin, Kenneth, Kingsley, Komidodji, Koola, Koumakan, Javed, Jamal, James, Juan, Justice, Lamin, Lancine, Lassana, Leo, Letizia, Lia, Madou, Maja, Makolie, Malang, Malika, Mamadou B., Mamadou F., Mamadou S., Marco, Margherita, Maria, Marina, Massamba, Massimo, Mathurin, Maurice, Maurizio, Michael, Michele, Mirza, Mohamed B., Mohamed D., Mohamed S., Mohammed N., Monzon, Mory, Mounirou, Moussa D., Moussa J., Moussa S., Muhammad, Musa, Musharraf, Mustafa, Nazif, Nfamara, Nora, Nour Eddine, Obinna, Oleh, Omar, Ousman, Paolo, Parkoo, Patrizia, Peter, Pierluigi, Prince, Razak, Redouane, Saidou, Salif, Salim, Samuel, Sandra, Saqlan, Seny, Serena, Shamsu, Sideeq, Sikhandar, Silvia, Silvie, Simon, Simone, Sofia,

Sokol, Soryba, Souka, Souleyman, Stefano, Stephane, Steven, Tamko, Tiziano, Touseef, Vincenzo, Yacouba, Yaya, Youba, Youssufa, Yssuf, and Wali.

At an institutional level, I am indebted to the refugee assistance department of the local authority and to the organizations that ran the center during my fieldwork. Nothing of this would have been possible without their authorization. Content-wise, I am especially grateful to Luce Beeckmans, Andrea Brighenti, Ester Gallo, Halleh Ghorashi, Anne Sigfrid Grønseth, Nick Harney, Pierrette Hondagneu-Sotelo, Peter Kivisto, Maggie Kusenbach, Valentina Marconi, Gordon Mathews, Aïssatou Mbodj-Pouye, Alejandro Miranda-Nieto, Karsten Paerregaard, Julia Pauli, Joris Schapendonk, Giuseppe Sciortino and Stefania Yapo. All of them, close or not so close in both geography and discipline, gave me the same valuable gift—reading and commenting on a chapter draft or another. By entering the center through my narratives, they helped me understand the human, relational and institutional commonalities between one inhabited place and many more housing environments for displaced, marginalized or dependent people. Many other colleagues invited me to present parts of the book along the way or engaged in lively and inspiring conversations about it, in several universities. These include Bergen, the Chinese University of Hong Kong, Florence, Gothenburg, Gottingen, Hamburg, the Institut Convergences Migrations, Malmo, the Max Planck Institute for the Study of Ethnic and Religious Diversity, Milano, Newcastle, Paris Science Po, Universidad Catolica de Lima, the University of Ghana, University of New South Wales, and University of Western Australia. As important were the meetings of international networks such as ECAS, ESWRA, IMISCOE, ISA, ISA-RC21, MSA, NMR and Thanatic Ethics. My thanks go to Marco Accorinti, Maurizio Ambrosini, Karel Arnaut, Loretta Baldassar, Eduardo Barberis, Synnøve Bendixsen, Alexandra Bousiou, Alberto Brodesco, Francesca Decimo, Hazel Easthope, Nancy Foner, Enrico Fravega, Andrew Geddes, Monia Giovannetti, Daniela Giudici, Christine Jacobsen, Shahram Khosravi, Thomas Lacroix, Paolo Maccario, Monica Massari, Jora Mato, Ruth McAreavey, Bruno Meeus, Friedemann Neumann, Emanuele Pastorino, Stefano Petrolini, Serena Piovesan, Violetta Plotegher, Alessandro Pratesi, Andrea Priori, Bruno Riccio, Victoria Sakti, Samuli Schielke, Mary Setrana, Simon Turner, Henrik Vigh, Zach Whyte, Maria Grazia Zanetti, and Stefano Zucali. I'm also grateful to Naomi Schneider, Aline Dolinh and Stephanie Summerhays at the University of California Press.

In practice, though, not a single line of this book would have been possible without the residents, volunteers, caseworkers and porters I met in one and the same house, one day, month and year after another. I mention again a few of them at the end of the introduction. Most of all, I am grateful to Cristina. It was with her, and thanks only to her, that everything started. Last, in a display of Italian familism that the young men in the center would probably sympathize with, I dedicate *Undoing Nothing* to my parents, as much as to Michela, Martino, Miriam, and Viola.

Introduction

ESTRAGON: That's enough. I'm tired.

 VLADIMIR: You'd rather be stuck there doing nothing?

ESTRAGON: Yes.

 VLADIMIR: Please yourself.

He releases Estragon, picks up his coat and puts it on.

ESTRAGON: Let's go.

 VLADIMIR: We can't.

ESTRAGON: Why not?

 VLADIMIR: We're waiting for Godot.

—SAMUEL BECKETT, *WAITING FOR GODOT*

I

"I'm doing—nothing," Ousmane said one afternoon, shrugging his shoulders with the air of saying a very obvious thing, as we came across each other on the doorstep of the center. He had been in his bedroom the entire morning, then gone for a walk and was now about to get back in, pray and prepare something to eat in his shared kitchen. Not much more seemed likely to happen until some potential employer would call him for a one-day job or some officer would decide about his appeal against asylum denial—and hopefully give him "the papers" for "two or five years," in the vernacular of the center. That afternoon Ousmane's response was enough to close the conversation, as I was heading back home and he was re-entering his temporary one—a former motel and student hall that had been downgraded to asylum-seeker accommodation. It was also enough for the starting idea of this book, which draws on a four-year ethnography (2018–22) with the male residents, mostly West Africans in their early twenties, of a temporary housing facility in northern Italy (henceforth, *the center*).

Ousmane is by no means alone in unwittingly replicating the apparently meaningless interjections of Estragon and Vladimir, the main characters in Samuel

Beckett's *Waiting for Godot*. Dozens of millions more have been doing the same worldwide, and increasingly so over the past decade, as a reaction to their predicament of enforced waiting as asylum seekers. The center itself is only one instance of the myriad housing infrastructures for asylum seekers in Italy and elsewhere in Europe, after the so-called refugee crisis of 2015. The contents and dilemmas of refugee housing and dwelling, as a domesticated variant of protracted displacement,[1] have increased scholarly attention. This is for the topic as such but also for its promise as a field to explore the experience and pathways of differential exclusions, along lines of race, gender and legal status, of young men from "third" and "unsafe" countries like the residents in the center. Each of them, whatever will happen next, has already survived the deadly obstacles against his transnational mobility set up by Europe and by the political regimes to which border control has been outsourced.[2]

The migration routes across the Mediterranean, over the past two decades, have resulted in millions of people effectively crossing to Europe but also in at least 30,600 human lives lost along the way, mostly in the central Mediterranean, per recent estimates of the International Organization for Migration's Missing Migrants Project.[3] This has turned the Mediterranean into an unacknowledged mass cemetery.[4] The unauthorized and dangerous migration routes across *mare nostrum* have taken traction since the early 2000s, have been accelerated after the Arab Springs and the Syrian war and have ultimately resulted, for Italy alone, in an estimated cumulative flow of about 1,083,000 people between 2014 and 2024.[5] Only a part of them, including the protagonists of this book, have effectively applied for asylum in Italy (as opposed to trying to move north or being deported). Their average acceptance rate has been in the region of 38 percent.[6] Their overall incidence on the foreign resident population in the country, though, has never gone beyond 6 percent.[7]

Once you become an asylum seeker, you should be in a safer condition, in a safer country. Being "here" feels like "being born again," Olusola and many others recount—or at least it should feel like that. If the metaphor held true, a reception center should be like an institutional cradle for their new lives. In fact, it looks more like a semi-abandoned parking lot. For the time being, the new life does not promise much more than waiting—an "activity"[8] that is the obvious and irrelevant background to everyday life in the center. Is it ever going to get anywhere close to the promised or aspired one? And what happens while it does not?

"I'm doing nothing," my young male interlocutors repeat in a daily, inadvertent rehearsal of *Waiting for Godot*. Their facial expressions usually cling toward resignation more than anger. On the face of it, a reception facility is precisely a place where nothing important happens—a temporary infrastructure where people are entitled to basic livelihood while their applications are processed, only to find out that this takes years of continuous, if provisional, dwelling. In the meantime residents may have little more to do than sticking to the rules or behaving as deserving (if not grateful) guests. In principle, they have an interest to hang out, learn a language, find a job and socialize with native people. In practice they may do without this, as long as they are formally entitled to hospitality. Even as they try to make a new life of their own, they encounter major constraints in times of increasing and racialized political nativism, enduring economic crises and intermittent covid-driven immobilities. As long as people stay in the center, instead, basic social reproduction is guaranteed, in a form of inclusion by marginalization—an experiential bubble of parallel normality.

Doing nothing, importantly, is no literary device. It does resound in the ways of being of the center residents. And it is in eerie resonance with the additional dose of stigmatization that informs public discourse on asylum seekers as supposedly bogus refugees, undeserving beneficiaries of a humanitarian apparatus, or possibly a business, that leaves them in idle waiting. While all sorts of derogatory labels are associated with migrants in general, the do-nothing one is a prerogative of people in "camps," even more if they are young, male, black and Muslim like many of my interlocutors. In fact, it is relatively uncommon for the people I met, and the place where they live, to be openly vilified as deviant, dangerous, out-of-place. Although this does occur now and then, it tends to be perceived as inappropriate and hence discouraged within the politically correct mainstream. More fundamentally and prosaically, both people and place are seen and treated as irrelevant, if not invisible. After reading so much about racialization, states of exception, hyper-surveillance and criminalization, I realized that an alternative category— a subtle and implicit sense of nothingness—primarily informs the (self-)perception of young male migrants like my interlocutors. The center itself is less a place of all-encompassing surveillance than of "attentional marginalization."[9] Its residents are implicitly expected to "act as to maximally encourage the fiction that they aren't"—that is, to contribute to their own social invisibility.[10] No worries about asylum seekers, as long as they stay in their temporarily assigned place within the "national order of things."[11] While exceptionalism and hyper-visibility dominate the public representation of high-risk forced migration and sea crossing, without necessarily producing better understandings or political responses, all that doesn't have to do with border "transgression" slides into collective oblivion. Silence, invisibility and irrelevance are the main markers of whatever comes after arriving in Italy, including the ways in which so-called people on the move struggle to recover a sense of normality.

For sure, dwelling in the center is only a transitional step in broader biographical and housing trajectories. A minor concern, perhaps, for someone who risked his life on the way to Europe and now prioritizes the search for a source of income. However, dwelling in asylum, no matter how fortuitous (since one ended up there after a dispersal scheme) or undesired, is more than an irrelevant parenthesis. You may end up spending years in the same place, under a peculiar condition of legal suspension and exposure to marginalization as well as, potentially, to new and unprecedented life possibilities.

As a way to account for this life predicament, *nothing* is more than a negative, antithetical or residual category.[12] It rather articulates a pragmatic habituation to living with undesired difference or in undesired circumstances. At least for a part of the native public opinion, "nothing" is the degree of interest for, and salience of, a social presence that is tolerated as long as it is virtually invisible. In a pandemic jargon, it should only stay home, assuming the center as a functional equivalent of home. No need to talk about them unless on episodic outbursts of protest or deviance or after pre-electoral stigmatization by right-wing political entrepreneurs.

Nothing, however, has an alternative meaning and use as well. It is a straightforward expression whereby my young male interlocutors articulate frustration and discontent for all that is not happening, or is happening with unbearable slowness, within institutional reception; put differently, a catchword for the perceived irrelevance of their own space and time. Nothing is thus evoked, respectively, as a way of framing (certain people and places) or as a way of feeling (whereby asylum seekers describe their perceived condition) out of the field of relevance.[13] Unpacking this perceived nothingness by revisiting how young men in asylum relate to their everyday timespace and struggle to negotiate what is relevant for them has fed into the urge to write this book.

II

The dozens of young Black and Brown men that appear in this book, and several hundreds more I cannot even mention, have been housed in the center for a few years. As residents, they are entitled to free hospitality and to some "pocket money," while being subject to minute constraints regarding, for instance, the time of entry/exit at night, the number of days in which they are allowed to stay elsewhere, or the sign-up register they must fill up every day. They are hosted in double rooms with their own toilets and shared kitchen facilities. In theory they may benefit from some psycho-social and educational support—if less and less so during the timespan of my fieldwork. And they have full access to the labor market, which does not mean that they will necessarily find a job.

From early 2018 to the middle of 2022, with a couple of short covid-enforced breaks, I happened to have free access in the center, spend time with them, listen to their narratives, participate in their routines, be hosted in their rooms. A reception center is also a house from which someone looks at the outer world and senses the incessant mobility of people and things, in contrast with his own immobility. As a housing infrastructure, it is not defined simply by what it lacks, by institutional invisibility or by its being instrumental to the governmentality of unwanted mobility. Behind its apparently frozen time and space, a swarming, emotionally thick and irremediably future-oriented social life takes and makes place. Things happen, and everyday life is reproduced, contested and sometimes innovated, in ways irreducible to the ordinary categories and moral subtexts about refugees as desperate and poor guests, victims, parasites, bare lives, resisters and so forth. After wandering for years in a place whose existence depends on external forces like high-risk migration, judicial decisions on asylum and public money for supposedly undeserving poor, I realized that "nothing" is not only a gross simplification of empirical reality. It is also an object of analysis, although not necessarily in an ontological sense here.[14] The point is rather charting, heuristically, the field of action that *nothing* elicits as a category in use: the ways of perceiving, evoking, making sense of it and implicitly refuting its existence by filling a spatial and temporal void with routines, rituals and relationships that strive to articulate and achieve what is relevant for each resident.

Researching into the ways of filling the timespace of enforced waiting is not only meant to contrast stigmatization. There would be little originality in pointing out that things happen, albeit not necessarily the desired ones or with the desired rhythm, and that "refugees are *not* lazy," as Olusola used to vehemently remind me. Admittedly, finding something meaningful, if not pleasant, to do was no easy task for some of his fellow residents. Always staying at home is "not a thing for men," my young male interlocutors would typically complain within a place that was inhabited exclusively, and hence oppressively, by men. Yet the sense of nothingness that emerges from their narratives and feelings is silently counterbalanced by a range of social practices. The place itself, as a built environment and a socio-legal infrastructure, does things to those who inhabit it, are supposed to benefit from it and frame it in all ways on a continuum between camp and prison;[15] or, as once Sani put it more creatively, a "chicken coop" where "you sleep, go out to eat something, come back and sleep again." If anything, a safer coop than anywhere in his country of origin, in spite of the systematic racism he encounters in town.

Approaching nothingness in an asylum center reveals ways of coping with time and space that resonate with many marginalized, temporary and heteronomous housing circumstances. In unveiling the fine-grained production of everyday life behind the apparent nothing, this book explores personal ways of *making* place rather than being simply housed in it. Once people's narratives are situated within their observed social practices, *nothing* is no longer there. Perceptions and narratives of irrelevance (of the place, of one's conditions, sometimes of human life itself) go pragmatically along with significant, if intermittent and unruly, ways of producing relevance; that is, of thresholding space and time by trying to attach emotion, meaning, purpose and engagement toward some region of the world around oneself. Most often, too limited regions, relative to one's expectations and desires. Even so, there is more to this than passive social reproduction. There are rather creeping, fragmented, partially inadvertent and disputed forms of place-making (and sometimes home-making).[16]

The struggle to carve out portions of an apparently empty and meaningless timespace[17] is constrained by major institutional, social and material barriers and by their long-term consequences.[18] However, it is also shaped by contrasting alignments, points of reference, expectations and prospects ahead. In the space that opens within these multiple pressures, asylum seekers are not statically in or out. Rather, they are in a constant process of re-positioning themselves in micro-spaces of encounter, sometimes of conflict, in which no position is necessarily better, exclusive or definitive relative to the others. This results in a multifaceted ambivalence,[19] within biographical fields that have shifting spatial, temporal, affective, aesthetic and moral boundaries. All of them rest on the bricks and mortar of the center but do not simply overlap with it. Asylum claimants like my young male interlocutors share a collective and yet highly individualized life predicament—they are together as much as alone. They are inside and outside, relative to opposite terms of reference. They are, and feel, still and mobile. They are living in a timespace that conflates a tangible material presence and a pervasive sense of absence. They inhabit everyday spaces that tend to be dilapidated and untidy but hold something of an inner order and care. In essence they are home and non-home at once. Faced with this ambivalence, Sani, Olusola, Ousmane and all the others struggle to set thresholds between what should be meaningful, controllable and worthy and all the rest. Put otherwise, they inform their timespace with unequal, shifting and contested degrees of relevance. Through the attendant social practices, they endeavor to address fundamental questions such as "What's in my power to do?"; "What matters for me?"; and "What should I care about?"[20]

My interlocutors negotiate what they construct as relevant on different scales, in relation to their counterparts, the rules and affordances of the center, and the structure of opportunities outside. As a result, most of them tend to feel lonely and isolated, even while being invariably together with someone else (see chapter 2, section 2.3). They take up different and unequal positionings between inside and outside, on multiple scales from nation-states down to their own bodies (see chapter 3). They are physically still and existentially stuck, if unequally so, relative to the geographic and existential mobility they have been dreaming of (see chapter 4). As diverse and weird is their experience of a dwelling arrangement that bears traces of what is present, as much as of the absent: on one hand, things or messages left by previous residents, along with one's belongings and uncanny memories; on the other, the absence of tangible prospects for the future, along with other forms of absence that become all too present (see chapter 5). Their ways of thresholding space and scaling relevance are especially conspicuous in the interior space they inhabit. This is dirty and clean, as a micro-battlefield between opposed expectations and moral assessments, depending on the scale of reference (see chapter 6). In short, dwelling in asylum entails a social condition and a self-perception that oscillates between home, in functional and sometimes emotional respects, and non-home, as estrangement, alienation and deliberate refusal to belong there (see chapter 7).

These ways of taking position and scaling relevance lie at the core of *Undoing Nothing*. They all speak to the importance and unequal distribution of place-making, as a catchword for the ways in which people negotiate what matters for them and struggle to exert control over it, in spite of their liminality. In doing so the young men in the center are not necessarily demonstrating their agency or articulating an explicitly political resistance. As long as they survived a risky migration journey, being there already embodies the deepest resistance.[21] More simply (in experiential terms) and more fruitfully (in heuristic ones) my interlocutors enact their own struggles for dignity, normality and the "good life"—the desire and obligation to move closer to their shared ideals of adulthood, manhood and family life as well as modernity and success. A real normality, as it were, unlike the bubble of racialized isolation and welfare dependency that separates the center from the outer world.

III

Undoing Nothing starts from over four years of participant-observation of everyday life in a place where nothing ever happens, or so people say, despite evidence to the contrary. It is of vital importance to understand what accounts for this sense of doing or even being nothing. This is reproduced by young asylum seekers themselves rather than being only a matter of external stigmatization (and potentially a self-fulfilling prophecy, the lesser the public investment in their activation). In practice this means exploring what people are actually doing; why they feel they are doing nothing nonetheless; how their routines and activities fare relative to what they would like, expect or dream; how, if at all, the real envisions the ideal and paves the way for it. Based on cumulative interactions with hundreds of residents as informants, friends or hosts, and with their institutional counterparts, my ethnography reveals their unequal ways of positioning themselves in a field of layered ambivalence. Such positionings articulate intimate suffering, frustration, dilemmas and unfulfilled aspirations. They also reveal recurring patterns of interaction and social configurations that add up to concepts such as nothing, relevance and ambivalence.

Undoing Nothing is all about a tiny number of young racialized men who struggle to achieve "proper" male adulthood. However, it is also meant to inspire comparative research on the lived experience of marginalized, heteronomous and temporary housing across generational, racial and gender divides, in light of the underlying societal mechanisms.[22] This book aims to scale its own relevance beyond the bricks and mortar of the center for multiple purposes: awareness raising (to nourish empathy and advocacy) and practical relevance (about the contradictions of humanitarianism and the prospects to sort them out) but also for analytical and conceptual purposes. The point is not simply that many more share the frozen temporality of the protagonists of this book, under worse housing conditions. More fundamentally, the residents' endeavors to threshold their timespace yield insight on more general ways of scaling relevance and on the contents and reach of relevance itself—what matters, demands care, justifies sacrifices and affords aspirations. There is a promise in taking up and reworking this framework across housing infrastructures that are more or less forcibly shared.

Starting from stories of refugees on welfare until further notice, expected to become autonomous soon and with limited means for that, *Undoing Nothing* explores questions that speak to many other marginalized and impermanent dwellers. These include how they see and make sense of themselves and the mainstream; how they manage the tension between normative expectations, future ideals and restricted scope for action; how they negotiate the reach of what commands attention and dedication in space, proximate and distant, as an example of socio-cognitive attribution of relevance.[23] In all these respects, I aim to highlight "trans-contextual patterns"[24] that reach beyond migration, refugee or housing studies.

Along the way I have been inspired by the burgeoning literature on place-making and home-(un)making under displacement and asylum.[25] As important has been the research on the lived experience of refugee housing against the background of asylum politics and policies in Italy. In a global scenario of temporal bordering and spatial externalization of asylum, moreover, large-scale youth migration has also emerged as a matter of generational struggles to achieve normative models of male adulthood. This involves questions of temporality, masculinity and race, as much as concepts such as nothing, ambivalence and relevance (see chapter 1). An essential presentation of the center, its residents and my fieldwork are likewise in order (see chapter 2) before exploring people's ways of *un*doing nothing by negotiating relevance through their ambivalent positions (see chapters 3 to 7).

IV

Before all that it is worth clarifying what this book is not about. Its field of relevance overlaps with the inhabitance of one particular asylum facility, to be reconstructed from the ways of feeling, telling, showing and doing in its bedrooms and corridors, on its doors and windows, across its inner thresholds, transitioning between inside and outside and mooring in. *Undoing Nothing* foregrounds the residents' ways of representing themselves and relating to others under the same roof, thereby illuminating their timespace as a meaningful, if segregated, segment of larger trajectories. The book does not address as in-depth what occurred in their past, unless to the extent that they spontaneously shared it with me and that it sensibly loomed there anyway. Dwelling in asylum typically entails an attempt to invisibilize the past and remove it from the normality bubble of the present. Yet whatever happened before is deep-rooted in the minds, bodies, souls and habits of the young men in the center. As a result, the past does emerge in *Undoing Nothing*, if only as a legacy or a weight.

Other questions relevant to young male migrants in general are also looming in the lived interiors of the center: stepwise (im)mobilities across borders and countries, ways and styles of consumption, claims for dignity and respect, and negotiations of masculinity, religiosity and race as well as peer relations and translocal ties with people living elsewhere. All these matters are refracted through the stories and practices of my interlocutors. Likewise, all that occurs once people leave for good is not addressed in-depth. Nonetheless, it sneaks through everyday life in waiting and hence across the pages that follow. The apparently narrow focus of my ethnography—one housing infrastructure in a specific time window—is then not so narrow after all. It covers a four-year span in which major transformations occurred, from the micro to the macro level. In exploring them *Undoing Nothing* defies the mainstream narratives about dwelling in asylum to reveal the underlying social mechanisms as well as the existential tensions embedded, invisibilized and temporarily protected inside it.

In sum, this book is less on refugee housing per se than on the ways of struggling for relevance therein and on their private and public significance. In this regard collective categories such as "they" or "them" are meant to stress some commonality between a number of young men from West Africa (mostly) and Pakistan (some of them) and sometimes between them and the native or long-resident staff. Of course, I also zoom down to individual narratives and practices whenever appropriate. Both the interpersonal and the individual level illuminate social, political and existential questions that cut across temporary and heteronomous forms of shared housing—and matter, beyond it.[26]

V

Undoing Nothing, as a story, is the cumulative outcome of thousands of microencounters under the same roof. It is also a story of rooms and beds, of blankets and sneakers, of empty timespaces and attempts to fill them, of presences and absences, of what is clean and what is dirty, of home and all that home is not. Throughout, it is a story of young men that fled their countries of birth, are categorized as asylum seekers, dwell in the center with their racialized bodies and engage in minimal, everyday mobilities in contrast to the accelerated and transformative ones they would aspire to.

All residents in the center are equal, but some are more equal than others. This holds not only for their unequal ability and luck in navigating the legal, job and housing markets ahead of them. More pragmatically, some have played an especially significant role for my fieldwork—as hosts within their rooms, partners in extended coffee sessions or walks in and around the center, or just friends. This means that, while drawing from all sorts of ethnographic encounters, I acknowledge the special contribution of a few young men—and the moral obligation to write and somehow save their "real" names, while using only fictitious ones throughout (except for Salim, for reasons that will become all too clear): Abdou, Aboubacar, Adama, Aladje, Alhassane, Assane, Babel, Bun, Chucks, Demba,

Douglas, Hassane, Iaia, Ibrahim, Ibrahima, Imran, Jamal, Javed, Karim, Kingsley, Komi-Dodji, Koola, Makolie, Massamba, Maurice, Mohamed, Mory, Moussa, Nfamara, Obinna, Omar, Peter, Prince, Salif, Salim, Sideeq, Souleyman, Steven, Yaya, and Wali.[27] These are the main characters of *Undoing Nothing*, if only as "ghosts," or "subjects that have been partially captured through the representational tactics" of an ethnographer, while necessarily exceeding, as human beings, the stories he has written about them.[28]

On the staff side, while being grateful to all doormen and caseworkers, I am most indebted to Cristina, Francesco, Nour Eddine, Ezio, Hassan, Irina, Letizia, Redouane, and Yusuf. As the following chapters illustrate, the formally asymmetrical power relations between them and their counterparts, controller versus controlled, have many nuances and interpersonal variations. They end up in different roles being performed, tensions being produced and accommodations being generally found. Contrary to an ideologically charged view of an asylum center as a carceral world, readable through a powerful-versus-powerless binary account, my fieldwork reveals interesting, sometimes unsettling, commonalities across the divide. *Undoing Nothing* is also a way of acknowledging them.

1

—

The Background

All subject matters, like all perceptual objects in a gestalt perspective,[1] are figures against a larger ground. They emerge and are framed as relevant under particular circumstances, reasons or interests.[2] For everyday life in asylum as a central figure, the background is simultaneously institutional, empirical and conceptual. There is a larger scenario and history of worldwide displacement, border tightening, externalization of asylum and routinized perceptions of refugee crises, as a backdrop for any particular case study. There is an extended, if dispersed, empirical literature on youth migration as a generational transition and on dwelling in asylum. And there is a conceptual backdrop in which notions such as nothing, relevance and ambivalence have a special promise to illuminate the lived experience of asylum seekers in waiting. So, enter the concepts, enter the protagonists of this book. Exploring this faceted background paves the way to foreground the center as an inhabited field of ambivalence, crossed by multiple tensions on what is relevant for whom and on the struggle to achieve it by *undoing nothing.*

1.1 FROM THE "REFUGEE CRISIS" TO ASYLUM-SEEKER RECEPTION IN ITALY

One in a million or so. Yet, one that embodies, displays and reveals something important about the 999,999 left. Of the almost 70 million "forcibly displaced people" reported by the United Nations High Commissioner for Refugees (UNHCR) in 2018, in a global estimate that has not gone unchallenged[3] and reached 120 million in 2024, about seventy at a time were housed in the center, on average for a couple of years each, during the timespan of my fieldwork. About seventy of the approximate three hundred thousand sea arrivals to Italy throughout 2016 and 2017, mostly from West Africa in those years, as opposed to the previous predominance of Syrians and Eritreans and the subsequent one of Tunisians, Bangladeshi and Pakistani.[4] Their constant oscillation in numbers is revealing both of the expansive consequences of wars and protracted crises and of the restrictive ones of European Union agreements with North African and Middle Eastern governments.[5] Back then as much as now, the formal figures on forced migrants from the Italian Ministry of the Interior are simultaneously an underestimate (as they do not account for unauthorized migration through the Balkan route, which is more challenging to quantify) and an overestimate (for a variable share of arrivals strive to move farther north, only to be categorized as "Dubliners" and potentially sent back if intercepted along the way). More fundamentally, it is an impossible estimate, as long as 4–5 percent of those who tried the central Mediterranean route are believed to have lost their lives in the past decade,[6] many of them also losing their identities and collective memories.[7] This is not to mention thoroughly unreported deaths across the Sahara and in Libya.

Even one death is too much, activists usually remind us, mid-way between indignation and frustration. Even one life is enough, I would add, to disclose stories, insights and concerns of potentially systemic significance. Following this premise, *Undoing Nothing* is about a few dozen young men from West Africa and Central Asia, categorized as asylum seekers in one particular facility. They are housed there, against a far larger (and yet highly self-selective) background of people moving for international protection across borders. It is only from in-depth engagement with lives and stories, though, that numbers are converted into human beings claiming dignity, respect and new possibilities. It is only from immersion into everyday life that a deeper and more humane understanding of forced migration can be reached.

It would be ordinary good practice, for a book about people who claim to be refugees, to situate the study in a larger account of the international asylum regime, from the 1951 Geneva Convention to the main steps of its implementation and diffusion.[8] More recently, circumstances of apparently massive displacement have led several scholars to argue for a radical reframe—ideally, for a radically new asylum regime.[9] For the purpose of this book, though, it is sufficient to be critically aware of the global, racialized hierarchies of inequalities protected by national borders and of the circumstances of open war, chronic crisis or massive impoverishment underlying large-scale displacement. It is enough to keep in mind the layered processes of border externalization and remote control, whereby rich countries worldwide try to keep unwanted migrants away from their borders,[10] while still formally acknowledging the right to asylum. It is enough to leave aside the dubious and yet "politically consequential" distinction between migrant and refugee by focusing, sociologically, on people "who have crossed an international border because of violence, including the threat of violence behind persecution, or those who are afraid to return in their country because of its threat."[11]

Not all the protagonists of this book, or hundreds of thousands like them, will eventually get an international protection status. All of them left for a variety of societal and biographical factors, including a degree of coercion, and exposed themselves to major life risks along the way. It is to their everyday life in waiting, more than to the institutional ways of processing it, that this book is dedicated. The micro, individual and semi-invisible non-events of *refugeehood*, as the lived experience of applying for asylum, prevail here on the macro, collective, and more visible events of *refugeedom*, as the complex arena of institutional relations between refugees, states and societies.[12] That said, a cursory overview of asylum politics and policy in Italy in the larger European Union scenario is part of the background against which the young men in the center struggle to *undo nothing*.

All that has to do with asylum seekers and refugees in Italy has long been framed as a matter of emergency.[13] A crisis-centered discourse has shaped public debate and policy since the institutionalization of asylum reception in the country, which only dates back to the early 2000s.[14] This has translated into a fragmented and territorially unequal system of hosting infrastructures, in which asylum seekers are theoretically entitled to free housing and a basic allowance (i.e., "pocket money"), only to receive little or no assistance if/once they get a formal status. Far more than in universalistic or continental welfare regimes, asylum seekers and refugees in Italy have to rely on their own informal networks as much as on sympathetic civil society.[15] After the territorial dispersion that follows their formal take-up in the national asylum system, their housing pathways oscillate between large centers with hundreds of residents and smaller infrastructures (including apartments) as well as more autonomous, informal and precarious arrangements.[16] This reflects a huge variation in reception schemes, regional public investments and local networks of collaboration and support.

Moreover, the institutionalization of asylum has come with the parallel establishment of standard hosting facilities under the supervision of local authorities and "temporary" or "extraordinary" ones, depending on the Ministry of the Interior. Such a two-pronged development has become especially visible after the 2011 "North Africa Emergency"[17] and then, on a larger scale, under the so-called crisis of 2015. This has fed into a relatively extended, if unequal, system of parallel welfare that has been significantly retrenched from 2018 onward, regarding both housing and educational, vocational or socio-legal support.[18] Even before that, and regardless of housing arrangements, refugee policy in Italy has been poorly integrated with mainstream welfare, educational or labor market schemes.[19] In essence it has mirrored the residual and unequal reach of local welfare provisions in the country, especially for immigrants as vulnerable clients.[20]

Importantly, not all undocumented newcomers to Italy have remained and applied for asylum. Particularly among ethno-national groups with stronger diasporic networks in central or northern Europe, intra-European mobility, while not admitted under the Dublin regulation and contrasted by neighboring countries, has long been the backside of asylum reception. As part and parcel of the European Union's southern border, Italy is bound to play the role of a first arrival country and hence, in theory, to be in charge for all applications from newcomers from third unsafe countries. It is also a central actor in the "necropolitical" field of migration through the central Mediterranean corridor, mostly originating from Libya and Tunisia, as mid-steps of larger migration corridors from Africa, the Middle East and East Asia.[21] Together with Greece and Malta, and in interaction with European partners and agencies, international organizations and NGOs, Italy has long been engaged in political and legal contention about search-and-rescue (SAR) operations toward people in distress at sea.[22] This has resulted in thousands of effective rescues but also in innumerable instances of right violations ranging from failed or delayed rescues to unlawful pushback.[23] A number of major shipwrecks and thousands of lives lost on the marine border have constantly marked the development of this field.[24] Most recently, predominantly right-wing national governments have engaged in increasingly tense relations with the NGOs that contribute to rescuing boats in distress. This is only an instance of a larger transnational social question on who bears the responsibility for migrant deaths, how the latter could be prevented and how people missing at sea should be given back the right to grieving and collective memory, if not to a proper burial place.[25]

Overall, despite the rhetorics of right-wing political entrepreneurs and their performative, if all too real, restrictive policies, asylum seekers and refugees have always made up less than 3 percent of foreign residents in the country, only to almost double after the 2022 Russian invasion of Ukraine. This resulted, across the European Union, in the prima facie recognition of forcibly displaced Ukrainians under the Temporary Protection Directive. As far as forced migrants from Africa, the Middle East and East Asia are concerned, racialized hyper-visibility has to do with the "border spectacle" of their rescue (or death) at sea,[26] as much as with poverty and protracted social and legal marginalization. Over the past few years, the constant outflows from both Mediterranean and Balkan routes have been increasingly approached under securitarian lines, with ambiguous and selective nuances of humanitarianism,[27] rather than through any rights-based approach. Young, male, Black men like my interlocutors are easily perceived as undeserving, if not bogus, refugees. A somehow alternative, if not unproblematic, frame has been advanced under analytical categories such as "survival" and "mixed" migration.[28] In fact, *mixed* should not refer only to diversity or indetermination in status, drivers of migration, and outcomes of the asylum procedure. The average asylum-seeker profile in Italy is also mixed in terms of ethno-racial and religious backgrounds, while being rather homogeneous in age (approximately 82 percent are between eighteen and thirty-four years) and gender (88 percent are male).[29] In practice once migrants apply for asylum, they hold a temporary stay permit that allows them to participate in the formal labor market, once two months have passed from the date of their asylum application. Unlike what would happen in other countries, the young men in the center can formally search for a job. This makes it no less difficult for many of them to get precarious or casual employment in the low-skilled and labor-intensive niches of cleaning, the catering and hospitality industry, retail trade and seasonal agriculture, among others.[30]

1.2   MOVING AS A NORMATIVE TRANSITION TO MALE ADULTHOOD

All the young men in the center are asylum seekers, juridically speaking. All of them engaged in protracted, stepwise, undocumented and high-risk migration pathways, mostly originating in West Africa.[31] This eventually allowed them to apply for asylum as they set their feet on EU territory in southern Italy. While the decision on their case is still uncertain, and typically comes after years-long legal battles, a fact is there—they made it to Europe. An individualized assessment of the credibility of their stories of persecution, risk and fleeing will determine their legal position and, in theory, their possibility to remain.[32] Nevertheless, this may not take into account significant aspects of their life experience that are irreducible to the claim for asylum and, indeed, to refugee studies. There is a moral and symbolic economy of attempted transitions to adulthood along gendered and racialized lines, which underpins their cross-border mobilities toward countries that have, and apparently promise, more.

Youth male migration from countries across the Global South is also a strategy, apparently the only one available, for "attaining markers of social adulthood" such as economic autonomy, a family life of one's own, the capability to care for one's kin—in a nutshell, a way to "pursue social regeneration" within uneven and fragmented "affective circuits" that are reproduced across borders.[33] For sure, this normative life-course transition and the struggle to achieve it, resulting in prolonged waiting, are no prerogative of African youth or, for that matter, of (potential) migrants.[34] However, it is especially among young African men that the "quest of social personhood"[35] through mobility has been explored, as a means to conflate two ways of *social becoming*: an intersubjective one, to meet kin-based responsibilities to provide for the family, and an intimately subjective one, toward better conditions and social status. Group-related obligations and individual success need not sit easily together, nor do they easily translate into practice. Nevertheless, there is no way to be in tune with my informants' accounts and make sense of them without acknowledging the underlying moral economy. This goes along with a peculiar, gendered combination of religious-driven fatalism and a relentless disposition to "questing for luck," or to fulfill one's own destiny by engaging with the uncertain and the unexpected, including the "back way" to Europe.[36]

An emphasis on ingrained habits and dispositions of mobility, as a part of the normative transition to adult masculinity, is not meant to obscure the coercive factors at the roots of large-scale youth migration (which are institutionally recognized whenever claimants do get protection status). It is to acknowledge, though, the emergence of a "global horizon" of perceived modernity or of "global awareness from below,"[37] underlying the diffusion and persistence of migration. Sociologically speaking,[38] migration is a mode of adaptation via "innovation" to the anomie between a cultural goal that has become pervasive (i.e., the achievement of modern personhood) and the persistent lack of institutional means to realize it otherwise. In practice, as Michael Jackson[39] poignantly remarks through the story of a young man from Sierra Leone in London, the difference between life or work conditions in Africa and Europe may have to do less with material improvement than with an unequal horizon of sense and hope. In a modern city or country, the promises of (future) progress, in a narrative of hard work and sacrifice, still exist. "There," "back" to Africa, it no longer does, or it never has.[40] To some this might sound like another unnecessary demonstration of the "compulsion to repeat toxic optimisms,"[41] a moral economy of collective illusion that involves the marginalized worldwide rather than only the declining middle class in the West. To others it would rather appear an embodied and resilient demonstration of hope[42]—a way of claiming rights and trying to fulfill aspirations across the Global South, challenging the position in which so-called structural violence, personal circumstances and unfathomable chance enforced (most) people. To me it is an unspoken worldview that creeps among my interlocutors, helps make sense of their life trajectories and demands respect, whether one's life is eventually up to its promise or not. Last but not least, an emically and existentially sensitive understanding of youth mobility toward "Eurospace"[43] contributes to deexceptionalize migration itself. Behind high-risk pathways that fall under a permanent frame of emergency lies the potential accomplishment of ordinary and morally shared goals, such as becoming independent, taking care of one's family needs, and paving the way for a "good life."

Part of the transition to adulthood is also an accomplished sense of masculinity, as a gendered declination of normative attributes such as autonomy, control, and responsibility to one's family and kin, along more or less patriarchal or conservative lines. Again, this is constructed as hard to achieve in a non-Western country but still at reach through the risk and sacrifice of migration. As it happens, though, little of this script is achievable under the protracted marginalization, dependency and uncertainty of life in asylum. The sense of not being up to these expectations is tangible in the narratives and practices of my interlocutors, inside an oppressively male-only environment. Forced migration as such can be seen as a masculinity crisis.[44] In the larger scenario of the global asylum regime, the protracted displacement of millions of refugees, whereby their survival is guaranteed but their entitlements are not, inherently "feminizes" them. The "long-term limbo" of humanitarian spaces encourages passivity and victimization as stereotypical attributes of femininity, regardless of refugee gender.[45] It also reproduces a binary coding of space whereby domestic space, including in encampment, overlaps with "feminine" vulnerability, as opposed to the less accessible public space of "masculine" autonomy, respect and self-achievement.

This "loss of masculinity"[46] feels even more paradoxical for youth like my interlocutors, who faced as "real men" the risks of desert- and sea-crossing and are now expected to become active providers, only to find themselves as or more dependent than back then. The main difference is that dependency, now, is related to an impersonal and bureaucratic authority that offers little control and sense-making rather than to an informal and patrimonial system of personal relationships that were familiar and predictable, if hard to navigate without the right capital.[47] On top of this, their racialized visibility as "young men arriving with backpacks and smartphones" easily lends itself to stereotyped or utterly hostile reactions.[48] The latter range from perceived undeservingness (for the genuine refugees would be women and children, ideally stuck in some poor African camp) to moral panic for their supposedly backward or hyper-assertive masculinity. That many of my Black interlocutors do hang out as "streetwise young men in baseball caps, low-slung jeans, and conspicuous jewelry"[49] articulates an aesthetic of their own, which may also be seen as a remasculinization strategy. In fact, it makes them no closer to the substantive adult identity they aim for, while possibly fueling—but certainly not justifying—a sense of racialized hostility, or at least of lesser sympathy, from the native population.

Along with masculinity, race and racialization also inform the demographic background and the subtext of intergroup relations in this book. Blackness matters, as my West African interlocutors periodically remind me, in a register that intermingles pride (Black is who/what I am), teleology (Black is what God wanted me to be), antiracism (Black is what I am discriminated against for), and disenchantment (You, the white person, cannot fully understand how they treat us as Black). In short, race is relevant and is sometimes explicitly foregrounded as self-perception and a claim of worth (of one's body and self, in relation to the native white ones). This happens in terms of overexposure to discrimination in the job and housing market, at a micro level; as a matter of selective visibility in a mostly white public space, at a meso level; as a demonstration of larger and enduring structures of life inequality, not always reducible to one's refugee status, at macro level. At the same time, race is interestingly downplayed in the discourse of sympathetic civil society. Due to the fascist legacy, it is also a historical taboo in the national political debate—aside from occasional, if uncannily increasing, right-wing outbursts. Nevertheless, race as a category of practice is salient indeed for Black newcomers like my interlocutors, including as a tool to make sense, if simplistically so, of their own marginalization. While being generally unreflexive about their own colonial backgrounds in West Africa, therefore, the young Black residents implicitly contribute to the uncomfortable debate on race in Italy. This has been emerging on the fine line between the heavy legacy of fascism's racial laws and the resilient, myopic and ill-deserved narrative of Italians as "good colonizers."[50] Last, the pervasive

view of migration as a transition to adulthood suggests the diffusion of a predominantly modern, linear and teleological temporality,[51] which invariably clashes with
the temporality of waiting in asylum. There is a temporal and generational side, as
much as a spatial one, to the lived experience of dwelling in asylum.

1.3 DWELLING IN ASYLUM,
BEYOND THE PANOPTICON

The young men in the center have very personal and intimate stories and yet have so
much in common with millions more, whatever the category in use for their mobility
pathways.[52] So do the infrastructures in which they are housed, despite large variations and inequalities between and within countries.[53] Some commonalities in refugee institutional accommodation, along the continuum between *camp* and *center*, are
relatively self-evident—residential segregation and lesser quality than ordinary housing, conflation of care and control (and of confinement and surveillance), and the
institutionalization of measures and routines that configure a "space of exception."[54]
Less emphasized, and equally ingrained in the lived experience of asylum, are questions of suspended temporality, everyday place-making and inner social order(ing)s.

Time in refugee accommodations is often perceived as different in quality and
less under control than in the larger society. It has a pace, a rhythm and a non-
linearity of its own.[55] This has in part to do with the predicament of asylum seekers themselves, suspended as they are between a *no longer* (the past, including the
suffering and violence that came along with migration) and a *not yet* (the decision
on their case that will shape their room of maneuver). By its institutional rationale,
moreover, a camp is meant to slow down the ordinary temporality of people's lives,
as long as they are entitled to little more than undefined waiting. This embeds a
form of power that is more subtle and grueling than simple surveillance.[56] Refugee
accommodation is part of a "temporal politics,"[57] whereby the formal recognition
of the right to asylum goes along with its institutional procrastination. In practice,
the "system" of asylum and immigration bureaucracies becomes "another sea" to
navigate anew.[58] To that extent an asylum center is a bordering technology[59] or a
functional equivalent of a state border aiming to discourage unwanted mobility
rather than preventing it tout court, by making border-crossing a slow, protracted
and risky endeavor.[60] As a result, the residents may end up with little more to do
than attending to basic social reproduction. It is no exaggeration to approach their
condition as "temporal injustice"[61] and their everyday life as "struggle for time."[62]

All this being said, the lived experience of time is not necessarily so empty or
invariably boring as the cursory glance of an outsider might suggest. While occupying a timespace that has the appearance of an isolated bubble, people engage in
routines and activities that differentiate it internally and reveal significant interde-
pendencies with the ordinary timespace outside. This can be fruitfully appreciated

through the scholarship on place-making and homemaking.[63] There is a promise in approaching in this optic camps, informal settlements, dedicated housing infrastructures and even particular niches of the public space.[64] Home matters, after protracted displacement, as a source of self-identification as much as of painful memories.[65] Its traces can be found in certain ways of approaching space and time in asylum.[66] While no center is meant or seen as a proper domestic space, its residents may operate selective and minimal forms of homemaking by carving out special portions of timespace and through functional and aesthetic readaptations; by enacting rituals, and producing material cultures consistent with their lifestyles, identities or ultimate concerns; and by attempting to improve and "reluctantly" take care of the everyday space around them (see 7.3 to 7.5).[67] These emerging pockets of special timespace have something of the "little islands of vivid, encapturing activity" in the "dead sea" of Erving Goffman's[68] "total institutions," having said that a housing infrastructure such as the center is far more ambivalent and open to negotiation than an ideal-typical total institution.

Overall, though, only a limited part of the scholarship on asylum accommodations has drawn on extended fieldwork within the dwelling space of residents themselves. This is critical to appreciate the inner interplay between narratives and practices, the accumulation of material cultures and the incessant negotiation between individual ways of boundary-making and place-making. This also reveals the emergence of subtle and contended inner orders with asylum seekers as active interlocutors rather than victims, or at best recipients, of the "system." Having said of the oppressive, disciplining and infantilizing texture of refugee accommodations, one fact remains—the lived experience of places such as the center of this book has little of a panopticon. Rather than a top-down exercise of governmental power, my ethnography reveals a "plural and layered" field[69] of micro relations that articulate contrasting views of what is relevant and unequal possibilities to achieve it. This calls for a novel conceptual repertoire.

1.4   ENTER "NOTHING"

Over the years spent in the center, the young male residents enter and exit it one day after the other, while staying in most of the time. In a similar vein, concepts like *nothing, relevance* and *ambivalence* should enter the scholarly debate on dwelling in asylum. While the residents will leave at some point, the concepts are worth retaining and reapplying in research on shared and temporary housing as an institutional, experiential and existential field.

Why un*doing nothing*

Doing nothing is an emic way to articulate one's emotional state and, to a lesser extent, one's practices, under circumstances that scholars would call "stuckness," "frozen transience," "permanent impermanence" or *waithood*—the "state of limbo" of young Africans who are neither dependent children nor independent adults but rather "waiting for adulthood."[70] "I'm doing nothing" pops us in a variety of tones as my interlocutors talk about themselves. It sounds normal and inevitable, if one has no better option than staying in a shelter. Why wonder or discuss it further?

The answer starts from the heuristic function of nothing.[71] As a negative expression that resounds with the empty, the absent or the missing, this is implicitly revealing of what is not there—the unaccomplished, the dreamt of, the potential turning point in one's life. The latter was precisely the expected outcome of migration,[72] one that has little to do with staying in a protracted waiting space. Whenever people state they are doing nothing, this is no invitation to further conversation. Yet, accepting the statement and the idea of nothing at face value is as unsatisfactory as undesirable, for it feeds into an unnecessarily passive and hyper-fatalist attitude—whatever one strives to do would make no difference. After all, people have no leverage on the timing and outcome of their applications, although they are encouraged to prove their "deservingness" by searching for a job, attending school or volunteering. What they do know is that at some point they will have to leave again. Doing nothing, then, will no longer be an option. Everything else being equal, the capital accumulated in the meantime will make a difference.[73]

What happens, however, when nothing seems to happen?[74] Rather than sticking to the narrative of nothing as a real thing, it is worth unpacking the cognitions, emotions and practices associated with it. "Nothing," I suggest, is used in relation to any way of being or doing that falls radically short of one's concerns and goals. *Undoing* nothing, then, should not just lead us to acknowledge the obvious—so many things happen anyway, as asylum seekers exercise their "agency-in-waiting."[75] More fundamentally, undoing nothing means to reckon with its opposites, a number of denied, non-existent or non-achievable "somethings," through the ongoing dialectic between things as they are (seen) and things as they used to be, should be or are aspired to be. Analytically speaking, nothing is a large, blank space between the register of perception and emotion—what I perceive or feel I'm doing—and the register of norms, moralities and aspirations: what I must, will or shall do. Undoing nothing means exploring the unaccomplished field of what *should* be there or should have gone differently (and perhaps could still go differently) but *is* not or does not. This is an inherently ambivalent field, which coalesces multiple lines of tensions between individuals and groups.

As I've realized in hindsight by revisiting the hundreds of "nothings" in my fieldnotes, the usage of this word illuminates different temporal, moral and practical aspects of dwelling in asylum. Content-wise, nothing is neither monolithic nor self-evident. Rather, it means different things to different people in different circumstances.[76] Each of its meanings and uses demands attention, prior to approaching nothing from the reverse—what the empty, the absent or the missing is about—through asylum seekers' ways of negotiating what matters for them.

Senses and uses of nothing

The center itself, as a liminal infrastructure with a supposedly temporary function, can be seen as an embodiment of nothingness. Nothing will be left of its instrumental relevance, one would think, once residents and staff end the segment of their housing or working careers that rested on it. Meanwhile, the staff habitually evoke "nothing" to articulate the lack of a temporal rhythm and direction in its inner life—as reassuring as depressing. "Nothing ever happens" until something happens elsewhere, in the asylum-processing system, out of their remit and control. With my young male interlocutors, in turn, nothing first comes as a synonym of no news about and no possibility to affect their asylum application and perhaps their search for a job. "Nothing *yet*" is the hopeful or perseverant variant of the same discursive repertoire. In practice, a number of residents do get a precarious and exploitative job sooner or later.[77] Likewise, some decision on their legal cases is bound to come. Meanwhile, this emerging sense of nothingness takes up multiple temporalities. It may reach into the future, as one has little idea of where he will live, or with whom, in a few months from now. However, it is also appropriated in relation to one's past life—a half-hidden wound that should not be exposed again.[78] Far from being a passive experience, nothing is actively produced[79] whenever one struggles to remove thoughts about the violence they experienced or, at best, witnessed. Nothing-to-tell is less threatening an option than delving into what has been and cannot be reverted or even only elaborated for now. Nothing of that should interfere with the search for the "good life" in Europe. It feels as if one is cautiously treading over a thin surface of nothingness that ought to protect from his own memories. In fact, these may emerge nonetheless under a variety of circumstances, like sudden and unpredictable cracks in the surface (see 5.4 and 5.5).

One afternoon, like hundreds more, I unexpectedly end up in Mbaye's room. I am strolling in the corridor right while he is cleaning in the doorway. One round of greetings, and he gently invites me in. Now he's sitting on his bed with a co-national who lives and works elsewhere, is more fluent in Italian, and starts talking about Mali. He's recently been back for a while, thereby realizing the intimate, if politically incorrect, aspiration of all my interlocutors. "It's a total mess, you know?" With the war before, with the terror attacks now, his hometown is "completely messed up—they could catch you anywhere." No need to play the victim role, for Mbaye's friend already holds a five-year permit. As he keeps talking, Mbaye gets stiffer and gloomier. He clearly doesn't want to talk or hear that. You need an outsider to transgress the taboo. While the outsider deftly intermingles stories from Mali and about his "good integration" in Italy, Mbaye seems to be apart from both worlds, just like the suffocating bedroom in which he is staying. "You can't kill like that, for nothing," says his friend. "I saw things you can't even imagine—eleven-year-olds who threaten to shoot you. . . . You were [in town] too, right?" His eyes turn toward Mbaye, who nods and shivers. "If you think so much," the other explains, "you'll see this like a movie in front of you." Enough of that for Mbaye: "I *don't* want to talk about Mali. . . . If only I think of what I saw—it hurts too much. You know, a woman, she was pregnant—." *Nothing* more about Mali. Trying to put his thoughts into words does not work any better than trying to push them away.[80] Yet for Mbaye or anybody else, *nothing* is not the last word.

In everyday conversation in the center, nothing is also used to lament the lack of useful things to do. "It's no good, no job, here always—I'm tired of playing all the time, just not to think of nothing." So Omokunrin murmurs in a joyless tone, whenever we chat beyond the conventional greeting threshold, and his mask of euphoric self-confidence starts falling down. "I've always worked in Africa—I've got nothing to do here. You end up thinking over and over. . . . It hurts, you know?" says Amadou, sitting with me in front of the entrance. "Four years with nothing to do—just sleeping, going around, say hello-how-you're-doing, and that's it," Kambanoo sighs, as I'm staying in his kitchen, sipping the fruit juice he offered me before preparing dinner. Each of my interlocutors tends to articulate, in an intimate and confidential tone, the same collective and structural concerns. You struggle to cope with a social space that is inherently void unless you find enough energy, contacts and good luck to fill it up.

In fact, a whole range of micro-practices do fill it, but are all too irrelevant to subvert one's sense of entrapment. So is the informal routine in Fatou's room, one of the most hospitable for me. We usually spend a few minutes in silence, each of us busy on his smartphone—and, in my case, in looking intermittently at the twenty-two pairs of sneakers in orderly lines on the bookshelf he shares with Sani. "I'm busy—call me later," Fatou says to someone, while he keeps scrolling his screen. Time goes by, nothing happens. Or, more precisely, each of us minds our own business and co-produces a shared sense of nothingness. At some point we'll start chatting—sometimes for minutes, other times for hours. Meanwhile, someone has finished cooking and starts eating in the adjacent kitchen. Every now and then Fatou laughs a bit—he must have seen some funny picture or video. "I'm tired of staying home doing nothing," he whispers at last, just before his prayer alarm rings. The time for praying has come. And then more phone scrolling and then some friends visiting him from another room or vice versa. And then another day is over, part of it spent doing nothing with me—with more freedom to do so, and less stigma, than anywhere else.

Perhaps doing nothing outside would be even worse. Most likely, it's not affordable. The center shelters one's nothing-to-do from any external gaze, as much as it perpetuates it. As surreal from outside, as weird from inside. Even grotesque sometimes, when I happen to be in Den's room while he's watching a Big Brother episode on TV. Unlike his roommate, Salim, who seems creative and stubborn enough to find some job most of the time, Den is often in—only to be reprimanded by the staff for the "disorder" in his room. "If I were there" in the reality show, he once exclaims in a burst of laughter, "they would kick me out, because I don't make up my bed!" Instead, he's here in a reception center. He'll be kicked out anyway two years later, but "only" for overstaying, after getting a humanitarian permit. For now his room and the Big Brother's, connected through his screen, articulate parallel life routines that feel equally fictitious, if radically unequal. As we watch the real-life show, we are doing nothing but watching other people who do nothing. Unlike Den, they are being celebrated and build their careers out of it. That's perhaps what I'm doing too, as extractive as any ethnographer is bound to be, a critical reader might object (cf. 2.4).

Nothing, in the ordinary jargon of the young men in the center, captures this form of undesired hyper-domesticity. However, it is also used in a different sense. *Nothing* is what "*they* know of how we live in Africa" since "they've never been there," says Fatou of the hearing commission that rejected his application. *Nothing*, here, stands for an essential wall to mutual understanding between us and them, Europe and Africa, white and Black (see 3.1). There is little space or interest, as we talk about asylum denial, for subtleties on the definitional criteria of persecution or for the proper refugee narrative they should have performed. Cultural differentialism gives a more straightforward response—the same that nativist actors use, after all, to underpin their principled opposition to immigrants or refugees. However, this use of nothing also holds a deeply moral subtext. It reveals a radically frustrated claim for expertise and good faith: "*Why* didn't they believe me?" Fatou and many others wonder, in ways widespread and emotional enough to suggest genuine surprise. The initial denial of asylum, hence of their credibility, becomes a denial of their own worth.

This points to still another meaning of nothing, as a catchword for all forms of undignified life—those one expected to leave behind. "In Nigeria," Olusola habitually reminds me, "there is *nothing* below. . . . They destroyed everything. That's why young people leave." As he adds, "My intelligence was there for nothing! I always saw the same people and did the same things. . . . Here, instead, I can grow up and thrive." Whether this prospect comes true is a different matter. You are still "nothing of a man," Gorko bluntly says during our coffee breaks, as long as your livelihood depends on the money of someone else. "As a man, you must not depend on Mr. Big. . . . Life is not like that," he concludes before getting back to his room and effectively depending on Mr. Big's allowance until he will find the next job. Living "out of your sweat" rather than staying here "getting money to do nothing" is precisely what former residents who did get a job stress to distinguish themselves.

Furthermore, *nothing* may refer to the scant material resources available to asylum seekers or to a devaluation of those they do have. *Nothing* is possibly the instrumental value of their skills and human or cultural capital, relative to those they need to develop anew. "How many languages do you know?" I ask Momo one day. It's just a well-intended way to feed the conversation, as we are waiting at the staff desk. "Five," he replies, including English, in which we are communicating. "Okay," a caseworker exclaims. "But the African ones—forget your *bambara* or whatever. That's useless here." Of no practical use and hence tantamount to nothing. Rude or cynical as the message sounds, it has a point. So do the staff's patronizing appeals for people to speak Italian among them, as they invariably do for bad words, mutual kidding or ironical mimicking of the natives. At the same time, some of their extant nothing-capital can be revalued through micro-homemaking practices that create continuity between present and past, here and there (see 7.3).

Finally, people in the center, as much as anywhere else, may discard as nothing all that exceeds their field of relevance: what is sensorially there but raises no interest in relation to one's perceived priorities. This often includes cleaning and maintenance chores and sometimes the needs and prospects of co-residents, on the asylum-seeker side. It may involve all the relational work that would exceed one's basic mandate, such as catching up with former residents, on the staff side. On either side the common space—all that lies between the bedrooms and the outer world—tends to assume the value of nothing, hence to be used only for transition, as time goes by, the asylum budget is retrenched, and the pandemic eventually turns an empty space into a virtuous example of compliance with new normality.

In sum, *nothing* does not simply articulate a negative or unwanted state of things. It rather stands for a process of doing and undoing.[81] It has multiple meanings, parallel to the ways of evoking, co-producing and effectively contrasting it. What its emergence reveals (i.e., what should or could be there in its place), and how its diffusion is un-done by the same persons who evoke it, are the questions to be conceptually introduced now and ethnographically addressed in the next chapters.

1.5   BEYOND NOTHING: ENTER RELEVANCE

How the young male residents see and negotiate the nothingness around them has to do with questions of relevance and ambivalence. Analytically speaking, irrelevance is tantamount to an attribution of nothingness to certain situations, places, memories or desires.[82] This evokes, by opposition, more questions: what is relevant to different social actors, with distinct interests and unequal resources, in the same social field; how far they achieve it; where/when they (dis)locate what they deem to be relevant. The production of relevance[83] entails singling out and foregrounding certain aspects of one's material and social space. I use *relevance*, rather than *attention*, to stress the subjective orientations, moralities and expectations that inform the foregrounding. These tend to be the same within one's group of reference. Moreover, relevance has to do with social practices rather than only with perceptions. Within any shared living environment, this likely entails friction between different ways of drawing the line between what matters and all that should stay in the background. Producing relevance is a socially and politically situated process—hence, a matter of unequal power relations, as becomes all too evident whenever this process fails, and people find themselves in a protracted and undesired position of irrelevance.

Each protagonist of this book, myself included, has his own structure of relevance, along with narratives to justify it and unequal means to (re)produce it. For sure, only a tiny part of one's field of relevance overlaps with the center or selected regions of it. These have primarily to do with the management of the common space and organizational tasks for the staff, within their working shifts; with generally tiny spaces of day-to-day social reproduction, as a part of broader translocal fields of relevance, among the residents; with any opportunity to spend time with people, ideally as a guest in their bedrooms, for me (cf. 2.4).

Relevance and the staff

As far as the staff is concerned, the center is as relevant as a workplace can be—one generally used for lack of better options. The bulk of relevance lies elsewhere, probably in some inhabited space they would call home, where they can get back after every shift, unlike their counterparts. Within the center their field of responsibility is relatively narrow. Doormen, in particular, have a uniquely bounded field of relevance: the entrance and the ground-floor hall beside their lodge, whenever someone is transitioning there. In the few square meters ahead of their checking window, in the few seconds it takes to cross them, all that is relevant occurs— allowing someone in or not. Relevance results in a micro-exercise of territorial sovereignty, along with little responsibility for, or interest in, what happens elsewhere. While that little field of intermittent relevance may generate tensions with residents or visitors, that is a secondary concern, relative to the major problem of all doormen—how to make time go by (see 4.2). That said, their field of relevance has a degree of flexibility. Now and then some informal conversation enlivens it. With the few who feel like talking with them, doormen occasionally engage in jokes and funny conversation, mid-way between fatherly recommendation and masculine complicity, beyond generational and racial barriers. As long as questions of sex are mentioned in the common space, this invariably is with them. Their perceived field of relevance may even reach into the courtyard, whenever they're having a cigarette and spot potential intruders on the opposite side, fifty meters away. They likely creeped in to dump their garbage or park their cars. In a sudden change in rhythm, the doormen run out to contrast the order violation. This would make little difference to place decor, but it would certainly be a lack of respect for them—and for that matter, for the residents. It actually defies the doormen's exercise of sovereignty over what is to happen in the courtyard—that is, as they say, basically nothing.

For caseworkers, in turn, the field of relevance tends to narrow down over the years. After the anti-asylum discursive and political turn in national politics since late 2018, and with local decision makers anxious to implement it,[84] the public money for refugee integration has plummeted. One year later or so, covid dries up the space left to promote sociability. Everything boils down to a suitable performance of law and order. Once caseworkers are sitting alone in the office in front of the PC screen, they will only need some eye work to re-focus on the entrance door, on the opposite side of the hall, whenever they hear a noise. As time goes by, that's their visual corner of relevance. Some female caseworkers strive to do more, in advising people or even only listening to them. Generally speaking, though, the budget and the salaries available afford little more than maintaining an apparent calm, itself a form of nothingness. "All calm, all full" (i.e., all beds occupied) are the catchwords they increasingly share with me and with themselves.

The less public authorities invest in refugee integration, the more relevance will be focused on being there as an aim in itself rather than as a lever to support and empower residents. In doing so caseworkers are far from omnipotent agents of surveillance. At most, they struggle to retain minimal order and cleanliness. As long as someone wishes to transgress, he needs to do so with a low profile, just like the Nigerian friends of Olusola and Ogwu who occasionally catch up on the backside to share some beer or brandy. One fall afternoon they're sitting there to chat and laugh together, while a newly arrived caseworker, whose name is unknown to them as much as they are unknown to him, is locked up in the office, waiting for the end of his shift. Someone must be there 24/7, per formal rule. No doubt he is doing that. All the rest need not be so relevant.

Relevance and the residents

What is relevant, in turn, for dozens of young men in waiting, and how do they negotiate it in practice? Much of this exceeds the bricks and mortar of the center, just as their identities, personal stories and ways of being exceed collective labels such as asylum seeker or resident. That said, it is from the timespace of a particular dwelling place that they struggle to undo the perceived nothingness around them. What they construct as relevant is by no means fixed or given, though. Rather, it is scaled across different timespaces.[85] It is also biographically relative, for it changes with their life course and those of their dear ones, wherever located.

I began to see the "relevance of relevance" thanks to a foreign-born caseworker with an educational background in mathematics. Unlike his colleagues, he strives to turn bedroom inspections into ways of befriending and doing things together rather than delivering recommendations from the doorway. "People here," he musingly says during a smoking break, "have different *ranges of their own*. Some take care of the kitchen and the space around, others of their beds and don't care for the rest, others care only about their bodies. . . . They're so well-dressed when they go out, aren't they? And yet their rooms are all messed up!" The residents, I rephrase, struggle to scale the range of what is important, meaningful and perhaps achievable and to threshold their time and space accordingly. Their ways of scaling relevance involve embodied emotions and emplaced practices rather than explicit statements. They are shaped by external circumstances, but they also articulate their own stories, aspirations and concerns.

Relevance has to do with the struggle to produce thresholds—that is, markers of discontinuity or difference in quality between what lies before and after, in space or time.[86] Thresholds are meant to set apart what someone feels, sees or thinks to be most relevant. As in any other built environment, material thresholds layer space between external, interior-common and interior-private.[87] Parallel to that, residents struggle to negotiate thresholds in their life routines to distinguish what they share with others, what they do alone but potentially in their presence and what they should do completely alone; in time, by making some moments more meaningful and oriented to an end than the ordinary circular timeline; in the ways of presenting the self to the others, as a balancing act between indifference, conventional greetings and protracted interactions; in the ways of telling fragments of their life stories for different interlocutors, occasions, and purposes; in the use and display of their dwelling space and of their own bodies. This, in turn, involves multiple thresholds: what they hide or show of their personal belongings, habits and lifestyles; how they get dressed, depending on the context and people around; who to approach, including female acquaintances and bodies, in the open space of sociability, online and offline, outside the gender-oppressive environment they live in. Most fundamentally, their lived experience of migration was expected to mark a moral and existential threshold between life before, made of stillness, dependency and childhood and life after, as a matter of autonomy, male adulthood and full personhood. This is arguably the most critical and uncrossed of thresholds.

Beyond the housing infrastructure, a larger but still territorialized field of relevance involves the surrounding urban space. That this may initially appear empty, unknown and rather hostile does not make it any less important. Learning to navigate the city is relevant instrumentally but also for purposes of sociability, as people unequally accrue networks of social support, acquaintances, friends and employers.[88] There is something of all this in the everyday life of Paul, a DJ and a singer, as much as an asylum seeker and a young man from southern Nigeria. Paul directs the Sunday service choir of his church, a few blocks away from the center. Singing, attending the church, and working whenever there is an African party are all sources of reward, sense-making and economic value. That is what matters to Paul, not staying *here*, in a place he sees with a mix of indifference and resignation. And yet it is staying here that makes anything else possible for the time being. There is hardly any relevant public field without a semi-private one to start from.

A larger, immaterial and diasporic field of relevance also exists. This is probably the most conflict-ridden, thick with memories and obligations, virtual connections and disconnections. All that has to do with the residents' past lives and kinship or affective ties is hardly visible in the center, while looming on it. However, in an era of potentially boundless and constant virtual connectedness, the diasporic field of relevance can also be one of deliberate irrelevance. Residents may have good reasons to disengage from it, possibly narrowing down what is relevant to the here-and-now. That their lived experience may disrupt the trope of the connected migrant[89] is a lesson I've learned from Larka. All across his daily routines, Larka displays a purposefully minimized field of relevance, overlapping with what appears to be under control at present.[90] On all that is not, silence is the only possible form of agency. We often have a coffee together on the bench outside the entrance. No news, "let's wait," Larka will comment after stating that he's "very well" right now. Since his arrival to Italy, he has enjoyed constant and free medical care to limit the consequences of his major disease. He has an accommodation for now and has recently found a job. Why bother or complain? *This* is the field of relevance. No point in discussing much else, one coffee after another. Future? No way. Pakistan or "home"? Even less. Whenever I happen to name the country, Larka takes a curious countenance, somewhere between disenchantment and superiority. "Pakistan is all a problem. . . . It's there, now I'm here." Full stop. He shrugs as I ask if he "sends," right in the middle of a conversation about money. "I don't care about Pakistan," he patiently repeats, with a hand gesture to push the country away. "I *don't* think—thinking is a problem," Larka grins, whenever I ask him what he's thinking about. The health, social and legal issues he has are enough. Sipping a coffee, listening to music, having some casual chats and getting back into his room is all that needs to be relevant now.

In fact, critical past events are bound to shape the present field of relevance anyway. The very fact of having made it to Europe has opened a field of new possibilities, as long as one is not deported. At the same time, what one has already lost along the way is going to affect whatever will come next. Once you have abandoned your dear ones, no subsequent separation will be as tough, Fatou explains one spring afternoon. He is on his last day of hospitality, with a two-year residence permit ahead of him and a number of suitcases and bags around him. "Leaving this place," he says with the slow and profound tone he uses with me, is "good and bad," the latter being about the friends he will be missing. "You can always leave," however, "after you've left behind your family, your best place." That disruptive event has structured the lifelong field of what is relevant. It discloses a kin-based moral hierarchy of worth—and an ongoing struggle to respect it from a distance. Yet, the grief of family disruption can become a source of self-determination. Once you leave home after sudden and unintended circumstances, you can't get it back anyway. And if you have already been on the verge of death, as everybody in the center has, you may give minor relevance to a number of concerns that "ordinary" people would perceive otherwise. In short, there is a biographical and existential side to the ways of scaling relevance of my interlocutors beyond their dwelling place. And yet, dwelling matters. The place itself demands relevance and so do other contrasting terms of reference, as time goes by and nothing seems to happen.

This reveals multiple forms of ambivalence that need to be navigated behind the appearance of nothingness, in the meanwhile.

1.6   AND STAY AMBIVALENCE

As long as someone strives to make their "backway" toward Europe, there is very little ambivalence. The aim is clearly there, no matter how much one suffers, is in danger or is still away from it. Crossing the Mediterranean was "life-or-death," Fatou and his friends remind me whenever they feel like sharing something of their stories. Either you survive or you die on the high sea or even before in the desert, as a few of Fatou's friends did—and "I was no better than them," he gloomily whispers. However, all that follows the boat arrival to Italy, and most visibly dwelling in the center, is deeply ambivalent. Opposite feelings, desires and prospects live along one another, just like Fatou's way of feeling "good and bad" upon leaving or, for other residents, the ostensible desire to leave "soon" and the silent resistance to do so when the time comes. In these and in several more respects, ambivalence is a promising and undervalued analytic to *undo nothing*.

As a Freudian conceptual legacy, *ambivalence* has long been used in social psychology and then in sociology,[91] although not so much in migration studies.[92] I understand it, here, as a perceived and protracted impossibility to take one distinctive and consistent direction, position or alignment in the face of opposite and equally relevant pressures or expectations. This may well be the condition of strangers who share the same housing space for free, for a while, for lack of better options. Forms of ambivalence such as Care and Control or Protection and Segregation are externally visible, widely discussed and probably inherent in asylum accommodation.[93] However, other less obvious modes of ambivalence emerge within, as my interlocutors struggle to set the boundaries of what is relevant for them, only to end up mid-way between opposing constraints and points of reference. None of these ambivalences is a prerogative of institutional reception or is necessarily sorted out once they leave. All of them, though, are especially striking inside it and illuminate the worth, potential and limitations of what people struggle to do.

Following this premise, my "tales from the field"[94] are structured along five coexisting fields of ambivalence, in as many chapters (3 to 7). While the main characters are the same over and again, the plot is analytical rather than narrative. Each chapter can be read in itself but is also part of a cumulative picture of enforced ambivalence in space, time, materiality, care and domesticity.[95] This is like a way of digging further into the biographical terrain of dwelling in asylum, under the uncanny and elusive surface of nothingness. Content-wise, it implies a transition from the most visible layers of ambivalence to the innermost, both in terms of lived experience and of analytical value. This gradually connects a dull and unnoticeable building with the personal stories and the societal questions and

BOX 1

Undoing nothing as a practical and analytical endeavor in an asylum-reception center

Practically (Dwelling in asylum)	Analytically (Researching asylum)
If *nothing* stands for . . .	
Having nothing useful to do Lacking jobs, papers and clear prospects Disconnecting with oppressive memories of the past	Perceiving the condition of forced irrelevance and the impossibility to re-establish relevance (in relation to the expected outcome of spatial and existential mobility)
Then *undoing nothing* means . . .	
Implicitly shifting from *nothing* (as a generic attribution of irrelevance) to *something* (what subjectively matters and is at reach now) Engaging in routines, rituals and relationships that are useful, meaningful or rewarding beyond mere social reproduction	Approaching dwelling in asylum beyond binary categorization (*or/or*) to find emerging fields of ambivalence (*and/and*): all that is not amenable to clear or exclusive courses of thought, feeling or action
Which leads to . . .	
Struggling to carve out portions of relevance (i.e., meaning, security, reward and care) from a larger and apparently empty timespace	Disentangling ambivalence in space, time, materiality, care and domesticity Exploring its drivers, sustainability and impact
With a view to . . .	
Making the condition of waiting more bearable and sometimes, in some respects, homely	Giving a deep, original and humane account of everyday life in "waithood"
Under the pressure of conditions to navigate . . .	
Getting a job, papers and a new bed in the short term Extending and diversifying the field of relevance in the long term	Bridging the gap between micro-personal issues and macro-societal questions Making text engaging and relevant to a larger audience
And hopefully reaching further by . . .	
Getting the "good life" for the benefit of oneself and for loved ones	Acknowledging the weight of forced irrelevance and the worth of unequal struggles to re-allocate relevance as existential and societal questions

dilemmas it is meant to enclose, invisibilize and perhaps normalize but certainly not sort out.

The first facet of ambivalence, "Inside, Outside" (chapter 3), involves the simultaneous relevance of opposite spaces and places, close and far, real and imagined. It unfolds along several coexisting scales, ranging from entire countries to cities and local communities down to a particular house and the racialized bodies that inhabit it. "Still, Moving" (chapter 4), instead, illustrates the friction between opposite institutional, biographical and subjective temporalities. This goes along with a sense of being literally still, while imaginatively, morally and virtually mobile. "Present, Absent" (chapter 5) delves further into the stories and memories of my interlocutors, revealing an uncomfortable juxtaposition between what is present, absent and looming in relation to the past and the far away. Next, "Dirty, Clean" (chapter 6) approaches the everyday negotiation of what should be taken care of and the attendant responsibilities and obligations, rephrased through the aesthetic and moral lexicon of dirt and cleanliness. Ambivalence between dirty and clean, on multiple scales, is uniquely revealing of questions of selfhood and decency, aesthetics and taste, personal dignity and renegotiations of worth. Last, in the deepest analytical and existential sense, "Home, Non-home" (chapter 7) unveils the narrative and practical conflation between contrasting locations, attachments, habits, memories and aspirations of home and non-home. Overall, these emplaced forms of ambivalence have consequences and raise dilemmas that deserve further elaboration along the fine line between accepting nothingness and struggling for relevance (Conclusion).

The whole frame of analysis rests on the social and material field of the center that hosted my four-year ethnography. Before entering it, it is worth outlining the process of undoing nothing as a set of social practices and as an analytical understanding of them (see box 1). There is a parallel between the ways in which my interlocutors strive to undo nothing across their everyday routines and my conceptual ways of doing so. For sure, the correspondence between practice and analysis about nothingness is far from perfect, given also our unequal positions and resources and our different interests and aims. Furthermore, different residents have different and unequally successful ways of undoing nothing. Nonetheless, the promise of undoing nothing lies there in the center and here in the pages of this book. Whether it is achieved practically or not, the life circumstances of each resident will tell. Whether it is achieved analytically or not, the readers will tell.

2

———

The Center

2.1 ZOOMING DOWN INTO ONE HOUSE

Somewhere in a city in northern Italy, away from downtown and yet at walking distance from it, lies the center (figure 1). It is semi-hidden in a lateral space bordered by a store of inexpensive shoes, a gas station and a fast-food restaurant. It is in this reception facility, a *centro di accoglienza straordinaria* in Italian jargon, that I was lucky enough to do ethnography between 2018 and 2022—longer than the average stay of most residents, across watersheds such as the covid emergency and the major budgetary cuts on refugee reception in the country. Once a motel, then a student dorm, eventually a place for asylum seekers, this four-story building has been set up to host up to seventy-five male residents, most of them young West Africans at the time of my fieldwork. The notes I accumulated over five hundred visits, initially in the common areas and then increasingly as a guest in private ones, are like a skeleton for this book as a body. What is, in itself, an inconspicuous and poorly maintained building, as such fully meeting the imaginative and moral standards of refugee accommodation, turned into an invaluable source of ethnographic insight. It did so by way of gradual engagement with its inner life, incomparably richer than the anonymous layout would suggest. A blurry night shot (figure 1) is already enough to convey a twofold message about it: (1) there is very little clarity and interest from the outside about what this place is or how it works, and (2) the place itself has a social life of its own—interior rooms lit up at night—which cannot be captured or understood from the outside.[1]

The place is institutionally and geographically set apart. While residents can freely move in and out during the day, outsiders would have little reason to pop in. However, suppose you happen to get in as a staff member, a friend of the residents,

32

FIGURE 1. A view of the center from the benches by the entrance. The presence of lighted windows signals that people are dwelling in the building. Photo by author.

a volunteer to give language classes in the time between one corona wave and the next, or possibly as an asylum seeker. What are you going to notice and why? On the surface of it, perhaps and once again, nothing—not too-blatant destitution, states of exception or hyper-surveillance. If anything, a couple of weird details are likely to stand out: a sense of carelessness and low quality that would be hard to phrase and yet soon emerges by contrast with the broader urban texture, along with little explicit markers of who is dwelling here. "University Student Dorm," the big metal plaque close to the entrance reads, invisible in plain sight.[2] This was the institutional function of the building until the outset of the so-called refugee crisis pushed the local authority for an alternative allocation—one more consistent with its decreasing housing quality. Nothing distinctive from the outside and so much in common with the downward housing history of institutional accommodations for asylum seekers across Europe.[3]

If one comes closer, all the way around a gas station that tends to invisibilize both the building and its residents, drawing a tacit color line between them and the external world, the actual function of the house becomes sensorially tangible. This is probably because of the uniform circulation of Black or Brown male bodies across the courtyard, up to the main street, against the surrounding, predominantly white and gender-mixed bodyscape. Possibly it is because of the detritus that lie scattered around in silent ruination—old rubble, bits of bicycles, older would-be flowerbeds with nothing in them, wet clothes lying somewhere to get dried. Sometimes there is just nobody in sight, not even Koné in his usual corner to repair bicycles or Bashshel, who tried to take over the trade once Koné suddenly left. Yet the bikes being parked wherever, including on the three big maples facing the entrance, are enough of a hint at what the place is for.

As one enters the doorway, invariably greeting the doorman (and implicitly asking for his authorization), he will probably have the sense of a cold and basically maintained inner environment, with a range of sounds, smells and dim lighting of its own (see 6.1). The place oscillates between a predominantly silent and sleepy atmosphere and intermittent waves of young men flowing in and out. They do so in variable rhythms, often talking loudly on their smartphones, with little mutual interaction beyond an essential greeting whenever their bodies get closer and enter the field of mutual relevance for a few seconds, before moving on in different directions. *Ciao! Comè? Bene* (Hi! How're you doing? Fine) is the ritual sequence that marks encounters, unless people feel so distressed that there would be no point in pretending otherwise. It will not take long, however, for the perception of an isolated and impersonal place to turn into fully-fledged familiarity with its rich sensescape, just as it happens to the staff and to residents. It is precisely by becoming a habitual visitor that I have started to capture the prevalent ways in which people spend time; display something of their life stories, dreams and nightmares; and possibly appropriate the place in unanticipated, even undesired, ways.

For young asylum seekers themselves, this is only the latest step of fragmented and multi-sited housing pathways. They took up the collective, equalizing and anonymizing identity of "resident" one precise day, as they were moved here from the hosting facilities where they had stayed for the previous year or two. Such a transition leaves little trace in their memories, compared to reaching southern Italy alive after sea-crossing—a date they all remember by heart, and a threshold of biographies as much as of relevance, for whatever happened before should not be recalled now. A new life has started since, or so people initially hope. No one ended up in the center or in the region where it is located by active choice. Rather, this was the random outcome of territorial dispersal policies.[4] Chance led them there—and, some would add by rephrasing it as fate or God,[5] let them survive along the way to Europe. Chance, for that matter, will account for the bedroom they end up in and the roommate they have to bear. Chance, if this is to be more than a basic shelter, will however no longer be the only force to drive the following steps—that is, searching for a job, papers, a bed elsewhere. Yet a degree of fatalism may always be of help, whenever one is in a particularly bad mood and needs to make sense of things nonetheless. "Life is this way because God wants it to be this way," Kambanoo usually reminds me at the end of our conversations.

Anybody who is admitted to the center is already an asylum seeker. He successfully made it to Italy and applied for international protection rather than being sent back at the border or eluding controls and trying to move northward. Once in, everybody is on the same, formally equal footing. This includes the benefit of formal residence as a precondition for local welfare access.[6] All residents are of age, or so they successfully claimed. Sometimes the staff would rather call them guests, a well-intended category that in fact alludes to their welfare and legal dependency. They may have different levels of vulnerability, but only in the case of a chronic disease or a visible impairment will this be taken into account. All of them are called by name or by what they claimed to be their name, in the seasons with most staff investment and dedication. Some enjoy the same recognition, while others are more of a "you" or a "he" whose name needs to be retrieved on the list for daily sign-up, the rest of the time. Throughout, all that has to do with their life histories lies in the domain of the private, silent and untold. It is as invisible and irrelevant within these four walls, as hyper-visible and critical for their status determination outside.[7]

From the day of arrival onward, the center is *the* background of everyday life, one unmistakably marked by a number of rules and constraints. Caseworkers or doormen are always in place, entitled to enter any bedroom if needed. All residents must sign up every evening for the service provider to be funded accordingly. Nobody is allowed back in after eleven o'clock unless for work reasons. No alcohol, no women and (since the inception of the pandemic) no external guests. For the time being, this is going to be the new normal. One can make sense of it, even while disliking it, much more easily than with abstract entities such the Asylum Commission or the police agency *Questura* that will report on its decision. Unlike these remote institutions, the center is visible, tangible and predictable. By staying in and complying with the institutional rules, one has access to free accommodation and basic economic support. Some might even call it home, for immediate and pragmatic purposes (see 7.1).

Overall, the facility as such has little that is remarkable or distinctive. This is part of its relevance, for its lived experience resonates with many similar infrastructures in Italy[8] and elsewhere, in Europe at least.[9] Indeed, this is not the worst of accommodations by the standards of institutional reception in Italy,[10] relative to emergency housing at the start of their housing pathways. "It's a hotel!," says a caseworker. "People are more well-mannered, and there are not that many animals around—just cockroaches." "It's like a harbor," a doorman adds—not the best of places but still a haven of sorts. What is remarkable and fortunate has rather been the opportunity for me to visit it one year after another, be witness to the constant flowing of everyday life inside, and befriend a number of residents and enjoy access to their narratives and practices. It is people's emplaced lives and untold stories[11] that make the place worth writing about—not its mere existence as an infrastructure.

For sure, the building per se shapes the life routines and emotions of its residents.[12] Just like any inhabited infrastructure, it embodies layers of memories, lifestyles and material cultures over time.[13] It might even be approached as a single house that affords studying phenomena of global relevance at the micro-level, through the residents' day-to-day emergence and reproduction.[14] To me, nonetheless, the center in itself has only been a relatively dilapidated assemblage of bricks and mortar. I missed people over time, as they were ending their authorized stay and moved elsewhere. I've never missed the place as such since I stopped going after over four years, basically out of saturation. All my key interlocutors were gone. Engaging with the newcomers would take fresh emotional energies and lengthy efforts anew, with apparently little new understandings to emerge by then.

Overall, I have approached the center as a stage where the residents' everyday life unfolds in apparently repetitive, frustrating and yet revealing ways.[15] It is toward these young Black and Brown men, categorized as asylum seekers, that my relational, emotional and epistemological investment has gone between February 2018 and June 2022. The flows of people moving in and out, their transitioning through the common areas and their ways of mooring—in short, their mutual ways of undoing nothing and negotiating relevance—are at the core of this book.

2.2   THRESHOLDING THE SPACE OF ACCOMMODATION

One day after another, across seasons and years, the center monotonously does what it is meant for—hosting for free people who have no alternative accommodation and, as many think, who should be grateful for that.[16] No need to call it with a particular name, as long as it works without major disruptions, people are entitled to be there and somehow stick to the rules. It may not come as a surprise, for an institutionally semi-invisible and semi-nameless place, that the interiors feel impersonal, decaying and neglected. Bad lighting, mold, dampness and a pervasive fustiness embody a perception of precarity that is shared by staff and residents, despite all the differences between them. Everybody sees themselves in transit, with unequal clarities of view and degrees of freedom on the subsequent steps. No one has much interest in the building as such, beyond basic maintenance.[17] Importantly, though, temporariness does not predetermine the lived experience of the place. Care for it, as a mandatory requirement or a spontaneous initiative, is not so uncommon (cf. 6.3). Likewise, the interior's perceived uniformity is just a perception. There is more to find out and make sense of, once inside.

For one thing, not all inner spaces are equal. A tangible boundary exists between the regions meant for transit and for more or less protracted stay. The former includes external surroundings and the entrance hall as well as corridors, staircases, terraces and the laundry and TV rooms. The latter overlaps with the bedrooms,

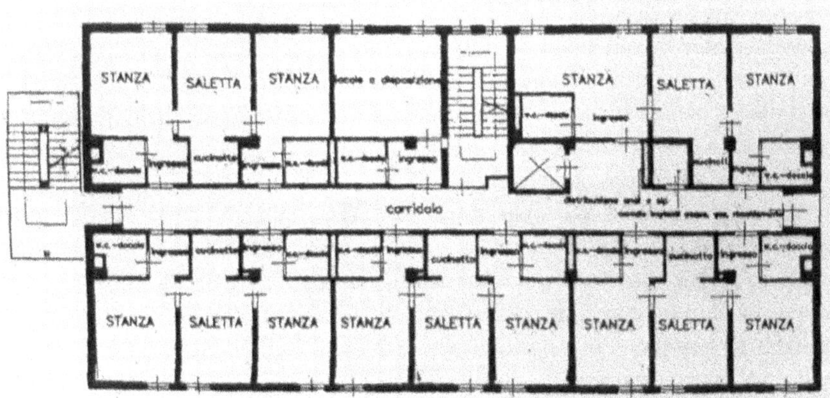

FIGURE 2. A map of the third floor, hanging on a corridor wall. It clearly shows the inner division between bedrooms and kitchens, as well as the presence of a little balcony on the right side of the floor. Photo by author.

although the doorman and the caseworker offices also have a degree of permanency. While the division is self-evident most of the time, it is not always uncontentious. Now and then the common areas are subject to attempts at beautification and functional improvement, whether by adding pictures and decorations or a table with some chairs and a small library, ideally for people to spend time there.[18] In a parallel and separate way, the residents may appropriate some fragments of the common space to have lunch, play or pray, alone or in a group. While these informal practices are typically ephemeral, they are revealing as far as boundary- and place-making are concerned.

The formal distribution of inner space is well captured by the maps available on each floor (figure 2). Silent infrastructures like maps and fire extinguishers lie here and there by default, just like the boards that were originally set up to spread the word on local initiatives for integration, only to end up filled with corona-related orders and recommendations. Just like asylum seekers themselves, a cynical observer might add, thereby capturing the appearance but not the entire story.

Each housing unit, inside, is made of two bedrooms (two beds and one toilet each) with a kitchen in between. The latter can be accessed only through the former. Whenever caseworkers or guests wish to get into the more neutral and unadorned space of the kitchen, they need to first cross the personal space of the bedroom, which includes one table and a bookshelf, as well as one closet and locked nightstand per resident. In fact, the same room space can have different functions and host different activities, not necessarily matching the expected ones.[19] As important, the boundary between personal and not-so-personal space does not overlap with the material division between the rooms—itself a permeable one, for the drywalls in between are easily crossed by most sounds.[20] Such a boundary may be redefined on different scales,[21] including through the distinction between *online* and *offline* life.[22] Moreover, other intangible boundaries such as those of perceived deservingness and moral worth are emically reproduced regardless of people's distribution in space, within and across national, religious or ethno-racial categories of belonging (cf. 6.3).[23]

Each floor includes two areas of transit, that is, stairs and corridors. These are typically less clean, the farther away from the staff office. On the north side (*left* in figure 2), the corridor borders an external emergency staircase. This is invariably empty, unless someone tries to get in by avoiding staff control. Residents are unlikely to stay there, in a position where the new building nearby—half offices, half middle-class apartments—is visible in detail (figure 3). From that particular position, the ordinary dwelling world is twenty meters away, while staying remote in legal, social and racial distance. In fact, indifference toward the other side predominates. I may end up peeping from the window, in an undue extension of my ethnographic role, more than my interlocutors would ever do. On their side they are far more prone to hide themselves from the neighbor gaze than to look into their places.[24] There is rather a parallel, I sometimes think, between the shutters down in many of their bedrooms, and the hoods down on many of their faces when they hang out in town.[25]

On the opposite side (south), the corridor ends up in a small terrace overlooking the parking lot. You may stay there for a cigarette or a phone call or just for staring out in the company of your own thoughts. You're alone for a while, having some sense of what happens outside while staying inside. This is even easier on the fourth-floor terrace, which offers a large view of roads and railways, buildings in the foreground and hills in the background. Close by, only some clothes lying to get dry, broken fragments of plaster and weeds popping out between the floor tiles. Sometimes there are also material leftovers from past dwellers. Much of this survives cleaning routines out of its irrelevance (cf. 5.2). Four stories below, instead, the ground-floor offices embody a unique sense of order, surveillance and potentially ever-emerging tensions about papers, pocket money or disputes among residents. The caseworker office is the key organizational hub of the center but not necessarily the most crowded inner space. Whenever people want to stay on their own, they'll likely avoid it, possibly getting into their rooms after quickly crossing the entrance hall.

As far as a reception center can afford any privacy, that's only in the bedrooms. Being in a room feels like being in a qualitatively different space, with a sensorial atmosphere of its own. This is not always or necessarily desirable. A room is the

FIGURE 3. The building nearby, seen from the left end of a corridor, showing how the residents have some visual access to the windows of the apartments and offices of the building. Photo by author.

closest approximation to a ghetto for someone who struggles to cope with people and institutions outside. It feels deeply unhomely for those who are alone with their thoughts and with no psycho-social support. It may have little of the personal markers of appropriation of an ordinary domestic space (cf. 6.2 and 6.5). At the same time, as in most housing arrangements, a bedroom is the main space for rest and retreat, even if you have to share it with your roommate, constantly treading the fine line between mutual detachment and attention. It is also a privileged ethnographic site, whenever I am lucky and trusted enough to be invited in.

Each invitation marks a threshold of deeper acceptance. As an ordinary guest in several rooms, I have become familiar with my hosts' ways of ordering space and time, amid meager resources, little interest in that place, external checks and rules and the need to make a home nonetheless.[26] The simple accumulation of visits, one year after another, has paved the way to a deeper understanding of their routines and even of their tastes, values and collective (dis)alignments. Prior to that, it's time to reckon with the ambivalence that has already been emerging, even from a cursory description of the center. All its inhabitants are together as much as alone.

2.3   DWELLING IN A PLACE FOR ASYLUM SEEKERS: TOGETHER, ALONE

Is there really anything special in an asylum facility when it comes to dwelling? As far as social reproduction is concerned, the lived experience of the center is not radically different from most forms of shared living between strangers,[27] if not for the weight of external regulations on sociability and intimate life. One might call it a community, albeit an accidental one. Everyday life is made of young men going in and out, sleeping and eating, taking care of themselves and com-plaining about their predicament or going silently along with it. Everybody tends to repeat the same routines under the same roof, with limited mutual interac-tion beyond the conventional greeting. "They couldn't care less about the others," murmurs a caseworker, while struggling to convince someone who was quaran-tined after testing positive that this is a form of *collective* protection for the sake of all. Why should they care, though? Perhaps corona-related solidarity is a white or middle-class luxury, some would rejoin, as long as they believe in the existence of covid. What is crystal clear, regardless of the pandemic, is that every resident is together, alone—in a group without making any group.

Learning the proper way of staying in the center means adapting to a form of civil inattention[28] that is ordinary in public space but feels weird in a self-sufficient living environment. One year after another, I have spent hours sitting on the same bench or on the same bed with three or four more people, each of us bent on the respective smartphone, only to alternate this with a quick greeting when exiting or (re)entering the scene. In each session of this ritual co-production of nothing-ness[29] our bodies and devices are there, but something else is missing—no encoun-ter between physical and affective proximity. You share the same sensorial niche, while being emotionally, relationally and cognitively apart and alone. People may stay long sitting close and far away from one another, whatever the location: per-haps a bedroom or the benches on the southeast corner outside, which joins a tactical privilege (no doorman camera covers it fully) with a meteorological one (more shadow in summertime). Even so, civil inattention-in-proximity does not necessarily lead to protracted isolation. Any moment, some joke, chat, gossip or complaint may pop up and give back some relational depth. Nevertheless, this way of staying alone together is so deeply ingrained to be the normal pattern of sociability. It is also the most visible facet of ambivalence and of people's ways to navigate and (re)scale relevance across it.

Nobody will ever find himself alone for long in the center. Even if one wishes to stay alone on his bed and keep the rest at a reasonable distance, he may still have his roommate a couple of meters away. Copresence is intermittent, if the other has found a job or likes spending time outside. It is almost permanent, if he shares the same need. After all, someone must always be present in the building, including a staff member. "You'll find us here 24/7!" a doorman exclaims one Christmas Eve. This is an unintended blessing from the egocentric viewpoint of an ethnographer. It is more of a mixed condition for those who are living there. You have no clue of when you'll get papers and a job. You know very well that there will always be someone to control you, though. It is already a paradox that a place that often looks empty, as far as the common areas are concerned, is invariably half-full with people.

The young male dwellers are objectively together, under the same roof, in the same legal limbo. Several of them habitually spend their time together, based on language rather than ethnic or religious commonalities (Italian works out as the lingua franca only when no other options are available). They may do so for different purposes: prepare food, eat, clean up, pray, have fun, go out to the supermarket or just stay there. Moreover, they are mostly seen from the outside in terms of togetherness, as a monolithic, single and possibly undeserving category. At the same time, everybody is intimately alone, just like the feeble light of the smartphone screen when someone goes up or down the stairs at night. No need to push the light switch, if the micro and portable screen reverberates enough to show a couple of steps ahead. The rest can stay in the dark, out of the shifting field of relevance. It is for deeply individual and biographical reasons, albeit tied to family moral economies and shared by many more, that everybody started their migration pathways.[30] Two or three years, sometimes longer, have passed since—by "doing nothing," many would add. Everybody went through distinct and often untellable forms of violence on their own. Alone he is in charge of the moral expectations of a number of significant others.[31] It is on an individual basis that the merit of his application for protection, or at least of his efforts at integration while waiting, should be assessed. And as a single individual he is struggling to find a way out and ahead by navigating the legal, labor and housing markets. All along the navigation he will probably rely on co-ethnic networks, only to find out that these tend to reproduce homophily and add little instrumental resources. Even as a form of reciprocity, being together may be not enough. Nevertheless, protracted togetherness, while accidental in its genesis, is real in its consequences. The center is also a node of sociability as much as immobility. While being an apparently static social environment, it is actually a coming togetherness between individual trajectories that are not so equal or fungible as they may appear. Some lives, at some point, suddenly speed up and move elsewhere, while most others stay behind.[32]

Some residents, sooner or later, will become friends—people one can relatively trust and engage with in host-guest dynamics.[33] It may be for sharing meals and food expenses or just for passing time. Yet "I respect everybody; I'm a friend of nobody" is the message I have constantly received from Salim, one of the most sociable guys in the center. No reason to expect that real friends will ever be more than a tiny fraction. Most others are bound to be accidental presences, just as one's own. They do not fall in the narrow field of mutual responsibility and care—in short, of moral and affective relevance. Rather, they invite an idiom of mutual respect and civil indifference. All that has to do with one's private life, and even the final decision on one's application is unlikely to be shared around. Silence is the most reasonable way of coping with suffering from the past and with the mistrust and anxiety for the here-and-now. It is by being silent that you can retain some control over your own memories and intimate concerns.[34]

At the same time, most of my interlocutors do not mind sitting side by side, one hour after another, as long as their neighbors do not elicit hostility, suspicion or simply antipathy. "I prefer to stay with the guys here," Suka explains on the outside benches during the long months in which no job prospects, not to mention the documents, are in view. "If I'm alone I think a lot," he gloomily adds, his right hand pointing up to the head as if to say, "I'm losing balance," or "I'm getting dizzy." Likewise, there are nights in which Fatou cannot sleep and has headaches "thinking and thinking" up to seeing the past again—including the tragic family circumstances that pushed him to leave. "It happens when I'm alone—not when I'm here with the others," he says before locking himself up again in his shuttered bedroom. Perhaps this time he'll sleep.

Staying together while feeling alone is not just a way of killing time. It is rather a collective effort to exorcize the aftermath of individual and intimate suffering, by staying with someone who knows what that means. Sitting around together might appear a weird form of protection by (self-)segregation—in a way, a self-fulfilling prophecy of isolation. In fact, sharing for a while the same bed or bench feels more normal and safer than being racially (over)exposed in the public, mainstream space.[35] It is less distressing than being alone at a bus stop and seeing the bus driver who skips it or sitting in the bus and seeing the seats around get suddenly empty, as some recount.

In sum, the young men housed in the center feel alone and in many respects are alone. At the same time they need to be together, if mostly through shallow interactions that draw on a constrained and homogeneous social capital. Interestingly, though, some tend to avoid these forms of sociability altogether. "I'm alone!" sounds almost like a blessing whenever it comes from Larka, as he tells of the rare occasions in which there are no roommates to disturb and often irritate him, whenever they do not clean up. Being alone also means to keep some tactical distance from the increasing number of Pakistani newcomers. Relative to them, "I'm up," Larka once exclaims, his right hand moving upward. Unlike the other

Pakistanis, he respects everybody, makes no mess and cleans up—or so his narrative goes. On this practical terrain, regardless of any shared ethnicity or religion, he does claim dignity and, indeed, moral superiority (see 6.3). Just like Larka, everybody has their own ways of scaling the reach and relevance of their ties and obligations, with all the attendant dilemmas.

2.4   ETHNOGRAPHY IN THE CENTER

Taking an asylum center as a research field means investing in a variant of *domestic ethnography*.[36] This is highly interactive, participatory and sensuous fieldwork by definition.[37] It involves negotiating proper ways of being in the dwelling space of others, in their own terms and rhythms, following subtle boundaries of (un)accessibility and (in)visibility. It means playing out dynamics of guest versus host(s) rather than of researcher versus participant(s). While being essentially a matter of legitimate guesthood, domestic ethnography relies on creative options such as home tours, picture-based research, object elicitation and mapping, among others.[38] Such a way of doing ethnography has its own complexities and ambiguities. Yet, it holds a unique potential in illuminating people's day-to-day concerns through their emplaced practices. It can be applied to an asylum facility as much as to any housing infrastructure, keeping in mind the limited reach of its inner domesticity and the relational and ethical challenges associated with research therein.[39] This has not to do only with negotiating appropriate ways of staying in or meeting the ordinary requirements of data protection and anonymization.[40] There is an extra layer of complexity inherent in research with people with a past of suffering and violence, a present of social and legal liminality and a future of uncertainty.[41] This may result in their strong reluctance to share life stories for any purpose other than the asylum interview, a well-known setting in which personal narratives are tactically reshaped and renegotiated.[42] In practice, an ethnographic approach does not necessarily lead to overcoming these narrative boundaries. It makes them more permeable over time, though, out of mutual habituation and trust-building. It also sheds light on the ways in which each asylum seeker sets the boundary of the (in)visible, (un)tellable and (un)appropriable.

A fieldwork account

I have conducted participant observation in the center, after formal authorization from the relevant local authority and managers, from February 2018 to June 2022. I was first introduced as an academic researcher, as well as a volunteer of the association that was then running the center. Within a few months, I silently turned into an ordinary part of the white facescape for many, a meaningful interlocutor to spend time with and possibly a friend for others, with an implicit expectation of temporal continuity in our interactions. "See you next time," "When are you coming back?" or, more intriguingly, "Thanks!" were the farewell words of my interlocutors whenever I left. Along the way I have fully gone through the "unbearable slowness of ethnography"[43]—unsurprisingly so, for a place institutionally meant to contain people in waiting. This has resulted in a constant tension between productivist wishful thinking, pragmatic fine-tuning with apparently slow rhythms and empty spatialities and the search for a position suitable to participate in something "interesting," if only by happenstance. "Little by little" was as much a category for my interlocutors to comment on their condition as for me to make sense of fieldwork, with our large differences in demographics, position, biography and structure of opportunities.

In a time span of major changes, politics and health wise, the center as such has not changed much, aside from infrastructural deterioration. "Once it's over" with asylum seekers, a doorman with a past life as a bricklayer forecasts, "it will need massive work." Whether and when it will be over indeed is more difficult to predict. Meanwhile, the residents cannot but change out of turnover, after an average stay of a couple of years (with quite a few cases of four or five). This follows a rhythm that is both slow and not fully predictable, in an awkward combination between contrasting pressures: dissatisfaction with one's dwelling conditions and, almost as frequent, reluctance to leave and face the strong housing discrimination outside. Overall, I have encountered around four hundred male asylum seekers and engaged in meaningful and ongoing relations, beyond the minimal threshold of mutual greeting, with about one hundred, talking either in English or in Italian. Most of them were in their early twenties and had been in Italy for one or two years before getting there. They were typically at a stage of appeal after an initial denial of their applications. Their countries of origin were mainly Nigeria, the Gambia, Ghana, Senegal, Mali, Guinea, Guinea-Bissau, Côte d'Ivoire, Togo and Cameroon, although a few of my key interlocutors were also from Pakistan. Witness to this are the national flags that some native volunteers painted one summer on the garbage bins close to the entrance (figure 4). Ironically, this intended act of beautification reproduces, to my eyes, an idiom of disposal—the same whereby a center is expected to host humanity in excess and, more concretely, some passersby dump their garbage into the parking lot, occasionally to be seen by increasingly angry doormen (cf. 1.5).

Over half of the residents would identify themselves as Muslims and the rest as Christians. Although none of them would ever be asked about this, religious alignments can easily be inferred from their demeanors, narratives and practices. Among their institutional counterparts, the dozen different doormen I have met over time were male workers, of both native and immigrant backgrounds, in their late fifties. They had typically been assigned there as a part of placement schemes for the long-term unemployed. There was more of a gender balance, instead, among the thirty or so caseworkers who have been employed over the years under different service providers. Interestingly, although incidentally, all those appointed as managers were women, typically exerting some more influence than their male

FIGURE 4. A garbage bin, no longer in use, decorated by some volunteers with African national flags, for "beautification." Photo by author.

coworkers. This was not necessarily enough to overcome the passive resistance of a number of residents to institutional rules, rarely bursting into open contestation.

On my side it would have been impossible to do this kind of fieldwork—being routinely accepted in the center and in many bedrooms—if I had not been a male researcher. Our shared gender identity created a common ground for people to vent out frustration for their passive and pointless domesticity. As an older man with an apparently decent breadwinner status, I was expected to understand what this means. By the same token, I was expected to be sensitive to the irritation of some for the prohibition to host women or for having to obey the orders of a female caseworker, or at least pretend to. In some moments of confidentiality, I felt addressed as someone who could well understand the daydreaming about engaging "soon" with a female partner, whatever her racial background, for those who had not one at present. As a husband and a father of three, I was supposed to make sense of the future family life project that most would articulate—a wife and "one, maybe two" children to be maintained by their hard work. All this being said, most people were as reserved on their sentimental lives as on their past biographies. Being private is a form of self-protection but also a demonstration of well-performed masculinity, one of the few available in a place that is hyper-feminized in terms of stereotyped gender prerogatives and hyper-masculinized in terms of effective composition. No more than one or two women would ever be present at once. Not much scope to play any stereotypically masculine role, if not, sometimes, by resisting the staff orders or rules. And so much boredom, I suspect, in having so many men around—and so little to do anyway.[44]

Leaving masculinity aside, I was as distant from my interlocutors in age as in class, legal status and ethno-racial background. None of this, I believe, has made a major difference to our rapport. Interestingly, and consistent with their constant labor to carve out an adult male identity, I was never asked for any favor that would go beyond the possibility of returning it at some point. No loan requests, for instance. And no reason to display a victimized attitude with me, unlike what some tried to do with the staff, in a guise that conflated suffering, frustration and a degree of creative, sometimes successful, manipulation. The perceived distance between us, however, was interestingly stronger when it would come to race. As a white man "you cannot understand racism," that is, "how they treat us Black," Sani and Fatou would periodically exclaim. Still, this almost ontological divide has not prevented them from sharing meaningful pieces of their stories or me from doing my best to make sense of them.

As already mentioned, within the time window of my study (2018–22), the asylum-hosting system in Italy has been significantly curtailed, after the rather improvised expansion that had followed the 2015 "refugee crisis."[45] The center management has been outsourced to three different providers under ever-worsening terms. This has resulted in decreasing relational support and counseling work, not to mention outreach with the mainstream educational, work and housing systems. Not by coincidence, the enforced deterioration of work standards has been paralleled with a changing composition of the staff, caseworkers being increasingly older and foreign-born rather than native, and with less formal education. In short, the ways of managing this particular house for refugees have mirrored broader trends in asylum policies in Italy. While the shift speaks the symbolic language of exclusionary domopolitics,[46] it has had all too real consequences—fewer opportunities for language learning, schooling, vocational training and psychological support.[47] On top of that, the advent of covid has undermined interaction with the local community and further affected labor-market participation.

Thanks to this partially serendipitous chain of events, I have done fieldwork across different organizational, political and even historical seasons—before, during and after the corona emergency. As it happened, once allowed in, I just kept attending the center by habituation, almost by inertia, with the benign acceptance of the service provider that took over (and my obvious gratitude to them, as much as to their predecessors). It is by being stubbornly and sometimes uselessly in place that an ethnographer legitimizes oneself. No particular capacities on my side or expectations about me, other than what I used to do—chatting and getting along with anybody who wouldn't mind doing so. Whatever my reasons for being there (which few seemed to be interested in) and as long as I complied with the routines of mutual respect, my hanging around was not problematic. It was actually part of the everyday ways of apparently doing nothing[48]—although a part marked by privilege and free choice rather than by lack of alternatives, as for my interlocutors.

This legitimacy-out-of-irrelevance has turned into an ethnographic asset. One month after another I became an ordinary visitor,[49] in a regime of tacit and "calibrated" reciprocity.[50] After a while it would be very clear what it was appropriate to talk about, what was a legitimate target of joking, what would require silence.[51] Only in a few cases, I realized, being in a bedroom revealed less an act of hospitality than a substantive indifference. My own presence, then, seemed utterly irrelevant as the formal occupant was hardly interested in anything other than his temporary micro-space—the physical one of his bed, the sensorial one of his ear phones, the virtual and affective one of his relationships with people elsewhere. In any case, once I was sitting on the chair or bed of someone who had invited me there, staying was not an issue. Crossing the doorstep—the ways, rationale and mandate to do so—was more of a tacit negotiation, open to different outcomes.

Dilemmas and prospects of reciprocity

For sure, this way of doing fieldwork rests on major power asymmetries. These would generally remain implicit, in the bubble of parallel normality around the center, only to burst it now and then, amid casual conversation on "how things are" or, as people would invariably ask me, "how's the family?" "I can't complain" was sometimes my answer, at least until Suka, one day, broke out, "*You* cannot complain! You have everything. . . . *We* can complain"—although, he would eventually add, recovering a timid smile, "We have God." Furthermore, I could afford to visit people in "their" place and not the other way round. This, however, worked only as a matter of spontaneous and hard-to-plan invitations. Even my close interlocutors were more or less inclined to host me from one day to the next. Prayers were a typical portion of timespace that some didn't mind sharing with me, while others would rather spend it on their own. Their doors would open or stay closed, and my fieldwork would oscillate between semi-private and common regions accordingly. Moreover, there were always people who had no reason, interest or trust to go beyond a quick greeting at best. Their dwelling spaces remained inaccessible to me. In many instances, furthermore, the threshold of privacy or intimacy had little to do with the boundaries of a room or a bed. As I illustrate in the next chapters, it can be much more of an interior, psychological, even spiritual matter. It is made visible and tangible only through the smartphone, as long as it is exteriorized at all.

All this being said, some field dilemmas require further discussion. The first involves extractivism. I was there, in a position to do ethnography, thanks to *their* presence. Put differently, I have been directly benefiting from the refugee industry, just like anybody else involved in the mobility, settlement, care and control of forced migrants. Each single visit was a source of ethnographic capital—chats, remarks, observation and fieldnotes—for me. Spending some time together, instead, was a rather irrelevant parenthesis in their everyday life routines. All interactions in and around the center fed into a long-term accumulation of original knowledge for me. They had little apparent added value for the residents, though. It was as if I were getting in like an empty bag, to be filled each time with new information, emotions and memories. The underlying rationale, however, did not fit with their ordinary expectations and ways of sense-making about white people around. More fundamentally, whenever our conversation happened to go in depth, what was most revealing for me could overlap with what was most painful for them, years afterward. Silence would then become an alternative form of communication—and a demonstration of empathy and respect, on my side.[52] Even so, I contend, familiarity and habituation have done their job over time. My presence has become frequent and ordinary enough to require no further justification, often opening up to spontaneous conviviality, including food or drinks together. Each of my intermittent hosts has been doing a dual gift to me—the explicit one of a cup of tea, a glass of water or any available variant of African food and the implicit one of shared time and chats.

How does reciprocity operate under these circumstances? There is certainly more to it than a respectful and non-judgmental attitude with people—the habit of staying with them without having necessarily much to do, in a house that no other white or native person would attend aside from the paid staff. It was rather a matter of practicalities ranging from help in translating documents or finding out welfare- or job-related contacts, to writing letters of recommendation, driving people around, or teaching them to drive. Nothing of this can be meaningfully formalized at a principled level, and yet it has effectively worked as our ordinary texture of reciprocity. As important, nothing of this could affect either my irrelevance for the most pressing concerns of the residents or their availability to me. I was no caseworker, lawyer or civil servant. I had no power over the place and over them—as a source of help, of control, or even a potential threat, whenever people would lose their entitlement to free hospitality.

At the end of the day, the main moral currency of lived, engaged and asymmetric reciprocity lies precisely in this book—a public statement about stories that matter in themselves and elucidate the suffering, dilemmas and prospects of displacement and asylum. Ethnographic writing is irremediably an objectification of a lived experience, or at least an abstraction from personal encounters to impersonal (hopefully, interpersonal) meanings and understandings. It may not do full justice to the thickness and complexity of fieldwork encounters. It produces its own "ghosts," while trying to do justice to refugee "voices."[53] Nonetheless, as long as the book helps make sense of people's lives and struggles and illuminates questions that cut across many temporary ways of dwelling, this may already justify the ethnographic intrusion and reward the author's effort.

I have written *Undoing Nothing* ex post, drawing on ethnographic material accumulated almost in real time.[54] Throughout, I use the present tense rather than the past as an endeavor to do justice to the lived experience of my interlocutors. This is certainly not meant to "freeze" or "de-temporalize" them in "any ethnographic present."[55] Rather, it aims to capture the unfolding of everyday life as over-concentrated on the "present tense,"[56] as opposed to any future horizon or looming past memory. The use of a suspended present tense is meant to portray and mirror the suspended temporality of the center, even while things obviously happen and change, with a lesser rhythm and direction than outside. In this sense life therein is in resonance with many other settings of care and control for asylum seekers, across migration corridors and pathways. As important, the center is no relic from the past. As I'm writing these notes, years later, it is still fundamentally reproducing, with different guests, the organizational and relational patterns I discuss in the next chapters. This can hopefully inspire further comparative research from within refugee facilities across Western countries—and beyond.

3

______

Inside, Outside

Fatou is in a weird position, as he often muses when we are together in his bedroom. He's unwell, and he's well. "Thank God, I have a bed. I can eat. I don't pay rent. . . . I'm lucky," compared with those who have nothing of this, let alone those who died on the way or are still in Libya with "the Arabs beating them all the time." Most enigmatically, "I'm no better than them." There is a sense of being both in and out across Fatou's lived paradox. While he can benefit from basic, if temporary, protection, his self-position on a hierarchy of moral worth and merit is bound to remain uncertain. Moreover, he is still visibly *out* in relation to the achievement of personal autonomy as a marker of male adulthood. No papers, no autonomous housing, no jobs, unless some calls for a day job now and then. All these in-out interplays are negotiated within the center, as a separate space with its own inner layers.

An asylum facility is set apart from the mainstream by definition.[1] As or more than ordinary housing, it is meant to mark the boundary between inside and out-side, although this is to protect the larger public space from its residents rather than vice versa (cf. 7.2). The young men housed there should not be overly vis-ible or perceived as a disturbance for the ordinary state of things outside. From either side, the built environment and the everyday rules and routines produce a tangible divide. It always feels weird when someone, including a native volunteer or supporter, lingers at the door. Perhaps they're making a phone call, chatting with someone, or waiting for somebody else. "Are you coming in or going out?" the doorman asks. Any unexpected occupation of a space of transition needs to be promptly addressed. It is a threat for the binary cognitive scheme, in versus out, underpinning institutional hospitality for asylum seekers.

A number of boundaries between inside and outside also emerge within the center. Its grayish and darkish corridors make for a liminal space that does not communicate with either the interior or the external world. Each bedroom in turn is like a separate region with its inner life that is hardly imaginable and probably even less relevant from the outside. Once people get in and lock the door, they are *in* and all the rest is out, for the time being, just as the center in relation to the city. Farther down in the bedrooms, each resident negotiates the same claim for separation through the day-to-day routines and material cultures around his body space.

All this notwithstanding, residents' lived experience is much too complex for a neat distinction between inside and outside. It rather unfolds within an ambivalent coexistence of spatial, symbolic and imaginative opposites. Each young male migrant struggles to position himself somewhere between inside and outside on multiple scales, ranging from entire continents (with the opportunities, imaginaries and inequalities associated with them) "down" to countries, cities, buildings, inner spaces and ultimately his own body. On each scale, people struggle to (dis)align themselves along hierarchies of moral, emotional and social value.

3.1   IN SPACE AND IMAGINARIES

"It's like I've been in Africa for two years," an Italian caseworker once tells me, looking back at her professional life in the center. Whether it does feel like Africa, unless for the inner circulation of African bodies and languages, is a question on which most residents might disagree. For sure, certain portions of timespace have more of an evocative atmosphere, such as when some gather to share a meal around one plate, "the way we do in Africa," as Fatou puts it. In fact, this form of thick conviviality is as ephemeral as the time needed to eat up the little food available. Other than that, there is little way to recreate Africa or to make sense of it by staying here. As little, some might add, as of their own past stories. As little, the silent fear goes, as young male Africans themselves might eventually be able to do after spending years "doing nothing." In any case, all that has to do with Africa is hardly visible to the white staff. It is present under the ambivalent guise of intimate emotions, memories and concerns, for their asylum-seeker counterpart (cf. 5.5).

The young men that inhabit the center with their Black or Brown bodies are simultaneously in and out of a social and symbolic space one might call modernity, for lack of a better notion.[2] They are physically situated in the rich, Western, modern world, while having scant resources to access it and only a temporary entitlement to dwell in it. At the same time, they have moral reasons and pressures to be obliged and stay connected to people in their countries of origin, whatever the circumstances that pushed them out.[3] Somewhere between these two terms of reference, each with its own power of attraction and repulsion, they negotiate their position and struggle to scale relevance through everyday life routines.

On one hand, being in Europe, albeit precariously, potentially opens much more than getting papers or a job. Questions of adulthood, the good life, consumption and self-fulfillment all have their roots in the same moral belief—things here are better or, if they are not, they will be. One afternoon like many others, days before the asylum hearing of Paul, I wish him good luck. "You should tell good luck to those in Africa—not to us," he replies. Here, whatever happens, he's in the land where life can change.[4] In Africa, adds Paul, echoing the view of all his friends, "no way," if only because there is no money, power or "connection," hence no prospect for improvement.[5]

On the other hand, physical distance from the countries of origin, in theory with no return unless from deportation, does not affect their moral and economic significance. Africa is a source of needs and claims, as much as an identity and lifestyle mold for all that comes next. "People in Africa think that once you are in Europe, you are okay," Gorko reminds me while he's counting the days left to the next pocket-money distribution. Being here is ontologically supposed to make a difference to one's position but not to one's obligations. You made it; you must have money; you must send it back. Your social and legal marginalization and your own sense of precarity are minor concerns. "I wouldn't have any problem finding a wife back there," Woikat reflects another day, "because they think we're full of money." And, he incidentally adds, it would probably work much better than with a European woman. Whatever the case, this novel status comes with higher expectations and responsibilities. "Most people must send money all the time," concludes Gorko. "It's the African culture, you know? If someone has, he or she must give to the others." *He or she* is a subtlety that does as much as his dress code—he often wears a shirt and jacket—and the new suitcases well ordered in his room, in distinguishing him from most co-residents, with their more informal dressing, jargon and record in formal education.

Whether regarding money, success or anything else, the reference to Africa as a parallel, remote and morally predominant world is almost invariably there. The texture of everyday life is woven with a thread of constant comparison between things on either side: the past deeply socialized frame of reference *there*, which needs to be denaturalized and questioned, and the present one *here*, with its stubborn demand for re-socialization. Africa and Europe, as essentialized constructions and separate worlds, make for one macro and imaginative scale within which my young male interlocutors struggle to navigate their way forward. In doing so they are simultaneously in and out of either term of reference, in different respects.

"No!" Fatou gently replies whenever I volunteer to help him clean up. In Africa a young person should never let someone older work in his place: "it's not normal." What is normal on either side, and how people negotiate the distance in between, opens a potentially endless field of conversation. Africa and Europe have "very different cultures," Fatou repeats. In Africa "it's not normal to look at someone in the face" while you talk together. You may quickly cross their gaze at most. "In Europe it's normal to look into the eyes—sometimes I do, sometimes I don't," he adds, smiling again, his gaze down to the ground. In Africa "men have power"—they do what they want and work out of the home, whereas women do everything at home. In Europe "women have power!" Like in a love story: "if a woman says it's over, it's over." In fact, he once points out, "the Koran says that women can do the same things as men." Women may go out to work. Men may stay in and help clean, which, ironically, is just what the center male residents should do. In Europe, Fatou ineffably adds, if the woman cooks, the man cleans. If the man cleans, the woman cooks.

In Africa "you always greet your neighbors—just like we do here," at least among Black people.[6] "There" people greet and help you even if they don't know you. If you want to visit someone's place, "just go." No need for appointments, something Europeans "can't understand." One greeting already makes a connection, Fatou believes. "We're united among us . . . and we like to mix up and do things together." In practice, the distance between here and there is reproduced through the line of color—somewhere between distinction and discrimination—between *you* and *us*, white and Black. "The white do not trust. . . . They need to know you first." In Africa people would always host you, says Fatou in an unusually assertive tone. Here, he shakes his head—"no way." In the Gambia, where he grew up, "they think the white" (i.e., tourists from northern Europe) are all good and rich. And then you come here. And even after that, they keep thinking you're rich. Otherwise, "why stay here?"

In Africa, adds Olusola whenever he feels like being my informal teacher, "there is no people like you" who don't believe in God, or so they claim. Back there "you have a different mindset—less rules and respect, less stress, more fun." Here "you have no time for nothing." There you always have the time you need. Leaving people aside, what he's missing from the homeland is "a life of joy," one in which, Olusola says, people have "the spiritual power. One can use it for you, or against you. It's serious, you know?" Once again, it seems as if white people can't make sense of it unless they have visited Africa. Once again, Black and white are parallel and hardly communicating worlds, just like the center and the city outside. It is from the threshold of Olusola's bathroom that we are making them communicate right now, while he's handwashing a T-shirt. Washing clothes is as good as any other moment for Olusola to chat, when he's in a good mood, including to warn against the center's washing machine—"it crumples your stuff," you shouldn't trust it. After a few years away, he concludes, the Africans seem to lose that power and "become like the white." Not a desirable development, judging from his tone.

What strikes him the most, and resonates in many other narratives, is however another thing: in Europe you cannot see if one is rich or poor. Even important people are dressed and move around like anybody else. In Africa, instead, the rich live apart and are afraid of the rest. On top of that, "politics is corrupted. . . . They take up the money and send it here, whereas we, from Europe, send it there!" Even

FIGURE 5. Africa, Europe and the sea in between: a detail in a picture drawn by Woikat to depict an ordinary African seaside scene at sunset. Artwork by Woikat. Photo by author.

worse in Nigeria. All of a sudden Olusola jumps down on the floor and twists his body in an awkward position, as if someone were torturing him. "This is how they treat you if you say certain things." Or rather, "this is how they treat us Black—*you*, the white, they'll always treat you well." Here, he concludes, "they protect you. In my country . . . no way." In a nutshell, as Olusola sees it, social hierarchy rests on different principles in Europe as opposed to Africa—more racism, less class-based interaction. Money counts less, or so it might appear, but race counts more. "You can't understand," Olusola and his friends repeat, what it means to be treated in a racist way—something they apparently had no clue of before leaving.

There is such a distance between Europe and Africa in the narratives of Olusola, Fatou, and the others. While they successfully navigated it in space, much of the legal, economic and socio-cultural distance is still ahead of them. Yet, *here* and *there* are invariably, if asymmetrically, co-present. They stare at each other and mutually compete in the lives that are lived and told in the center. No full separation ever emerges in the pictures Woikat, a young Senegalese man, likes drawing for himself and for all those who ask for one. Closer to the viewer lies an African natural environment made of Black people, wild animals and lush vegetation, all of them apparently at peace with one another. In the middle is the sea, with a small fishing boat. Beyond in the background is a land with little details, decorations or shade (figure 5). "That's Europe," he points out smiling. While that part of the picture seems bound to stay blurred, what is clear is that it lies there, within one and the same horizon.

3.2   IN A COUNTRY OF EUROPE

The young men in the center are in and out, likewise, in relation to the country in which they are currently settled. This holds in a legal sense, for their temporary right to stay is connected to the asylum procedure and conditional on its output. It is also true in a more existential sense, as long as they are mostly jobless, economically dependent, and single. There is both an infrastructural side and a lived dimension to their ambivalent positioning.

What does Italy mean?

Italy, in the subtexts of my interlocutors, does not necessarily stand out in comparison with other European countries. They have reached so far and might move farther or get settled for the years to come, depending on circumstances that are out of their control. This does not mean that they do not feel somehow integrated in Italy. After two or three years spent there, and despite all frustration, they learned the language, if unequally so. They did make (again, unequal) efforts in schooling and vocational training or even in getting a job. Unsurprisingly, they'd be reluctant to start from scratch elsewhere. Some highlight, and appreciate, the relative permeability of its legal boundaries, while associating with the country the same fuzzy sense of Europe as one cultural zone they'd probably attach to any location north of it. That said, Italy, in their narratives, first comes as a collective category for those that "saved our lives" after the Mediterranean crossing, only to leave migrants in protracted waiting at a later stage. "I'LL NEVER FORGET THAT DAY" reads the title of another of Woikat's large pictures in the kitchen. A ship and an overcrowded boat are coming close to each other. A rescue team is about to carry over a number of Black people, "women and children first," he explains after saying that he really needed to portray them. Once on a safer ship, and then on the mainland, one is physically in. And, at least at the outset, he has all the reasons to feel grateful. Working with the recently arrived was "the best thing," says a caseworker who seems to miss his previous experience in emergency reception—the first step after newcomers' dispersal across Italy. People had just escaped from Libya, where "they whipped them day and night." They said thanks for all that you gave them. No complaints. However, "after a while they start telling you: Don't want this sweater, it's not branded!" he adds, mimicking a disgusted look. It does not take long for asylum seekers to become "ungrateful."[7] *Afterward*, perhaps as a matter of months, means raised expectations. Afterward, as a matter of years, means rising disorientation.

Even in hindsight, Woikat is not alone in saying "thanks to Italy" as much as "to God" for rescue at the end of his life-or-death journey. Making it to Italy was like being born again, recounts Olusola in his occasionally poetic and consistently metaphorical mood. *Born again*[8] relative to the risk of losing one's life at sea but also to the social death perceived in Africa.[9] Covid did not hit the continent so much, Gorko tells me one afternoon as we are chatting by the entrance, our face masks oscillating up and down. His tone is of paramount detachment, as always when we talk about Africa. The point is that "there is no control. . . . You are free to move around." However, he soon adds, "the state does nothing for you." "What if someone is in need—no places like . . . this one?" I ask, looking back at the building. Gorko grins and shakes his head quietly. So, what if you're poor? "You die poor—or you leave for Europe." People cope "by the grace of God," he adds staring fixed ahead, a self-made cigarette butt in his hand.

Against this backdrop, the construction of Italy as a savior sits uneasily with the years of waiting that have come since. There is an emotional and moral tension but also a fundamental struggle to make sense of this. Seen from the rooms and corridors of the center, Italy is an assemblage of faceless, hard-to-decipher institutions that seem to hold the power to decide on one's legitimate future. The institutional differentiation and division of labor between asylum commissions, ordinary courts and local authorities in charge of reception, and NGOs that run asylum facilities are all too complex and unnecessary. What is weirdly clear is that the same state that first rescued you is now leaving you in undetermined waiting. Rather than exerting discipline, it confines you to irrelevance. "If they're people that care about you, they don't do this—no news, as if you're deaf." So repeats Kambanoo while he is slicing up onions for dinner, before asking about my family—no point to say more of himself. Even less, I realize, to add what I immediately add: "There are so many people around like that, no?" "I think for myself, not for others," Kambanoo bluntly replies. "I know it's like that for me." Why should he care about the problem being also of many others—and ultimately about the others? Whatever the answer, the moral geography of asylum reception does not seem to make much sense. As long as people retain a sense of gratitude or moral obligation, this can hardly be toward the center as such—having spoken of the benefit of free accommodation, opposed to an external world where you've got nothing for free, as the past residents point out.

"Italy is crazy, crazy, crazy," Suka periodically blurts out during the long weeks in which he has no job options at hand, not to mention papers, and tends to spend his days moving up and down—bedroom to courtyard and back. While his frustration is crystal clear, the meaning of "Italy" is not. Is he referring to public authorities, people, the country as such, or his own condition? One afternoon I retort about the Gambia. Isn't it crazy too? Generally speaking, the judgments of my interlocutors on African politics are even harsher. There's a difference though, Suka explains. There, "when you want to do something, you do it." You're free in your day-to-day business, as long as the structural conditions allow. Here, "forget it." You do want to work in Italy—that's why you came, albeit you wouldn't be supposed to state it loud. However, you cannot. It is "life without work" that is "crazy," he gloomily concludes. "Here you only send CV, CV, CV . . . and no work." In the meantime he's waiting for the decision on his appeal, but he's unlikely to mention that. All that has to do with legal arrangements, hence with long-term residence perspectives, is less salient and often appears rather accidental.[10] Work, instead, is what dignifies you—as much as, in a longer perspective, marriage and children—that is, a "normal" family life. For now, whether in Italy or wherever, for "you never know" where you'll end up, one thing is beyond doubt: "You can't live with no work," Suka repeats, as he pushes down the visor of his cap and moves back in. You cannot live as he's living right now. Meanwhile, no trace of the friend he was supposed to meet up in the courtyard. *"Dai, prendilo!"* (Come on, get it!), he exclaims on the phone—no reply. Enough with that—back to the rap music he was listening to before.

"I'm cold now. I'll go back in," he says at last, as usual ending our conversation with some explanation of what he'll do next. It looks like a form of politeness, a common and tacit norm among my West African interlocutors, more than a way of accounting for what he's about to do.[11] In any case, no doubt Suka must be cold. He's hanging around in mid-November in his "bedroom suit"—shorts, soccer-team shirt, flip-flops, cap. And the mobile, of course. And a pissed-off look that commutes between the smartphone screen and the void around. "Italy is crazy," Suka mumbles again on the staircase. In fact, as long as he dwells in the center and gets his allowance, he's *in*. He can move around, dressed any way he likes. When it's summertime, it's not uncommon to see people straddling the corridors half-naked, as in one's domestic space. "I'm home!" Omokunrin playfully replies to a staff member who reproaches him for doing so year-round. And it is in the courtyard that Omokunrin, once he has finally bought his much-dreamed-about secondhand car, can afford to move it around a bit. No driving on the main street, right beyond the fence, as long as his license is suspended.

You are in (only) if you have a job

Both Suka and Omokunrin, in a sense, are home. Are they also *really* in Italy, besides their bodily presence? Feeling effectively in the country depends primarily on having a job, as opposed to "staying home." "Sleeping all the time is no good," people usually say. Less frequently, somebody could comment on one of the center's public secrets: if you get only a "little job," a few hours per week, you may gain even less than staying here to wait for the pocket money. So, why bother? If you get a relatively decent job, instead, you'd better get paid under the table, lest you lose resident eligibility due to "excessive" income. Even so, no alternative to a very badly paid job for, as Sani once reminds me, "my father didn't leave me any job."

As long as there is no job, however, one could do so much with his free time, a well-intentioned outsider might think.[12] For one thing, why not do volunteering? This is precisely what caseworkers used to propose to every newcomer. Yet, as

FIGURE 6. A handwritten scribble, "ALWAYS VOLUNTEER—ENOUGH OF IT," in basic Italian, on a blackboard frame. The phrase suggests a pervasive sense of frustration with all those volunteering activities that do not end up as real jobs. Photo by author.

time goes by, even those who enthusiastically joined the invitation are increasingly reluctant to do so. "It's good for you, and for your CV," the staff used to say. To an external observer, this probably sounds reasonable. Not to the young men themselves, unless it does turn into a job. "ALWAYS VOLUNTEER—ENOUGH OF IT" someone wrote on the wooden frame of a blackboard in the TV room (figure 6). It is in (basic) Italian, for the staff and everybody else to read it. Indeed, anybody would easily notice it, if they found it of any relevance. As it happens, they do not. The writing has survived three years, as irrelevant as the blackboard and, for that matter, the TV room. One day the frame fell down and ended up in a garbage bin, along with the message on it.

As an ambiguous condition whereby you do something for someone else without being paid back, volunteering or even internships appear hardly sustainable over time, unless they make for real jobs. The question seems straightforward: working or not means being in or out. "When there's work it's okay—when there is no work, it's not," says Larka on our first casual encounter, which ends up with a shared plate of rice with pepper chicken after his gentle invitation. Work has irremediably popped up at the end of a few chats on the windowsill of his ground-floor room. Work or, more often, lack thereof. Either a thing is there, or it is not. In the latter case, you can still expect it will be at some point, whether this means just waiting, such as in the asylum process, or doing one's best to get it, as everybody claims they're doing when it comes to work.

"No job, no papers," is however a most common statement in everyday interactions. Again, work is the source of security and self protection, far more than legal status. The latter sounds like a procedural issue—a matter of unreasonably long paperwork—rather than a terrain of rights, institutional recognition or membership. Work, instead, is as much a necessity as a dignified and morally appropriate state of things, unlike the passive condition of welfare recipients or volunteers. Work means being willing to accept almost any paid task for, as Gorko puts it, "I'm not at home. I'm not in my country. I must adapt." We all need a job to live, right? "Italians or immigrants, it's the same," he concludes, throwing his cigarette butt over the hedge. "The same" is less a claim for equality than for normality, I realize. And also for relevance: *having* a job is what matters, regardless of the terms of it. Before the integration budgetary cuts in 2019, some basic vocational training was part and parcel of a caseworker toolkit. Don't get any sort of job, try and focus, take your time! Then, with fewer caseworkers and more corona-produced unemployed, the point is getting a job whatever. It always has been, probably, out of the caseworkers' wishful thinking.

In short, work is the most visible and obvious embodiment of an accomplished masculinity. "You must have a job if you want to be somebody in this country," exclaims Chinedu one fall afternoon, in the middle of an informal drinking session in the back courtyard. No way to make progress otherwise, whatever "being somebody" means.[13] However, he instantly shifts from the volitional to the fatalistic: "I wish myself I can find a job . . . but it's not in my power. Only God knows. I pray to God."

It is for the lack of a job and out of weariness for waiting that some occasionally leave on their own. No notice, just the hope of making it elsewhere in Europe.[14] Unless for that, Olusola rhetorically wonders, "Why move away? People don't want problems, no?" If one could work and earn his own money, that would be enough. One summer afternoon, in the middle of a soccer match we are watching together, Ibrahim tells me that his court appeal will take place in two years. "What can I do meanwhile?" As it seems, just wait. "And if I don't have a job, I think too much. It hurts." A few weeks later he will leave and try somewhere else, north. For the bulk of my interlocutors, however, one has already traveled enough. "Three years—and nothing yet," as Cheikh wraps it up with a sigh, does not generally mean that one would be willing to start again from scratch. Time to get settled, if only there is a chance (cf. 4.4).

There is little surprise in seeing work as the key lever for achieving migration-related aspirations. However, contrary to the master narrative in the center, a job need not be enough to move beyond one's ambivalent position. For now, people *are* in a country, while feeling emotionally and morally out of it and somewhere in between, juridically speaking. Even once they hopefully get a job and a stay permit, being *in* will also have to do with softer language, relational and navigational skills—the pragmatic abilities one needs to build a "good," or even only a "normal" (family) life. Much of this informal capital can only be accrued outside, and yet it critically depends on having a place to start from. The center itself, as embodiment of a basic welfare scheme, elicits a sense of being simultaneously inside and outside.

3.3 IN A HOUSE OF PROTECTION, SURVEILLANCE, AND SEPARATION

Rather than living in Italy tout court, my interlocutors are living in one particular asylum facility. Most of them have little familiarity with the rest of the country. Rarely do they leave the town where they ended up after state-led dispersal. In practice the center is the main stage on which they position themselves on multiple scales, for the time being.

In versus out

As a separate place with its own rules of access, the center is meant to discipline and watch over asylum seekers, as much as protect them. Both the institutionalization of surveillance and its entanglement with protection are general patterns in state-driven housing for refugees.[15] In this case, the low fences and hedges around the courtyard mark a clear separation from the outside and facilitate an atmosphere of mutual irrelevance. It is uncommon and surreal for the two parallel worlds to communicate across the fence, within the same sensorial field—one that, seen from the upper floors, includes transient people, cars and even trains in incessant mobility, unlike the residents. One summer afternoon, while Cheikh is muttering about the two-hour-per-day job he has found so far, two foreign tourists are entering a brand-new rented car on the other side, five meters away. Enough of a distance to make for a separate world—the same I'm embodying whenever I'm sitting along with him. Meanwhile, Cheikh is mildly complaining, as he could have done months before. In the worst scenario, he'll keep doing so up to the end of his stay here—so close to the affluent world in geography, so far away in biography. On another ordinary afternoon, a group of five is sitting on a bench under the tree shadow and a car stops nearby, behind the gas station. A man seems to notice them, unlike most passersby, only to ask if they know where the station attendant is. Khame, precariously sitting on a bicycle with his shorts, tank top and flip-flops, is the closest. He briefly replies, "No—we don't know nothing of this." Indeed, people in the center know little about their neighbors. They would see no reason to know more, just like the former do with them. A few more seconds and the man has moved farther on his way, unlike Khame and the others.

While the city around them is generic, full of markers and brands, and mostly white, the center is specific, anonymous and almost only Black or Brown. This is the place for young male asylum seekers. It is the occasional white visitors, instead, who need to justify their presence. The place has its own address, which is often used in lieu of its formal name.[16] The residents' identities, however, are invisible from the outside. As much as the material environment protects the social reproduction of their bodies, the lack of external visibility is supposed to protect their privacy. In practice, the center is irrelevant enough to mainstream society for identity protection to be no issue. On the inner side, people obviously know one another's names. So do regular visitors like me. In covid times, even the names of those who tested positive and are quarantined are a public secret, for rumors circulate on their own. For sure, all that has to do with asylum applications and the past life is confidential indeed. However, one's declared identity is no secret, as long as someone is interested in it at all. Irrelevance matters, and wins, over privacy.

Better in or out?

As much as it protects insiders, the center sets them apart from any other needy migrant that does not meet eligibility criteria. Relative to their predicament, the sense of emptiness and unfreedom inside feels like an unintended blessing. There is so much freedom, and so much lack of protection, outside. Within the parallel normality of asylum reception, the young male residents are not blatantly poor. Each of them is formally in the same position as everybody else, although the unequal distribution of technological goods in the rooms is telling of the difference between the employed and the jobless. The real poor are in Africa, as people repeat. And the real poor are outside, including co-nationals who lost the right to protection, while retaining some expectation of reciprocity. Some do pop up now and then, possibly screaming *Bro!* and hoping that someone may come out with a dish in their hands. No way for them to be formally allowed in, unless in exceptional circumstances, under staff discretion. It is of his own goodwill that a caseworker, one December afternoon, welcomes in for a while a Somali young man who had received a temporary status in Italy and then applied again in Germany, only to be sent back to the place where it all began ten years before. Time has made some difference to his fluency in Italian, but no apparent progress in other respects. In turn, the short time of a coffee together in the hall is as moving as it is weird. "Call me next Sunday. You can come to my place for lunch," the caseworker says. As long as he wishes to help, he can only do so in his private capacity as a citizen with a job, a family, a house.

As a rule, the poor outside are to stay separate from those inside. When outsiders encounter insiders on the doorstep, however, their interaction is as surreal as revealing. Insaan, a Pakistani in his late thirties, was expelled after a number of misbehaviors—thereby becoming irrelevant for the center and the staff—only to go homeless. He will systematically return, looming out of the entrance, for a few months. "This is my place," he tells caseworkers, who oscillate between repeating he's no longer allowed (if men) and ignoring him (if women). Whenever Insaan tries getting in, the doormen stand up: stop! After a while, if he is staying quietly out in cold or rainy weather, a doorman may partially give up—"Come in. Sit there. Don't move." An empty chair in the hall turns into the internal border. Things are "so-so," Insaan tells me, if only because I'm the only one who wishes to talk to him. "Away from home," he adds, pointing to the building around us. "On the road." What people should do and how they should relate with someone who should not be there is not self-evident. What is clear is that whenever Insaan shows up, he disrupts the envelope of normality around this place. There is something grotesque in struggling to get back into a house whose residents look forward to leaving, or so they say. "This is no longer your place," the staff repeat whenever he comes to pick up some clothing from his old suitcase. "If you don't carry it away, we'll throw it away." No reply. Well before being expelled, Insaan was unlikely to chat much. He had a routine, though, and a way of ordering space and time,[17] which are lost from the first minute he's out. Perhaps his obsession with return has to do with that more than with the need for shelter. "I want to stay here," repeats Insaan one afternoon, in his disconnected way of murmuring, to the police officers who were called to expel him. "I've done a lot of things. Now I've got nothing." "We all have our problems," a police officer replies, before getting harsher on their way out of the center. "For those like you there's only the homeless shelter—or you want to sleep under the stars? Either this way, or you go back home—*not* here." *Here* is not home, if anywhere ever was, or will be (cf. 7.1).

When it comes to people like Insaan, the in-out divide is meant to be as rigid as possible. However, not all former residents are equal. "I'm poor!" sounds more playful whenever Olusola screams it out, the first months after his final exit, hoping that a Nigerian "brother" on the third floor will hear him.[18] If you've ended up outside with no place or a job, you are bound to reappraise the center as a lost haven of security and decency. Which is not to deny the obvious: as long as you spend the bulk of your time in the refugee place, there's little chance to get a job and access the mainstream. Once you are in the labor market somehow, and until the next job loss, your position, self-esteem and reputation will rise above those of anybody who's stuck waiting.

In and out, within

In between the city and the semi-private domain of each bedroom, the common space of the center is nobody's space. People, sounds and smells moving in and out make intermittent connections across it. It is an obvious ethnographic temptation to approach it as an ongoing, 24/7 front stage[19]—one, however, on which the main characters perform quick crossings in and out, more than extended scripts. No point in staying longer than for a greeting, unless to chat with some, argue with others or clean up when the mandatory shift comes.

There is certainly a common space, and there are hardly any commons. All that is spatially shared feels as empty and bleak as irrelevant. Nobody would trust leaving personal belongings in the corridors, certainly not the sneakers that caseworkers often notice, and complain about, on the windowsills. Likewise, day-to-day affordances like the portable drying racks on the upper terrace tend to silently end up in the kitchens and bedrooms. If personal or useful objects move in as much as possible, so do people over time, revealing a constant tension between communal affordances and private use or appropriation. The dwelling story of the TV room is a case in point. This had initially been conceived as an informal space of conviviality, with sofas and books around. As time goes by, most residents start to withdraw in their rooms or in friends' ones, as long as they have a TV set in. Only newcomers and apparently lone wolves keep staying there and, a caseworker says, use it "as their own bedroom" to sleep, drink, smoke or just stay alone. After some more months of well-intentioned beautification, the staff will remove the sofa and lock up the room. Anybody is still allowed in—they just need to ask for the key. Unsurprisingly perhaps, nobody does. "It's so clean now!" the staff remark. As clean as a place that has become irrelevant. Whenever I get in again, micro-traces like cigarette butts, old chewing-gums or betting-agency receipts[20] are the only witness of some past use, if one stubbornly searches for them. Far more visible are a number of novels, comics and newspapers, waiting for a non-existent reader—just like people in the center are waiting for something meaningful to occur outside. Yet, little or no communication between things in waiting and people in waiting. The best decorated and equipped inner space is the least inhabited. No point in staying there with the others if one can do things on his own—as alone as in all the key steps of his legal and work trajectory.

All this being said, the common space is more than a transitory background. It also hosts selective and intermittent ways of carving out privacy, autonomy and conviviality that are not necessarily in sync with its intended function and create new boundaries. Prayer activities are a case in point (see 7.3). A young Muslim just needs to lay down a rug in the right direction, at some distance from the rest, to turn an empty space into a part-time prayer room. Even when the prayer takes a collective form and a ritual rhythm, the temporary use of place is critical to make it acceptable to the staff and less intrusive to fellow residents (figure 7). Sometimes, moreover, people do stay in the common space for more than a mere transition. Perhaps they are chatting, having tea, trying driving-license tests together or exercising up and down the stairs, the free equivalent of a gym. Daokaate, more than anybody else, fills his existential immobility with continual physical exercise. This usually means jogging around in the neighborhood, as a late afternoon ritual. "Paolo, come on—join me!" is his ordinary, gentle and hopeless greeting, as we come across each other. Other times, instead, it is enough to exercise on the fourth-floor stairs, away from the bedrooms. This way, he will not "annoy" the others—"Perhaps they're sleeping."

People may also carve out some special timespace in the courtyard. This offers a dual advantage—less surveillance than inside, more control than the mainstream urban space. Moving the benches to the right corner is enough to set up a temporary sitting room and open it to outsiders, other migrants as male and Black as the residents. It may be easier to create pockets of domesticity there than inside. After all, one may well be in the mood to have fun, just like anyone in his early twenties (see 6.5). You might reclaim a right to fun, as much as to protection. Whether you achieve it, and for how long, is a different matter. In practice, you spend part of your time outside, for somewhere you must stay and something you must do, even while you feel you are doing nothing. Whenever more people do the same, some regions of the courtyard turn into a semi-private space to chat, joke, have meals or drinks, celebrate a birthday, pray or sit alone together. You end up being segregated twice—the center from the external world and your own ephemeral place from the center—which is precisely what you want. The courtyard, then, is more of a space of irrelevance than surveillance. You don't care much about the others, and vice versa, as long as you don't go too visibly against the rules. Wherever you are, you'll keep feeling inside and outside—intermittently included and excluded, depending on your mood, on how things evolve, on your terms of comparison. You just have to live with this, even in your bedroom.

FIGURE 7. Turning an empty hall close to the laundry room into a part-time prayer room. Both rugs will be unfolded when a few Muslim residents gather to pray. They should be folded again at the end of the prayer. Photo by author.

3.4   IN A SHARED BEDROOM

One's bedroom is the innermost section of the center, but not necessarily the most intimate or private. As a rule of the care-and-control game, staff members are always entitled to do inspections. If and when they do, they generally knock on the door, like any good visitor. Nonetheless, under a polite guise of guests, they are rather the hosts, with their passe-partout key and the prerogative to (try to) enforce discipline. Moreover, and unsurprisingly for a welfare infrastructure, dwelling is rarely a solo experience. Someone else is around most of the time, which turns every room into a layered and contended space. Roommates' boundaries of space and time need to be fine-tuned accordingly.[21]

Whenever a resident gets back, he can move straight into his room, lock it up and leave everything else outside. As long as you are in, you can be a bit more of yourself—no role to perform for a public audience. You can (un)dress the way you like and take care of your body with suitable ways of washing, perfuming and dressing. You can lie on a bed to sleep, roam, chat, watch TV or play games on a PlayStation. You could even have a cigarette or a joint—preferably in the kitchen, out of courtesy for your roommate. The staff, whose potential or interest in surveillance falls short of the formal rules, is unlikely to find out.

Once inside, you are relatively in control. It is up to each resident to decide who to allow in. One day, during a lively conversation in Den's room, someone evokes Matteo Salvini. As a Far Right political leader, and (at the time) minister of the interior, he's an intriguing catalyst of weird fascination, as much as anger and frustration. "*He* must get out of this room!" Den exclaims, as joking as assertive. "That's just politics. Why talk about him? We don't care." Here, the subtext goes, is the place for us to mind our businesses—no matter how deeply these are shaped by the opaque, farraginous and exclusionary political complex that Salvini embodies. And no matter if sometimes there is not much business at all. Here, *it's our place*—not just the place for *us*.

The discursive opposition between refugees and nativists is only a variation of the ordinary ways of thresholding between one's personal space, the rest of the room and the adjacent kitchen. It goes without saying that all non-perishable food should stay in the bedroom, rather than in the more contended kitchen space. The personal, or rather the pragmatic concern of avoiding robberies, overwhelms the functional. In this, and in many more respects, co-presence between strangers demands tacit mutual adjustment. It also calls for a tactic use of the material affordances available, such as the chairs Olusola and Tvel have positioned one meter from the respective beds, to mark the space around their bodies. A decent-enough cohabitation rests on these tangible signs, as well as on an ingrained attitude of mutual indifference.[22] Whenever one is eating or calling someone on his bed, the other can only try to disregard the rich sensorial field in front of him. Sounds, as much as smells and lights, are indifferent to any attempt at bordering. This means that ordinary civil inattention need not be a form of hostility. It is actually the best possible embodiment of mutual respect.

Such an ongoing balancing act is not without frictions, albeit, as everywhere in the center, the power of irrelevance tends to win out. It is also out of fear of these tensions that people voice their own preferences about (un)desired roommates. Whenever someone leaves, his roommate—by then a longtime resident—is likely to argue against potential newcomers with a certain ethno-national or religious background. People from *there* are too noisy, unreliable, dirty, smelly or utterly

FIGURE 8. The micro-sovereignty area close to one's bed, and on and around the nightstand, where a resident can store personal belongings and objects of everyday use. Photo by author.

wicked, the argument goes (see 6.3). So, *NIMBR—Not In My Bed-Room!* In practice these moral hierarchies have little importance, since all decisions are up to the staff. Even so, they are sociologically revealing. A number of shared rooms may already be enough as a micro-lab to make sense of what nativism means or how it works out, on far larger scales.[23]

Within each room, moreover, one may scale down the in-out boundary to his own bed. This is probably the most private and least visible of places in an ordinary domestic space. Not so much, instead, in the center. It is common, among my West African interlocutors in the same room, to sit or lie down on any bed available. Even so, *one's* bed is a special place. Some treat it with special care and order,[24] sometimes with forms of personalization ranging from a new and colorful blanket to a teddy bear. For everybody the bed is the core of one's micro-sovereignty area, around which personal belongings such as papers, smartphones, and hygienic and beauty products are allocated, ordered or hidden (figure 8).

On my side, being invited to sit on a bed is a critical step to normalize my guest role. It is always at the end of Den's bed that I end up sitting when I come and see him, during the months in which he feels suspended between the impending decision on his case, the fruitless search for a job, and the loss of confidence in vocational training or even only in basic education. "Life is very difficult," Den repeats, just like thousands more would do. His head is on the pillow, looking down, his right hand depicting a circle to show how he feels with his mind. A few more seconds and he'll be chatting on his phone again, intermittently commenting with me about soccer—certainly not about the others around. "I don't know nothing of them," those in the same predicament and yet fully separated in their inner experiences and memories. This protracted way of occupying a bed engenders irritation in the staff. It gives them an uncanny feeling of dealing with old, sick or dependent people. Yet the bed is there. It accommodates one's sense of discomfort, while doing nothing to overcome it—just like the center at large, the less local authorities invest in refugee integration.

To some extent, the bed itself marks a threshold against the world, including fellow residents. Any bed in the center is potentially a place of conviviality as much as separation. It often happens, when I'm in Bashshel's room with his roommate and friends, that he gets back at some point, whispers an undifferentiated hello gazing down to the floor and jumps on his bed, his back to us and the face down on the pillow, just slightly inclined to watch his mobile. While Bashshel is carving out his own space, the others around do not necessarily feel out of place. It's simply a matter of parallel living, with intermittent interaction. In a similar vein, I may end up in a room to chat or eat with someone while his roommate is resting under an all-encompassing blanket—as isolated as his condition affords. Parallel worlds stay and breath together in a single room, as much as in the larger city or country.

One afternoon I've come to see Ousmane, who welcomes me in, still in his bathrobe. We start chatting as usual while he's getting dressed, the shutters down and a stuffy atmosphere around. Contrary to my initial perception, Ousmane is not alone. His roommate, Ogwu, is there, wrapped up in his red blanket on the bed, his music popping up across it. If it were not in that room, it might feel like someone sleeping roughly. In there, under the dim light, it looks like a way to domesticate an approaching risk of homelessness, as he is due to leave soon. I'm not in a position to greet him unless he first does so. Nonetheless, everyday life around Ogwu keeps on without much variation. So does my conversation with Ousmane, between jokes and bittersweet remarks about Italy and the Gambia, face masks and the people around, along with a sequence of *not-yet* when it comes to his search for a job or his appeal against asylum denial. After a while Ousmane is ready to exit, "five layers of clothing" on, a coffee thermos in his hands to cope with the cold outside, a daily routine of hanging out to "meet friends and change negativity into positivity."[25] Meanwhile, Ogwu's body has stayed immobile. After all, he is only doing his business, like all of us. He can do so, though, only as far as his red quilt affords. As he's lying there with his body fully covered he is, once again, *in* (a sheltering space) as much as *out* (of any space of substantive privacy, let alone autonomy).

3.5   IN ONE'S BODY AND MIND

Sometimes, when even the proximate space raises little interest or commitment, my interlocutors are implicitly scaling down the in-out divide—the reach of what is relevant—to the boundary of their own bodies. This is the innermost space that matters and demands care, even when the surrounding one does not. The body is the only scale on which almost all of them are really in control regardless of external circumstances, including the unavoidable proximity with dozens of other young, male and racialized ones. One's body makes for the primary, most basic and portable home.[26] Taking care of it is no simple matter of social reproduction. Rather, it is an assertion of sovereignty and dignity (cf. 6.6).

While the imaginary of refugeehood and its institutional recognition presuppose the demonstration of a suffering body,[27] there is much more than victimhood or bare life in the bodies of the young men in the center. For most of them, one's Black or Brown body is a fully intact, enduring and unalienable capital. It is relatively salient within the prevalent bodyscape outside, while being unremarkable inside (where the few white bodies stand out as an exception associated with power, insidedness and nativeness). Sometimes it bears scars that are silent, if tangible forms of absent presence (cf. 5.5): the past nobody wants to re-evoke or disclose, and everybody should emphasize, as "proof," in asylum hearings. In either context the body, as the cumulative product of one's biographical transformations, testifies to resilience across life-or-death migration. Its simple existence is obvious here and now, but it was not along the way. "I'm fine," Kambanoo reluctantly murmurs whenever we end our conversations. Although his virtually jobless life is "hard," he's in good health and has a bed for the time being. His body should now be the lever to try and achieve his aspirations through hard work and dedication.

Moreover, a body is like a stage on which everybody displays their tastes, alignments and lifestyles.[28] You can present it in different ways to different interlocutors, just as you do with your life story. In fact, at least in the center you can afford to say little or nothing of that. Keeping one's story private is already a demonstration of mastery and sovereignty. It nourishes a reservoir of identity and intimacy that, while not unproblematic (and probably edulcorated in one's memories), cannot be torn away. Likewise, everybody in the center has incomparably more control over his body than on any outer portion of space and time. Importantly, higher control translates into higher care. The predominant dedication to physical fitness, as an expression of youth as much as masculinity, playfully emerges whenever someone comments on my middle-age fattish appearance and warns me to get more exercise, as they do.

The ways of feeding, dressing and presenting one's body are also affirmations of mastery over space, albeit on a minimal scale (see 6.6). As far as the little money available affords, a resident can choose and cook his own food, hence be in control of what his body ingests. The same goes for the clothes he likes wearing, the caring products he uses, the music he listens to. In all these respects, tastes and styles mark a boundary in relation to those who have different ones. And just as for anybody else, dressing styles embody a boundary, and possibly a hierarchy, between contrasting circumstances and groups of reference. There are remarkable differences between the basic clothing one keeps in the center and more accurate outfits to go outside. Likewise, those Muslim youth who attend the city mosque on Fridays keep their *dishdasha* with care and carefully separate it from ordinary clothing.

Music is another effective, if ephemeral boundary-maker. Whether rap or pop, international or local, loud music from the earphones or portable speakers marks a sensorial boundary between the body and the rest. It is like a portable extension of one's comfort zone and realm of influence—in a way, of the body as a minimal home on the move (see 7.3). However, extending one's comfort zone, sensorially and temporarily at least, requires enhancing the boundary with the outside world. No way to have one thing without the other.

The bodies that stay or circulate in the center have also a strong power of boundary-making through the senses, including smells.[29] There is a stark contrast between the sensorial background of stale and musty, intermingled with some spicy food flavor, the soapy smell that comes from the bodies and the vivid scents they often bear upon entering or exiting (see 6.6). The scent traces in an empty corridor are the only mute witnesses to one's daily trajectories of micro-mobility. Stale, clean and perfumed smells overlap in the same space, while staying distinct from one another— the interior space of a corridor (or for that matter, a room) versus the body that inhabits it. The good, relevant smell is for oneself (and for mutual respect with friends in the center, and for protecting one's reputation outside). The bad, irrelevant smell is for the housing infrastructure in which one ended up. Underlying this unequal smellscape is a politics of smell that the racialized bodies in the center articulate in multiple respects: as a field of distinction (*My body is not smelly*, against all racist stances, and perhaps, unlike other bodies); as a form of dignification (*I'm sovereign over my body—I can treat it the way I like*); and of course as a tool of boundary-making (*My body matters more than the place I'm in*; ultimately, perhaps, *My body is my place*).

At least in these regards, everyone has control of his body-space. No resident, though, is in control of how his body is perceived and treated outside. Certain things, Sani once tells me, change over time. Say, using the bicycle lane. You've no idea of this at the beginning, for "there is nothing like that in Africa—maybe some day they'll make it." Car drivers honk the horn, you get scared at first but then you learn to use it "properly." Other things, instead, remain the same—struggling to get a job, waiting for the papers. And people looking down at you. It happened "at least ten times" during the first lockdown, as he was going to his workplace by bike, that a car driver would stop and spit at him. "We escaped from Africa because we could no longer stay there—there are those who shoot you down. . . . What would you choose between a spit and a shot?" The answer is his everyday life experience. "If you were Black for one day, you could understand," he bluntly concludes. No way to do so, as a white. Likewise, I cannot fully grasp what Fatou has gone through, or so he seems to feel while recounting his multiple attempts to make it to Europe. My body would not allow real understanding in the former case. My life story—my good luck or my privilege—would not allow it in the latter case.[30]

Yet, like any ethnographer, I'm trying my best to make sense of what my body has not experienced or cannot experience. This includes the embodied ways of mediating the aftermath of displacement, violence and risk. You may happen to feel, as it were, physically *in* and psychologically or imaginatively *out*.[31] "Thinking all the time" makes you tired. It even "hurts," people invariably warn, including Olusola, one day, while he's moisturizing his hands and is about to use his hair gel. You would not feel so "tired of doing nothing," perhaps, unless the memories of your own past were looming there. "I've so many things in my mind," says Ogwu, another day, to the caseworker who has just reproached him for not signing in. There is a minor breach of the rules to repair with his humble smile, just while he's about to receive the pocket money. However, there is also an attempt at sharing the same question—being in one's body, while feeling out of it. In practice, it's easier to retain control by trying to forget all thoughts or by avoiding the circumstances in which they will emerge again. This tactic, with the emotional work it requires, is part and parcel of one's ordinary self-presentation in the center.[32] It's important to feel in control of your self and body, as you display them around. Whether the others will buy into that presentation—or even only care about it—is a lesser concern.

Showing mastery over one's troubles has both a moral side, for it is consistent with an appropriate model of masculinity, and a pragmatic one, related to the need to protect one's reputation. Sticking to normative masculinity, and hence ensuring respectability,[33] is especially important in the most critical transitions. So Olusola explains during his early months out of the center, when he is couch-surfing between the places of his Yoruba "brothers" here and there. He's run out of money, some friend may be helping him, but he doesn't want to feel like he's begging. A "gift" is okay, because "I can return it, although I have less money than you." But that's all. "I must be hard," Olusola repeats one afternoon, as we are sitting on the backside bench, in mutual indifference with the staff around. After a couple of phone calls, it turns out that his "sisters" in the reception system are helping him with lunch—just as he is helping them with writing CVs. "No more help," though, otherwise "I'll lose respect." It happens when men and women get too close. When it comes to help, instead, "it must not go beyond my power." As I rephrase it within myself, impression management is critical,[34] and reciprocity must be properly calibrated.[35] "Of course I'm suffering, but I mustn't show it. I must be happy and joke. . . . That's my life—I'm poor but I'm smiling. I don't want the others to see me suffering."

3.6   THE IN/OUT DIVIDE, UNPACKED

"Visits from external guests have been suspended since 25 February [2020]", reads a notice in the ground-floor hall. The hopeful sense of temporariness of the earlier pandemic stage has been overcome by inertia, as the prohibition has just stayed there. That the divide between in and out is stressed further in times of covid is no surprise. In practice the effort at prevention will be as necessary and insufficient, just as in any collective housing environment. Even an asylum center has multiple connections with the larger society "through flows of bodies, through social media and through the knowledge and practices" of those who run it.[36]

Whether a young male resident sees full isolation as a dream or a nightmare, he still won't achieve it. People may strive to lead parallel and separated lives, but they are bound to do so within the same sensorial field. Along with the circulation or mooring of their Black and Brown bodies comes the diffusion of sounds and smells—across walls, from one floor to the next, between inside and outside. While nothing important seems to happen, the inner, endogenous life of each room goes on and oozes out somehow. It all feels empty, but now and then, potentially any moment, a loud TV or music suddenly starts, a scream, a song or a laughter bursts out, a pungent smell emerges somewhere, and more will follow. People are in and out, then, as long as they are routinely exposed to sensorial co-presence as an outcome of infrastructural limitations rather than of purposeful conviviality. Coping with forced proximity requires, once again, civil inattention—hence, a degree of mutual irrelevance, what anthropological research into West Africans' experience of displacement, but also into housing infrastructures such as the French *foyers*, has called *sutura*, as an ingrained way of "displaying respect for the others and for dominating norms in public, with inappropriate behavior reserved to private spheres."[37] This goes along with some pragmatic tolerance, for instance, in naturalizing sounds that would feel improperly loud elsewhere, from the staff side. "They're just boys," "it's their place"—no point complaining too much for a caseworker or a doorman. Their shifts will soon be over. And just like those being controlled, the controllers make up their own bubbles by watching TV or listening to music. Each of these sensuous bubbles stays on its own, until it collides with another. As a result, the center is as much an institutionalized bubble from the mainstream city as a container of makeshift bubbles. Yet, all bubbles are short-lived—inside and, over time, outside.

Along the borders of the building, windows have a key and ambiguous role of mediation. It is up to each resident, in a minimal exercise of power, to leave a window closed or open, the shutters up or down, the light on or off.[38] While a number of windows stay obstinately shut, some, especially on the ground floor, are rather channels to share music, meals, chats and gossip. One afternoon I'm passing out of a ground-floor kitchen, where Issa is about to have a plate of rice and meat. After our ordinary round of mutual greetings, I can stay on his windowsill, making my way across mosquitos and pigeon droppings. I'm bodily outside, and inside his eating routine. Things, Issa says, are "so-so." In fact, "It's all bad," he soon adds with a bitter smile. "Can't stand it any more." Three years have gone since he arrived in Catania and soon moved north: "no work, no papers, no nothing." He has appealed twice against status denial, "the lawyer will tell." No job in sight, unlike "Germany or France" where he'll actually move some months later, after a final denial. Finding a place to sleep wherever is not a problem, he points out. Work is.

As Issa shares his frustration, I'm feeling slightly idiotic in focusing on tiny details inside his room, including the sneakers orderly laid out beside the dining table. Little of what lies there matters to him, relative to the struggle for a job and papers. Yet, while talking to me, Issa has started to clean up the kitchen. He's effectively taking care of a place for which he couldn't care less, possibly as a way of taking care of himself—of his own rhythms, routines, lifestyles. "Thanks Italy!" he ironically concludes, interrupting my silent musings. "I'm with headache all the time," he adds, only to recover the appearance of a smile one minute later as Den joins us. It seems you are in a better mood whenever you chat with a Black friend rather than with any native white guy. You can have more fun, as much as mutual support. You have a reputation to protect and little to claim—just the opposite of everyday interactions with the staff. The entire conversation has been right across the windowsill—Issa inside, Den and myself outside. It could have equally taken place in his room or outside. To that extent, being in or out does not matter much, as long as one wishes to share something. What matters the most, and will shape one's future, lies beyond the horizon of life in the center anyway.

Everyday forms of sociability in the courtyard also contribute to blurring the inside-outside divide. So do the clothes or sheets laid out to dry on the balconies or the sneakers airing out on the windowsills—ordinary affordances of living *in* that visually trickle *out* and may transgress the imperatives of decency and invisibility (see 6.4). Moreover, the in-out divide is as blurred in space as in time. Even former residents, who left their duties and privileges behind, may be not totally and irreversibly out. Some keep coming in search of residual traces of ethnic and social capital—friends to stay with, caseworkers to ask for advice, bubbles to be ephemerally remade in a place more familiar than the larger cityscape. As time goes by, with the turnover of residents and caseworkers, this emplaced social capital gets thinner. It may always happen, though, that a former guest shows up, now supposed to act like the adult who got rid of oppressive and infantilizing rules. An especially creative example comes from Omokunrin one February afternoon, as I'm strolling around the fourth-floor terrace for lack of better things to do. Some hurried trampling from the emergency staircase, a jump around the security door,

FIGURE 9. A "KEEP THIS DOOR CLOSED" sign on the fourth-floor
balcony door warns that the door should always stay closed. However,
it is usually open, as this picture exemplifies. Photo by author.

and he appears on the stage again through the "back way." He has always done
so, in a sense, since he left Nigeria. "It's okay," "Little by little," "We're men—aren't
we?" and "Always forward!" are his usual mottos. Omokunrin is back to see a
friend who seems to be nowhere. However, he doesn't want to "see them" again.
It's not too cold, as we stay at the terrace entrance, right before the emergency door
that should always be closed—so a notice reads—and is always open (figure 9).
Not much to do or get for Omokunrin now. If anything, he finds someone to spend
time with, until he's fed up waiting and gets out, same way. Time to go back coping
with a number of divides that are far more critical and hard to negotiate than an
emergency exit.

Whether that means moving forward in more than a literal sense is hard to predict or generalize. Each young man in the center has his own story and a limited

degree of control. That said, the unequal language, relational and employment capital one has been accumulating does make a difference. At some point it could turn the always-ahead moral mantra into a tangible, if ever-reversible, achievement. Omokunrin's own story is constellated with new *outs* that emerge whenever he hopes to be *in* at last, and perhaps free to be fully himself, for instance, in his ways of clothing and of consumption. *Here*, I'll do more or less what you want me to, was the subtext of his ways of dealing with the staff over his five-year stay. *After*, I can do things my own way—thank God. In fact, as Omokunrin finds out whenever he starts a new job, the outer world can be far tougher and less compassionate. Even leaving aside the discrimination that his skin color and national background elicit, there's no way for him to keep a job as a cook assistant unless he's properly dressed. Or to work in a construction site if he doesn't buy suitable shoes beforehand. There may be as many in-out divides to negotiate as every new day in your life out of the center. And there are people's ways of preparing themselves and envisioning their prospective trajectories as a matter of moving ahead or staying still, as the next chapter illustrates.

4

Still, Moving

"Three years and five months with fucking nothing to do, just eat and sleep," Koné bursts out one day while we're alone in his bedroom. No question or input from my side—he just wants to vent this out in an improvised monologue, before getting back to his ordinary demeanor of placid resignation. "I'm sick of this shit. I've done volunteering and training all the time. What's for? My friends have got their papers, they're working—not me. I can't stand this country any more. Nobody helps me. . . . I'm young!" Koné exclaims. "I can do so many things! If I get a new job, I'll learn in one week—forklift driver, carpenter, stockman—but that's it. . . . In Côte d'Ivoire, all bad. In Libya, all bad. In Italy, all bad. . . . What on earth have I done to Italy?" He pauses, with a bitter sneer. "I'm tired, I swear it. You can't stay home all the time. . . . I'd better die in the water. I came here, my life was supposed to change." No change, instead, unlike those who have apparently made it. Just stuck in a place for asylum seekers, no clear idea of why or until when. What Koné does know is that a lot of patience is needed, and he no longer has it.

There is a moral and temporal subtext to migration, as a transformative turning point in biography, which can help people to cope with, even make sense of, whatever they will face. Once in the center, the loss of any clear sense of the future is the most frustrating thing. Most residents feel *still* in time—not just *immobile* in space. They occupy a biographical position of pause, or liminality,[1] in which it is clear who and where they no longer are but not who or where they will be. Being still in the here-and-now is bitterly ironic for people who are portrayed as hyper-mobile, and for their own imaginaries of spatial, biographical and existential mobility. As the years go by, the young men in the center keep feeling stuck at a child life stage, as opposed to the adult masculinity they feel they must achieve. They are still, in relation to their ingrained aspirations and in stark contrast with the upward mobility opportunities they perceive around themselves. Stillness gives them a degree of predictability over the everyday—sometimes only in terms of "nothing to do"—which is in tension with the unpredictability of what will come next. This may generate unequal reactions, from active engagement with the mainstream community to self-seclusion and pragmatic adaptation to things as they are. It is important to unpack this ambivalence in time and hence the temporalities of (un)doing nothing and renegotiating relevance, by looking at the multiple facets of the still-moving dialectic: how people cope with their time, engage in place-making and hopefully, somehow, in future-making.

4.1   (IM)MOBILE, (UN)PROTECTED, IN-BETWEEN

Everyday life in the center tends to feel like a pause in a pathway that should lead upward elsewhere. Yet, this is by no means the first experience of immobility people went through. Common across their narratives of the past is a pervasive sense of being stuck in their countries, with no tangible prospects in sight.[2] "The only way of improving was to leave," as the ordinary statement goes. Little new or original in this, apparently, as a rationale of migration. If only one delves further, however, more complex and surprising stories of aspired mobility will emerge, along gender and generational lines, in friction with present disorientation and undesired immobility.

Some leave because "they must," says Fatou, out of personal and family circumstances. This was his case, as he presents it. Many more leave because "they want to live the good life"[3]—that is, "get along well with the others, respect, get respected." People leave because "they want to live like in Europe"; in Fatou's words and smile, "make money" and become "big men," entrepreneurial guys who can afford whatever they like. They can even afford a new house, maybe a compound for the whole family—nothing to do with his house in the Gambia. "Some make it," he adds, with a more serious expression. If the conversation reaches out to another generational viewpoint, such as that of an older doorman of African origin, it takes a still different bent. "These boys" have "no project," he argues. "Many of them sleep, eat, get stuff dirty, and that's it." Not all of them, of course. Yet "you should always ask yourself, why did I leave? . . . Well—they've no clue." Again, not everybody. "Some" understand that "if you can sleep and eat for free, you'd better do something good out of it." Others, "no way—they don't speak nothing Italian. . . . C'est la vie."

Regardless of this hypothetical distinction, many feel stuck and temporally still in the here-and-now. Many also share a still image of Africa—one anchored to the past, with no viable futures ahead. The sense of stuckedness has an ineluctable, almost ontological tone in some narratives, as a matter of social death.[4] It is more connected with a realm of "bad politics," if loosely defined, in others. Well before being and feeling marginalized in Italy, people feel like outsiders back "home"—existentially outside the narrow field of those who matter in wealth, power and age (leaving aside gender—the only attribute they share with the powerful). Out of the systemic corruption in Nigeria, Paul repeats, only the old and wealthy shall be in power and stand above the law. "If you don't have money, you don't have power," "if you don't have money, you can't talk." No way for youth like him to "compete." "We're small men," he says laughing, his hand down to emphasize low stature. Put otherwise, in Africa we "can't be vibrant," a thorough bodily vibration coming along with his words. "That's why young people leave, no?"

Following this premise, and a variety of structural constraints and personal pressures, hundreds of thousands of young men like my interlocutors go through informal, fragmented and dangerous migration pathways, with no point of destination given in advance, to hopefully achieve better lives;[5] in fact, to reach some form of protection by risking their lives along the way, as a typical paradox of forced migration.[6] Now, in a safe country, their temporary protection as asylum seekers depends on staying still—dwelling in one reception space and complying with its institutional rules. No matter how inhospitable, an asylum center gives shelter, a basic livelihood, an address and a place to be, socialize and hang out—with all the friction that may come along. However, it is a mode of protection that risks disempowering people as soon as they have to move again, unless they have enhanced their social and employment capital in the meantime. If institutional hospitality turns too protracted, short-term protection may turn into long-term *dis*-protection.[7] This is not simply inscribed in institutional reception, though.

Far from being an impersonal dispositif of surveillance, the center is a very personal, if implicit, mechanism of downward selection. "It's always the same—the good ones go away," a doorman once says, nicely capturing the mechanism in question, albeit with a moralistic subtext. I often have an uncanny sense of this perverse effect, mentally phrased as "still here," whenever I come across people like Bashshel, who entered the center in the early months of my fieldwork and is still in four years later, with an equally limited mastery of Italian, little or no jobs done, an invariably melancholic gaze when we exchange our conventional greeting. Whenever limited extant resources interact with little social, legal and psychological support, temporary protection does not take long to turn into its opposite. This is something doormen would call "holing up here the whole day . . . so strange for young lads." This is something people themselves rephrase as "being tired of staying home with nothing to do." This means being temporally still, in ambivalent coexistence with literal, metaphoric or at least potential mobility.[8]

As long as one stays still, though, he is temporarily sheltered and maintained. "Here you can stay in your room the whole day doing nothing. Outside, nobody will pay for that! You have to gain your money." So Paul reflects in the middle of a lively discussion with Olusola and Sani about what will come next. If one is "motivated to work hard," says Paul, he'll make it outside alone. If one is "lazy," troubles will come. "Lazy," here, is no phrasing from anti-immigrant right-wing supporters.

It emerges from Paul's own career as a welfare recipient. Yet such an account is as honest as eerily (over)individualizing. As he puts it, the question boils down to personality, even to one's ultimately good or bad moral nature—in essence, to (un)deservingness. The hard worker will make it, the lazy one will pay for laziness. This leaves little space either for biographical determinants (e.g., intergenerational poverty, lack of education, precarious living conditions, exposure to trauma) or for societal ones (including the decreasing support to refugee inclusion). It reflects the relatively narrow perceptual field of an asylum seeker who sees people like him around, one day after the other. The societal determinants of this condition are far less visible and more complex to decode. As for the biographical roots, they're too painful and intimate to be uncovered again. Bringing down the issue to individual attitudes or behaviors, in an ironic replication of the predominant neo-liberal mantra, is more straightforward. It is also more reassuring: if I'm dedicated and committed, no doubt I will make it.

Along the way, the argument reproduces a narrative of passivity that some would call "blaming the victims" and many more would see as a blatant demonstration of non-deservingness. Such narratives touch deep chords in the lived experience of institutional waiting, which has a perversely reassuring side to it. Nothing so bad will happen until the case processing is over. Better staying in than sleeping rough, an outsider might say. Better finding something useful to do outside than staying here, residents would reply. The question is rather what "useful" means and how it can be achieved. What is clear is that, aside from sheltering, all that matters the most—job, papers, accommodation, sense of autonomy and freedom—is out of the reach of this place. Indeed, the longer one stays still, the harder to get rid of a sense of doing nothing. Sooner or later, things are bound to change anyway. Once the final asylum decision is taken, people *must* leave. A tangible, if possibly ephemeral sense of freedom will come along with many more responsibilities and risks—ultimately, with a more pressing demand for adulthood. The "meanwhile,"[9] though, is too important to be discarded as a parenthesis in people's lives and in ethnographic ways of recounting them.

4.2   STILL, NOW: STRUGGLING WITH THE ONLY CAPITAL IN EXCESS

One afternoon like any other, Omokunrin is standing on the third-floor balcony close to his room. He seems to be staring outside, somewhere between the parking lot, the gas station, the street that leads downtown, the unnoticeable buildings ahead of us. He keeps on like that for a while before greeting me in a gentle and dismal tone, as I'm getting closer. "How're you doing? Family, work?" All right, as far as I'm concerned. "So-so," for brevity and reluctance to tell more, on his side. Behind us, the door of his room is half closed. Enough for a glimpse at the cooking stuff piled on his desk, around the large TV screen that has long been broken.

No money to repair it. And then, his closed suitcase standing permanently in front of the window. As we keep talking about the weather and the shops down in the street, Omokunrin repeats the same phrasal circuit every five minutes or so, like a chant. "It's not easy" to find a job in Italy. So many Italians with precarious jobs, so many immigrants looking for a job. But it's important to find one. "Then I'll get the papers." "Then you make your life little by little," *piano piano*, as he slows down his own rhythm. At that point, he considers before continuing, you can stroll around and "go on holiday," perhaps Sicily or Naples. "I want to see them," he adds smiling. At that point, I mentally rephrase, you feel you are *normal*. For now you must wait and pray to God. "God is great," says Omokunrin, "if you pray for something, he will give it." God will help me "if I do the right things," he adds, stretching his arms in parallel to depict the right way, his gaze dreaming and disoriented at once.

Meanwhile, the budgetary cuts on caseworkers' support have only made things worse. As we are talking, my eyes fall on the tattoo of Lady Liberty on his right forearm—the American dream, embodied. She's surrounded by stars. "NEW YORK", reads the cover of the book she's carrying. Now, Omokunrin says, "I'll have a shower. I'll go to the Wi-Fi," a street corner with free access on the main street. "I'll have a stroll. I'll go to sleep." Down on the right corner of our visual field lies the gas station. He used to work as a lorry driver before leaving Nigeria. It was dangerous. He had to drive at night. And he had three smaller sisters. "I'm going now—see you next time." I'm always left in doubt with Omokunrin. Is his story deliberately vague or just hazy as such? Perhaps its circular and reiterated structure is more revealing than the contents. Reiteration, as a way to fill time and make sense of one's story until something new is in sight. "Today—this way," says Omokunrin another time, somehow more playfully, while we're eating together in Paul's room. "Tomorrow—this way. It's always this way! Nothing ever changes. . . . You get up, eat, stroll around—and that's it." No money, no jobs. And "no wife," he stresses with a laugh. "You have a wife, who cooks for you when you're back home, right? I don't!"

Not all of Omokunrin's fellow residents are without a female partner, and not all would necessarily subscribe to the same gendered subtext. Most of them, though, share a problem that becomes increasingly common among the staff too—how to make time go by. One and the same temporal plot cuts across the lived experience of the center. Whenever I don't find much to do or people to see around, I may end up spending a couple of hours with an uncomfortable, if short-lived sense of doing nothing. Whenever a staff member is in the same position, the sense of doing nothing may last up to eight hours. He knows he's being paid nonetheless and may have some chats or make some phone calls, watch TV, or find something else to do. Now and then caseworkers have a look up at the clock on the wall in front of their desk. Little by little the hand turns around, until one day the battery runs out, the new NGO that runs the center does not pay for a new one, the staff do not wish to pay for it. As a result, time is literally still. Even then, one's private and family life goes on as usual—it is just waiting outside the bubble. Whenever a resident doesn't find much to do, instead, he has fewer resources and opportunities to cope with a major risk—spending months or years in the same predicament.

A sense of stillness does emerge across the narratives of my interlocutors. However, it is also embedded and reproduced in the temporal working of the place they are inhabiting. Nothing seems to ever change, aside from the turnover of residents and staff, the external changes in seasons and atmosphere or the internal ones out of infrastructural decay. To be sure, an asylum facility is also an institutionalized mechanism of time management (see 1.3) or a biopolitical dispositive whereby a public authority exerts power over its subjects by leaving them in undefined waiting.[10] Aside from the basic rules of institutional hospitality, nothing much is necessary or even only relevant in this temporal bubble. This may leave people with a creeping sense of immobility that is existential as much as physical.[11] In a larger biographical perspective, this is only the latest example of the friction between unequal rhythms and contrasting perceptions of time along the course of displacement.[12] While past disruptive events, such as fleeing one's country or sea-crossing, may have come with an accelerated rhythm (at least in people's stories), the rhythm of intermediate stops and moorings, including in Libya, feels much slower. Now, relative to the immediacy of sea rescue and the urgency of finding something useful to do, the waiting time for papers feels invariably too long.

On the institutional side, saving human lives in distress at sea, such as those housed in the center, demands accelerated time lest the rescue fails, as is not infrequently the case.[13] Once the life has been saved, the time for processing its worth of protection need not be so accelerated. Although formal law provisions and reassurance of public opinion would require precisely that, in practice there are no resources, infrastructures or particular reasons to rush. Time can decelerate again. The cost will fall on asylum seekers themselves, and only marginally on the mainstream society (i.e., the relatively low costs of keeping basic institutional reception running). Once a final decision on asylum is made and a resident is expected to leave in a matter of days, however, biographical time suddenly runs fast again. By contrast, the time needed for education or vocational training is often perceived as unreasonably long, against the urgency of making a respectable livelihood through a "real" job. And given the brief duration of most jobs available, Fatou's two-year permit for humanitarian reasons ironically feels like "a long time." This he remarks, with no irony, when he lets me know about it, with far less emphasis than on his new three-month job in a cheese shop.

In the here-and-now, time feels circular, changeless, recursive. In spite of the routines and expected tasks that structure it, including the evening sign-up and the periodical cleaning shifts and pocket-money delivery, it does not flow as fast, smooth and goal-oriented as outside, in the mainstream society or among those who apparently made it (i.e., found a job, got papers, moved elsewhere). Nor is it as linear, progressive and cumulative as in one's aspirations. As long as one stays in, there is much that is predictable in the flow and sequences of people moving out and getting back, in their ways of greeting one another, even in their self-narratives. So repetitive and perversely reassuring, the current everyday life. So unpredictable and obscure, from the timing and outcome of the asylum application to all that will follow, the future life.[14]

All this being said, the center timescape is neither still nor empty. My interlocutors do try to stratify it, with variable intensity and fortune. This results in mundane but meaningful activities and practices that enable them to bring some temporal fragments under control. There is a parallel between their ways of bordering space and the attempts to order everyday time by isolating some special moments of it. Going out to search for a job is only the most obvious of these attempts. It is also a reminder that temporal and spatial semi-immobility need not entail physical immobility. Aside from pandemic restrictions, each resident is free to go out wherever during the day. Many do, whether for active job seeking or just to break the oppressive inner atmosphere. If staying put feels confusing and baffling, going out does something to "defeminize" one's position, as long as one has a purpose, whether to meet friends or spend his pocket money in a Pakistani or Chinese grocery. Going out, generally after extended rounds of body washing and care, makes time linear and goal-oriented again. For sure, this is no guarantee that one does find a job or gets access to mixed or mainstream networks that would blur the color line around his body. Nevertheless, bringing time under control is easier with external anchors to rely on—a job position, a school class, a meeting with friends or native supporters. It is also easier when one has ingrained routines or ways of sociability and conviviality to nourish.

Most notably, praying affords to carve out some time, as much as space; put differently, it contributes to producing relevance (see 7.3). Particularly for young Muslims and during Ramadan, praying holds its own inner temporality. It is a time benchmark to follow, in synchronicity with so many more, on the same footing as them. Praying makes for a micro-suspension of the ordinary timeline in the center, just like the latter feels like a suspension of the mainstream timeline and of the normative transition to adulthood. I feel in a special and suspended time whenever I'm a witness to the prayers of Olusola, Halebugor or Fatou, sitting behind them, after they come out of the bathroom and lay down their rug. There is something mesmerizing in the rhythmic alternance between sound and silence, murmuring and chanting, kneeling down and standing up. During the silent interludes, a few seconds per time, the soundscape is filled only with the cars passing down and the birds tweeting outside the window. And then, cyclically, another round of murmuring prayer.

In short, time within these windows feels more focused, rewarding, ultimately progressive. Nonetheless, all attempts at stratifying time are also temporally shaped. If you have no or bad news about the asylum application, the job search or the invisible unfolding of family life back home, your way of coping with empty time may lose vigor or enthusiasm. There is a downward temporality in the reactions to institutionalized waiting among the young men in the center. "What's the point of going out if you've nothing to do," says Kambanoo after three years spent apparently "doing nothing." "Better stay home," for somewhere you must stay, even while you have no reason to feel attached to it. Taking care of it, if only in terms of cleaning routines, may already be a way of undoing nothing and of making a difference, though (see 6.3).

4.3   "BEING HERE," UNPACKED

Being in the center involves repeating the same patterns of interaction, for staff and residents alike, with apparently little scope for variation or mutual surprise. Someone, however, may always transgress the norm by moving beyond the ordinary greeting. It's enough to add, "I'm here," or at best "We're here," to the usual "okay" in response to the usual "How are you doing?". Unlike "okay," which sorts out the interaction in a matter of seconds, "I'm here" means that someone devotes some extra time to the question—marking it as relevant to some extent[15]—without necessarily addressing it in depth. Perhaps one is having a cigarette or a coffee or would like to stay a bit longer in the common space. Whatever the case, his response comes with a silent and self-evident message: look at this place or at the facial expressions of these guys—it's all too obvious how we're doing. Indeed, "I'm here" is also an emic way of saying "I'm still," relative to any dream of existential mobility. Yet, it does not articulate only pragmatic resignation. "Being here" may hold a more positive subtext: we've made it, thus far. We exist, *here*.[16] You can see, hear, touch and smell us (although the latter verb would hardly be used, body smelling being both an intimate and political field—cf. 3.5 and 6.6).

By simply being in-place and by virtue of the basic rights and needs associated with their presence, the young men in the center are making a public and political claim.[17] No matter how invisibilized an asylum facility, it is no longer possible to disregard their presence thoroughly. Even in the pandemic years of enforced domesticity, turning a blind eye does not work as much as it would before their physical arrival or, most radically, as it would in a regime of remote control of border management, which prevents people from entering the visible field, the collective awareness and the territorialized rights regime of a rich country (cf. 5.4).[18]

As time goes by, and despite delays or denials on their cases, "we're here" also means "we're not going back." "We will not give up until we are in our promised land!" Ogwu exclaims one afternoon in his bedroom, almost hilariously, as if to exorcize his imminent eviction. The land may not be as promised as in one's dreams,[19] but it is tangibly here, in one's sensorial reach and hopefully, over time, in one's field of social relationships. Being here, bodily within the boundaries of a self-professed democratic state, is enough to claim for some recognition. For sure, the time spent in waiting is wearying, and the legal decision may eventually be a negative one. Nonetheless, time may also operate as a self-feeding mechanism of legitimation. This is more easily the case if someone proves "deserving" of staying in light of what he has been able to do (e.g., getting a job, learning a language), regardless of his past circumstances. In short, being still can pave the way for a positive claim rather than only for increasing frustration.

Moreover, resistance to leave the country under any circumstance is consistent with common and practical sense. "They only came here for work. They only know they can make money. They don't care about anything else," a night doorman, West African himself, once tells me in disenchantment. "But now they are here. . . . They can't send them home." Regardless of the asylum decision, large-scale enforced return is an unlikely scenario for a country with a notoriously weak infrastructure and record in deportation, political rhetoric notwithstanding.[20] ("We all know it's easier to stay in Italy!" Woikat once giggled during our McDonald's lunch to celebrate his five-year subsidiary protection.) "They're already here" means it is too much, or too late, to substantially reverse the flow. Too much, my interlocutors would add, to start from scratch again elsewhere. Too little, at the same time, for many to achieve their aspirations, even only the basic ones.

All this being said, "I'm here" may also be another way to say or anticipate, "I'm doing nothing." "What on earth do they want from us!", Daokaate exclaims one afternoon as he's getting back into his room. It's still early for his running session outside. We can stay there and chat. "With no work and no papers, we've got nothing to do." What about Italian classes or a vocational course, I try. Daokaate shakes his head, well tucked under his blanket: "We've already done that." Full stop. Back to his smartphone, under the surveillance of a white teddy bear that is sitting on his headboard ("my mascot," he comments with a smile). "Health wise, I'm okay," says Amadou, another time, as we've come across each other on the staircase. "All the rest is not. . . . You can't stay in here all the time, right?" My murmuring feedback is meant to be empathic, but it doesn't really work. For once Amadou suddenly stares me in the eyes: "*You*—do you always stay home?" No, I don't. "You see? Me neither." Where are you going though, he slowly adds, as if he's weighing each word, "if you've nothing to do? What are you going to do all day long? Nothing," he concludes, as placid as disenchanted. At some point a job call may well pop up. Someone invites you to go out, some class to attend, a new internship perhaps. And at a later point, when the final decision comes, this will be over anyway. Meanwhile, Amadou is not alone in occupying an interstice of nothingness and in feeling tired about it.

In sum, the opposite of nothing, or what is perceived to be absent, missing or denied, is not just having something to do. It is rather and primarily a job, as an instrumental resource and a dignified, gendered way of filling time. Work is as much a need as a gendered demonstration of decency and self-worth. "A man is supposed to work . . . to do what he wants to achieve in life," repeats Gorko in the long pauses between one short-term job and the next. "The problem here," he adds in an unintended echo with Paul, "is that you're idle. You've got nothing to do, just be home the whole day. This aches you; it aches your mind. It makes you think too much. . . . Some people have mental health problems. . . . And their body hurts too." Not being employed is more than an instrumental problem. Rather, it is demeaning and stigmatizing in relation to the normative register of masculinity.[21] "Slow violence," an academic would probably rephrase[22] what Gorko, Paul and many more are experiencing through their bodies.

However, while Gorko is repeating the same message as most, his serious face suggests he's not sure I'm really getting it. "How can you spend your days this way? . . . A man must live out of his work. . . . You go to work, then go back home, you eat, take some rest, and then you work. If you stay here you sleep and eat all the time. That's not good." Masculinity, autonomy, self-worth as part of the same moral repertoire. "You work, at the end of the month you have your salary, and you can sort out one or two of your problems." Meanwhile, there is the pocket money, I retort. Gorko snorts, his gaze still fixed ahead. "Of course, it's important . . . but it's only for you to eat." There would be so much more to be done. And you would need much more money anyway. Some, he adds after a pause, "use it to send home—if your father or your mother need to go to hospital, you use it, okay, that's important"—if only that "you stay hungry here!" As long as you haven't a job, money is bound to be too little (although it may remain too little anyhow). Moreover, this is not money you really gained. "Here we depend on the local authority! If they say stop, we are left with nothing." Dependency is the problem. And dependent people would be a more accurate category than residents, although nobody would use it. "You must work if you want to be somebody," Gorko sternly reiterates, before deciding that he's done with me, for today: "I'm going in to relax." To relax, I repeat within myself.

Whether for Gorko or anybody else, *nothing* comes with an implicit reference to what is missing—nothing perceived as novel, meaningful, tangible, fruitful, future-oriented or anyway relevant. Yet, at least when it comes to a job search, "nothing" need not be the last word. One may just keep trying, which sometimes turns a job search into an occupation in itself. Sani, with his daily round of CV distribution in town or in the countryside, is a case in point. "I'm not staying here all day sleeping or watching TV," he points out to me. And he's asking for no favor. "I've only asked you if there is something wrong in my CV, which I should correct." In fact, his CV has nothing incorrect. The point is that it holds very little, just as for hundred other young men like him, along with the real discrimination against them. "I left so many CVs," repeats Sani. "Nobody ever called me, not even for a trial period. . . . Is it because I'm Black? Or because I'm Nigerian, and they think Nigerians are all in drugs?" Perhaps, he adds, "My suffering must continue here too. Like in my country."

There is so much frustration around, Olusola will comment later on, as the three of us are sharing a plate of meat and spinach with fufu. "They'll never look at your CVs—it's no use," he warns. You must do your training, he says, turning what he's trying to do into a patronizing recommendation. Otherwise, unless you're very lucky or know somebody, no way. "Nobody gives you nothing out of this place— you must help yourself." "That's what I'm doing," Sani resentfully says back. A few tense gazes between the two, with myself in the middle, and then they depart, each on his own, as long as the little space and the huge available time allow mutual disregard. A few more hours and the tension is over. A few more weeks and Sani will find a job indeed—a very exploitative one for me, a better-than-nothing one for him. In fact, a success story, enough for him to be kicked out of the center—he's become too rich by then—some months later.

4.4   VIRTUAL MOBILITY: A WAY OUT OF STILLNESS?

The everyday ambivalence between experienced stillness and desired mobility— being bodily still and imaginatively, even morally, mobile—is constantly mediated by the use of smartphones. In principle, this enables connections with places and people worldwide. In practice, virtual connectedness does not necessarily facilitate access to the labor market, a legitimate legal status, or adulthood. There is some risk of over-celebrating its emancipatory power by way of technological determin- ism. At the same time, smartphones do shape everyday life in multiple ways, well beyond the striking contrast between the material boundaries of bodily presence and the immaterial unboundedness of online communication.[23]

Smartphones are invariably there in each bedroom, including those with fewer material belongings. Owning and using a smartphone is as ordinary for a young asylum seeker as for anybody else.[24] Yet it may seem weird to (naif) outsiders, for the apparent contrast between a relatively expensive good of consumption and the poverty of its owner, or for the habitual scene of young men alone, or alone together, bent down on their devices. To my eyes, the everyday use of smartphones holds a special analytical value. These are powerful tools for people to relocate relevance—hyper-concentrated in physical space, just around a tiny and generally well-kept device, much more dispersed and potentially boundless in the virtual space. So many practices, meanings and functions come together in one artifact, at the core of private life.

As people who are bodily still use their mobile phones, are they also mobile in some non-literal sense? What about grand narratives of time compression and space annihilation, within the microcosm of a place for asylum seekers?[25] The first and most obvious response is that time keeps flowing slowly, and external space is hardly any more accessible with a smartphone in your hands. Virtual or imagina- tive mobility need not come along with any better capacity to bring sensuous prox- imity back—to reach certain places, own certain goods, meet the dear ones again. It simply takes the shape of icons popping up intermittently, depending on the Wi-Fi quality, on a tiny screen. As in Zygmunt Bauman's[26] famous rephrasing of the poor as "flawed consumers," people keep strolling around the images of all they cannot afford, right out of the virtual window shop of global, branded and racialized capitalism. This, however, does not make virtual mobility any less important. Even unfulfilled consumption desires are revealing about personal tastes and (dis)alignments with the normative ways of being youth, male, religious, and possibly African. More fundamentally, there is far more than daydreaming to their online lives, including the multifarious connections they can nourish or re-establish. Virtual contact, including with family and friends elsewhere in the world, may well be the most real contact possible—the deepest form of (non-literal) mobility—in the everyday life of displaced people.[27]

Moreover, as the recent scholarship on the entanglement between offline and online life has shown,[28] there are meaningful parallels between the care and decoration of a smartphone, as a material artifact, and the care and decoration of domestic space. The former may be a functional equivalent of the latter. There is something more homely in one's mobile device, hence worth taking care of, than in the anonymous and heteronomous space of an asylum facility. More than one's temporary bedroom, the smartphone is private, intimate, exclusive. More than any physical environment, it obediently responds to one's commands, embodied in fingers moving fast on its surface, as long as one can afford some data traffic. More than any physical location, it is a place of power and control. It stores contacts, videos and pictures, hence personal memories and meaningful relationships. Its relevance is affective as much as instrumental. Besides opening up to a potentially global virtual space, a mobile device has more pragmatic and immediate functions. People obviously need it to be constantly available for short-notice job calls. They use it to participate in collective prayers, try a driving license test, perhaps attend a language class—all the way being exposed to institutional and social media from Italy, as much as from elsewhere.

The homepage of one's smartphone, often decorated with a selfie, marks the deepest threshold of privacy in the center. Some may well share something of their ways of surfing, even with me, if only out of boredom for their everyday routines. One day, as I'm intermittently chatting with Ninu on his bed like many other times, he starts a video call, the peeling wall of his room as backdrop. He turns the smartphone screen toward me—a young woman in a nightdress, a clean and bright room, a lovely toddler close to her. Some chats in *kriolo* between them, a quick greeting in Portuguese as we wave our hands, *amigo*, and the scene is over. Ninu's virtual roaming is not, though: online videos with young Black bodies singing, playing rap music, partying. Things are no different when we catch up outside, if he's in a good mood. One afternoon, on a courtyard bench, he's murmuring something on his smartphone, as if he were talking to it. In fact, he's struggling to read an online mortgage offer he's fished up by chance. After that, a new commercial picture every few seconds—sound systems, bicycles, watches, sneakers. At some point, as he shifts to his Facebook account, he shifts his body too—

no more space to be shared with me. This is for him only, although in less than ten minutes he's done and moves back in. It's like an ongoing temporal swing: upstairs and downstairs, indoor and outdoor, online and offline. Moving somehow, while staying essentially put. Meanwhile, time goes by.

"Look at it—so beautiful!," Suka says, another time, of a watch that virtually lies in front of us. And then on and on, in a virtual and global "cultural supermarket"[29] in which his facework is more telling, to me, than the flowing brands under the semi-broken surface of his screen. Suka slowly reads them and tags a few. Some players of Manchester City, "my team." A whole range of black or golden watches, and the cheaper version of a smartwatch, fifty-nine euros, "too expensive." Some BMW cars. Pictures of Mecca. And a post with three pictures, "from Allah, for Allah, to Allah": a fetus, a praying man, a shroud. Suka nods in approval. And then another moral teaching: "When you have a place to go to, that's home. When you have someone who loves you, that's a family. When you have both, that's a blessing." Perhaps *if* would be more appropriate, I think to myself. After reading it thoughtfully, Suka concludes, "I have a home, but not yet a family." And then some posts about the Gambia—soccer players, rappers, beautiful and not-too-undressed women—the latter two categories, almost invariably Black. And then a warning message against sex tourism on the Smiling Coast. And then the show goes on, as it probably would among many other twenty-year-old males wherever.

By roaming within the global supermarket, hours go by until something happens, someone arrives or one goes to rest, with the smartphone at hand. In the meantime, something emerges about people's tastes and lifestyles and possibly about their personal lives. Even a casual roundup of comedy videos can open to something else, when a Gambian journalist asks native young people what they think of sentences like "woman means home" or "woman is the homemaker." While the interviewees nod with a smile, Fatou gives a sly look to me: "Here, little by little, you change your mind." Over and again, facetious images intermingle with more serious ones—Islamic celebrations or preachers, TV news, reportages. Sooner or later, with Fatou, more personal images emerge too: hanging out with his friends, playing soccer, swimming in the lake. Sometimes intimate tales about his mother or sister appear, supported by their own pictures (see 5.7 and 7.4). Even a Ramadan dinner on the balcony, as rare as a video as an event. An old rusty grill, a table with lots of food and drinks, and a powerful instantiation of endogenous order—what people do through their own group-making. In the midst of the video, some exchange good wishes about the future—that is, about work and papers.

Sometimes, African politics eerily comes in. On another room visit to Ninu, his "sit down!" on an old and re-adapted school chair comes with unusual sounds from his smartphone. Lusophone news, politicians speaking. "Coup!" says Ninu, without losing his mild smile and low tone. This is Guinea-Bissau, seen from a place for asylum seekers in Italy. The makeshift video of the "jury ceremony" of a new self-proclaimed president in a hotel. Neither the parliament nor the international community recognized him, says Ninu. "Now we have two presidents and two prime ministers." Nothing good. However, no need to be especially worried. His family is in a village, away from the capital. Everything else is all too far from his life. Even so, a smartphone would already suffice for him to be reasonably well informed. In a group or alone, one can well stay updated on what happens throughout Africa. This does not mean that, in practice, they do, nor that the transnational communication flows with family members are constant or smooth. The opposite is more likely the case, after the relational disruptions of displacement and the fragmented pathways that followed.

4.5   MOVING: OUT, ON, FORWARD

Even in a regime of temporal stillness, the young men in the center are not literally immobile. However, their pervasive uncertainty about the next developments goes along with little scope for moving in the short term. In part, this is a result of the rules of institutional hospitality. In part, there is little alternative unless one makes the most radical choice, as sometimes happens—try and restart from scratch elsewhere.[30] At some point, though, institutional hospitality will be over. You have to move *out* (in search of new accommodation), as well as *on* (in the life course) and hopefully *forward* (in struggling for better conditions). Each of these ways of moving deserves discussion.

Moving out

"Here it's only a matter of time," Fatou replies, soft-spoken as usual, as I tell him that "at least" they can stay until, *inshallah*, they get papers. Here they counsel you somehow, he admits. That said, "better on your own. But you must be set up." Whether people are "set up" on their way out from the center is far from granted. What is certain is that they must leave the field of relevance of institutional assistance and navigate life on their own—just as they used to do before, but ideally with more practical expertise, richer social capital and more focused aspirations. Interestingly, most caseworkers do the same every couple of years or so. And just as it happens with their resident counterparts, those who stay longer seem to be those with lesser employability.

Moving out means anything between an obvious and unremarkable step in one's housing pathway and a prospective eviction that looms for a while, encounters passive resistance and is made effective at last. Whenever one leaves spontaneously, as is mostly the case, he may still frame it as a demonstration of dignity. "I don't want them to kick me out," says Fatou, having in mind Sani, who was expelled by the police one night, while he was sleeping in their room. "It's a question of self-respect," he explains, slicing up the onion that will end up in the frying pan with chicken thighs, beside the big plate of cold pasta he will share with his new roommate. "I have my own mind set. . . . We cannot stay here forever. At some point those who help you tell, 'We can't help you any more,' and you must go—it's the law." Fatou won't end up in the street though. "If you live out you may have the necessity to do bad things—I don't want to do bad things. . . . I have never been out, not even in my country, and not here! I will make my plans and ask my friends . . . and will have to distinguish the true from the false ones." As it happens, Fatou will leave on the day agreed, doing precisely what he had anticipated: "I will greet them, say thanks and apologize if I hurt them or did something against the law." As I look surprised, he explains, "We all hurt people sometimes, even if we don't know or they don't tell us. . . . It's normal, we're human. So, I will apologize. Maybe sometimes I did not do the cleaning I had to do!"

Leaving the center, from a longtime perspective, is one housing transition among many more. Nevertheless, in the here-and-now it means much more than losing a bed and searching for a new one. On your way out, you are crossing the moral boundary between heteronomy and autonomous responsibility. "Here they tell you what is good and what is bad. Out there, all do their business," says Olusola, once he has transitioned outside. Nobody is expected to either control you or care about you, whether you leave spontaneously or not and whatever your means by then.

Moving *forward* indeed, rather than simply moving *out*, has all to do with getting and retaining a job and some accommodation. This will obviously be more expensive, and yet it promises more freedom. No limitations on the times of entrance and exit or on who is allowed in. No gatekeepers staring at you or checking to see if you cleaned up. Ultimately, no more relevance attached to you. Either you'll make it on your own, or you'll end up in some form of homelessness. Even then, and even if the asylum application is rejected, one is very unlikely to move back to "his" country, unless in the rare occurrence of an assisted return plan. The embodied rationale of being here can only be forward-looking, whether one lives up to it or not. "We are moving ahead," albeit "little by little."

Moreover, even a status rejection may be framed as a minor concern, relative to the adversities one has already come through. This is what Ogwu helps me understand as the final decision on his case comes, after four years of institutional hospitality. That decision has a paradoxical tinge, if one connects it to perceived deservingness. "I know guys who got [papers] and have done all bad things. . . . I've never sold drugs. I've never hurt anybody. I never did something wrong. . . . And I got negative." Within this frame it does make little sense. However, Ogwu proudly says, "I will always be myself—I'm good with everybody. . . . The document is only a material thing." In adverse and apparently inexplicable circumstances, the claim for dignity and self-respect is all the more urgent. The moral geographies of people like Ogwu need not overlap with those embedded in the reception system. Claiming back one's purported value is also a form of agency, albeit insufficient to avoid eviction.

As for the next steps, there is something fundamentally true in the "point of reference" that Olusola murmurs beside me, whenever we have an informal driving lesson in my car. While putting the car in reverse, he's been taught to focus on a certain point behind as a "reference"—which he diligently (and, in my perception, slowly) does. Moving the metaphor out of a parking lot and reversing the movement (ahead, rather than behind), the next steps have much to do with the variety of points of reference available and with one's mastery in interacting with them. Whatever the next place, this is part and parcel of the eventual transition to adulthood.

Moving on (and perhaps forward)

As long as you stay in the center you are protected, but you are not really seen as an adult. Nor do you perceive yourself as such. This is ironic for a facility that is targeted to "autonomous adults" (as opposed to individual newcomers or asylum-seeking families, who have hosting infrastructures of their own). The well-meant, if increasingly elusive, mission of the place is precisely facilitating the transition to "full" autonomy. "You're an adult by now!" the staff periodically say, if only to exhort people to take up everyday chores. In practice, the emphasis on adulthood and the initiatives for "activation" go along with discourses and practices that instantiate infantilization.[31] While this is often inscribed in asylum-seeker reception,[32] another fact is perhaps more surprising: top-down infantilization touches deep chords in the emotional and moral repertoires of people themselves.

If migration is expected to enable the transition to adulthood,[33] life in the center is a demonstration of how limited, slow and contradictory the transition is. You're not an adult, as long as your livelihood depends on institutional welfare and on the staff delegated to represent it. You're not an adult, anyway, because you have no say on the routines and rules that shape your everyday life. There is an irremediably infantilizing subtext in rules that do not allow residents to be out after eleven o'clock on weekdays or twelve on weekends, unless for work reasons. There is also some sad irony, since many of them would hardly hang out anyway. You're not an adult, moreover, because sometimes the staff see your ways of undoing nothing as unnecessarily infantile. "Stop being a child!" some male caseworkers exclaim, whenever they see someone who's lying in the bedroom the whole day, keeps complaining about his body that "aches" or appears indifferent to their sexist jokes.

Yet, not everybody would object when a well-intentioned female caseworker says that she feels like "a mum of seventy children" and should take care of them accordingly. Since their parents live so far away, who else is gonna do that? Indeed, as Olusola once tells me, caseworkers should be like "mum and dad"—listen to them, take care of them—something the newly recruited staff, with a decreasing budget and an increased work burden, are unlikely to ever do. Admittedly, most fellow residents would never subscribe to this view, publicly at least. To their eyes caseworkers are only an unavoidable and irrelevant presence. However, the view speaks to the fact that infantilization is no one-way process. Rather than simply creating infantilization from scratch, institutional hospitality reveals the ongoing friction between expectations or aspirations of independence and actual dependence, even need for care. This is what the teddy bears that are sitting on a number of beds, although not in most, tacitly suggest (cf. 6.5). Young men like Olusola do suffer from the protracted distance in space and time from their loved ones. Perhaps Olusola is only more reflexive and open-minded than others in this respect, at least with me. This may call for a private lexicon of semi-childhood, as much as for a public one of semi-adulthood.

Overall, though, it is "the system" that prevents you from reaching adulthood. You're not an adult yet because, generally speaking, you do not work enough to maintain yourself, let alone those in Africa. And you are not perceived as an adult, in day-to-day communication, whenever your broken Italian invites your counterpart to a simplified, childlike lexicon. It always feels weird, with my Nigerian, Ghanaian or Gambian interlocutors, to shift back to Italian—their mode of interaction with the mainstream. Some have actually achieved a good mastery of oral Italian and navigate the conversation accordingly. With many more, speaking in Italian makes communication poor, hesitant, even pietistic, regardless of face and body language. One language shift is enough for me to shift down my perception along the biographical gradient. Before, I was speaking to an adult. Now, I feel like I am speaking to a child. Nothing bad in using an elementary lexicon with people with little language mastery. However, the resulting infantilization is weirdly at odds with adult bodies, adult (if mostly unaccomplished) life projects and more-than-adult life histories.

The same ambivalent co-existence of childhood and adulthood emerges in written texts, such as a short essay Woikat prepared for his eighth-degree school test—a stage that most of his fellow residents have not (yet) reached. At the end of a one-page history of Senegal, from "France in power" to Léopold Senghor, Woikat explains that a volunteer, "who's like an aunt for me," helped write that down. "I do not know much of recent history . . . [because] I haven't studied it since I left school." If I were to read the text alone, I might attribute it to an early teenager. As it happens, this is the lived experience of someone ten years older, with his own adult mindset and body. Much of that experience, however, Woikat articulates through drawings rather than words. He has specially prepared some new ones for the school exam. This turns a formulaic assignment into a powerful channel for storytelling. Unsurprisingly, his drawing-based narrative is as intimate as didactic. The first drawing, "When they shot at me in Libya," is about a beach with a small and overcrowded shelter (figure 10).[34] "It is of the owner of the wooden boats—we gave him the money" to leave. "Libyans," he recounts, kill "Africans" for no reason.

FIGURE 10. A visual translation of an episode recounted by Woikat. While in Libya, in a shelter close to the seaside, he was shot by someone from there, apparently for no reason in particular. Artwork by Woikat. Photo by author.

That day Woikat had come out of the shelter with a friend to buy some bread. A car passes by; someone calls him in Arabic, "Friend!" Woikat gets closer and the guy shoots him down, wounding his leg. All of this is portrayed in a style that may not give the sense of a potentially tragic event. Yet his story becomes tellable, and powerful, only by conflating oral, bodily and graphic formats in the interaction with someone like me.

Overall, for Woikat and the others, adulthood is not just a horizon that keeps shifting ahead. It is also a matter of unequally distributed and effective ways of anticipating it through everyday practices of future-making. These have to do with people's navigational capacity outside the center, hence with the uneven networks of trust, friendship and support they build—the more mixed, the more (instrumentally) valuable. However, even while dwelling inside a place of dependency, one can find ways of playing out an adult identity that lives up to the predominant expectations. Care for one's body and clothing is also a way of asserting this identity. Likewise, spontaneously sticking to Ramadan rules and constraints, without any complaint (and possibly offering food and drinks to guests like me), is a way of reproducing and displaying a version of achieved male adulthood. Much of the rest will have to wait outside the center, though. Once people are out into "real life," as Olusola calls it, being mobile again is no guarantee of becoming adult. However, it disrupts much of the scope available to being anything else than that.

4.6   BEYOND THE STILL-MOVING BINARY: GLIMPSES OF THE FUTURE

"For me there is no destination!" Ousmane cries out in the courtyard one autumn afternoon. He's in the mood to chat for a while, beyond the usual "nothing new," before going out for his usual stroll in town. "I could be anywhere," he says, waving the hands around. "I'm here now," beating his feet on the ground, "but tomorrow I could be in a different place." There is no destination, as a legitimate and accomplished place to be, until he has a job and then papers, "even only one or two years." The former, in Ousmane's moral view, is a precondition for the latter. You will get papers if you work hard and thereby "if you're useful—not useless." As Suka often reminds me, "Here, if you don't have a job, you are useless."[35] "I'm praying for a job," Ousmane repeats, just while he's waiting for the final decision on his case. If he gets a job, if he gets papers, he'll finally be able to go back to the Gambia, even only on a short visit, "after five years." You have your family there. You keep in touch. You send money if you can. But it's a lot of time, even while you want to move forward, as he says, and literally does, getting out of the park.

"I could be anywhere," Ousmane maintains. Yet he has been literally in the same place for four years. Time has left its own traces—including in his everyday routines—and perhaps some reluctant roots.[36] It is no coincidence that my interlocutors stress that they wish to stay in Italy rather than moving farther, if only they get a formal status. Enough of uprooting and readapting to new places, languages, people and circumstances. For sure, moving farther would be a minor cost, relative to those taken up already. However, the idea of a settled, ordinary life or of a selective immobility of choice seems far more attractive, with a view to setting up a family of one's own, as yet another dimension of adulthood. At least when it comes to narratives, my interlocutors' dreams of a stable home may be not too different from those of their native and sedentary counterparts. Socialization, habituation and perhaps inertia have their own weight.

Nevertheless, from a here-and-now of suspension, talking about the future—what one feels he cannot tell—is hardly less challenging than talking about the past—what one does not want to tell. More often than not, future talks take the self-performative tone of principled statements. "I'M BUILDING UP MY FUTURE" reads the title of another drawing in Woikat's room. This is no mere rhetorical statement, though.[37] Improving the future is part of the moral texture of migration, as much as "helping our families and building our house," Woikat repeats. More fundamentally, the future may emerge as the ultimate reason why "*we* left—we did it, no Italian has ever called us here," as he reminds those who complain of Italians' racism. At the same time, what the future will carry along is hard to envision, unless by concluding that it is "in the hands of God."

Beyond the surface, more insights on the future emerge out of casual conversation. One afternoon in the staff office, a caseworker and I are chatting with Olusola in front of a large world map, on which he struggles to recognize most countries. It seems as if Italy is "carrying the weight of the whole Europe," he mulls, looking at its position. "But I know it, I want to stay, and when I'm older I want to do like you." That is, "travel during holidays," but otherwise "stay here," he adds, beating with his fingers on the map. For him, and most of his fellow residents, the emplacement of the future is not in question—"here" in Italy or anyway in Europe. In fact, such an emplacement is not guaranteed as a right, as of now. Beyond the short-term horizon of jobs and papers, the future is as vague in terms of navigational strategies as it is predictable in terms of a desired point of arrival. At some point, as the prevalent imaginary goes, people should have a job, a wife and some children, a house. Everyday life should flow around a fixed point of reference and control (put otherwise: a home)[38] to start from and get back to. Perhaps one could "do something to help the poor," Olusola adds, for "there are poor people everywhere." Leaving that aside, these future narratives sound as unremarkable to an outsider as they are remarkable to someone used to the parallel and demeaning normality of refugeehood.

How far people will become "like everybody else" is of course difficult to say, based on the here-and-now. It need not be so exceptional as the predominant discursive register on refugees and their "bare lives" would lead us to assume, though. Regardless of the next steps, the obligations toward those in the country of origin are also likely to persist—or at least, the moral pressure from their side. "How on earth can you send money all the time!" complains Woikat on his way out of a money-transfer agency. You earn little, if at all. You're struggling to build your own future here. Even so, "there are those who send all they get—I don't." In practice, most feel they are expected to send. The moral pressure to do so is one of the forms of absent presence (see 5.7) that loom on everyday life in the center. As clear, though, is that uncertainty need not be the last word on the future. "Sooner or later we'll all return anyway," murmurs Woikat, before changing the topic of conversation. No point or way to add more.

As a matter of fact, yet another view of the future lies deep in the narratives of my interlocutors and somewhere ahead of them in time. While staying and struggling for the good life is the goal for the conceivable future, it may not be the last step. Moving *back*, to spend old age or even only be buried in Africa, feels like a moral obligation or a way of reestablishing the natural order of things.[39] This is typically an implicit assumption, which occasionally pops up in intimate conversations or along critical transitions. One day, as Fatou is leaving the center for good, he's around to say a quick farewell to those who happen to be there, including Bashshel, as melancholic as ever in his continual wanderings out and back in. As most fellow residents do, Fatou approaches him as a younger brother. Bashshel looks back in hesitation, before asking one question: "When are you going back to Africa?" Fatou smiles back, as he jumps on his bike: "Let's go back together!"

FIGURE 11. Salim as an ambassador on a civil-service poster that reads "FOCUS ON YOUR FUTURE." The poster is from a local campaign for youth civil service. Salim was himself a volunteer in civil service for a while. *Source*: Civil service department of the local authority. Used with permission.

However, Bashshel gets serious and looks down to the ground. "No, I'm not going." Already on his way out, Fatou is taken aback. "You don't want to return? You *don't* want to return?" Bashshel silently smiles and goes back in.

As all that has to do with the countries of origin, return is unlikely to be openly discussed. In a short-term perspective, it would only be seen as a failure that frustrates all risks and costs faced so far. Upon deeper reflection, though, "Africa" and "home" keep looming within (see 7.4 and 7.5). This is what Cé reveals, when he periodically comes back—he's got papers and a temporary accommodation elsewhere—to meet his friends and pray with them. As we chat on the bench outside, his attitude is invariably more reflexive and his language mastery better than most. Whatever happens, Cé states, "everybody must return to his country. One must die in the place in which he was born. . . . So I will hopefully do."[40] Nothing to add, unless being aware of the dissonance between the promise, lure and potential of making it in Europe and the moral obligation to stick to one's essential(ized) identity—hence, go back to Africa, in a rather literal homing.[41] This should be the last step of a morally good, ultimately circular life pathway.

As it happens, the moral ideal of homecoming may be all too practical and concrete. "Nobody comes here for no reason. . . . My reason is to work hard and help everybody," Salim tells me one afternoon in his room, before saying, as many do, "I'm looking for my future and my own life . . . but I don't know where." His expression is gentle and slightly defiant—the same expression he "lent" to a public campaign for youth civic service that included his picture along with an exhortation, "Focus on your future!" (figure 11). Four years later, as I'm writing these lines, his future is all too certain—as long as it exists at all. Right after getting his papers, and after a short journey back to Guinea, Salim fell prey to a severe illness and passed away in a matter of weeks. The future of his body is back to his village, where he has been soon repatriated, as per his desire, thanks to a fund-raising initiative. The future of his life, and of many lives like his, can also go through storytelling and ethnographic writing—still another way out of still another form of nothingness.

5

Present, Absent

"This is no Christmas," Ninu repeats one mid-December evening, as we are strolling under the glittering decorations in the streets. While these are in stark contrast with the bare interiors of the center, they raise little emotions for an immigrant Christian like him. No reason or way to celebrate as long as his family is in Guinea-Bissau. And as long as he has no way of helping them to leave, nor any intention to get back to Bissau, where "there is a problem," about which he wants only silence. While his mother passed away, his siblings are present there and absent from his life predicament here, no matter how frequently they get in touch. "God knows— he'll do the right thing for my future," Ninu concludes, "the right thing" being "a job and the papers" as a precondition for whatever may come next. For now, all that is literally present is a number of mundane objects around his bed and around his body. His family is far away in space (and time, in the case of his mother), while being present in the moral economy of his private life.

Absences that matter, presences that do not matter and uncanny "creepings" of the absent into the present[1] all go along with one another in the center, which is meant to guarantee, by its very presence, something that would be absent otherwise—a basic protection during asylum assessment. Migration itself was expected to afford something that was absent before—a safer, more dignified and forward-looking life. Now, in a place of confinement and waithood that might still pave the way for a better future, various forms of presence and absence are mutually entangled. No neat separation exists between presence and absence and between past and present, in the ways of feeling of my interlocutors. The materiality of a sheltering infrastructure is present. Any clear idea of what will happen next is absent. The memories of past life and of the circumstances that pushed people here

97

are both absent and present. They should be kept at bay and occasionally emerge nonetheless as "ghostly matter" that keeps "haunting."[2] So does the ongoing, fragmented field of emotional attachments and moral obligations with loved ones living elsewhere. This also takes the ambiguous shape and the dragging weight of an absent presence.[3]

As I weave together the analytics of chapters 3 and 4, it is time to explore the ambivalent relation between presence and absence (in space) and between present and past (in time). In an analytical sense, *undoing nothing* means unraveling the entanglement between what is literally present, including what is no longer relevant, and what is materially absent and yet present in the realm of emotion, memories, affective ties and moral obligations. The exploration starts with the unnoticeable material cultures that the residents accumulate and leave behind. Most of these objects end up in the realm of irrelevance as soon as they lose instrumental value, while still leaving some trace. It is worth approaching them as embodiments of existential liminality,[4] and as markers of the gap between what is there and what is not. After an overview of what is present, I chart, through people's practices and narratives, all that is absent and matters nonetheless. This calls for reflection on questions of silence, invisibility, troublesome "floating" and eventually two forms of absence—what no longer is and what still could be.

5.1   (UN)DOING PRESENCE

You probably wouldn't be there, if you could afford anything else, and yet there you are. Most of the time, for the time being, my young male interlocutors are present in the center with their Black and Brown bodies. However, much about them is absent, including any common knowledge of their past life circumstances. Legally speaking, this is not in the remit of institutional hospitality. What the staff is expected to know amounts to basic data such as their declared name, country of origin, date of birth (often fixed on January 1 for lack of certain information), date of arrival to Italy (this being always impressed, instead, in people's memories). These are the only official traces that will stay once people leave. Meanwhile, people are in. Whether they're visible or not and whether or not someone cares about them, they probably feel, and are perceived, less out of place than elsewhere in town. This is the place where they have a bed, some pocket money, the right to get in and out during the day—in short, the best available approximation of home (see 7.2), subject to compliance with the rules of hospitality.

As for any infrastructure of a migration industry, their presence is the ultimate raison d'etre of the place itself. "*We* are the structure!" Olusola once cries out, while reclaiming more affective proximity from the staff after the 2019 budgetary cut and turnover. The very existence of the place is justified by their presence. As in any residential infrastructure,[5] the length of stay is a source of local expertise, if not of self-legitimation. Several "old" residents know the place better than the most occasional staff members. Moreover, their presence leaves traces.[6] As little as these may mean to residents themselves, they are stubbornly and inertially there. As they suggest, dwelling in the center is like a still in an open-ended film—that is, a larger life and housing pathway. Even when it emerges in an empty and apparently immobile present, one's presence is inscribed in untold biographies that exceed it. Rather than being a fixed and self-evident state of things, it is continuously made and unmade in relation to several forms of absence.

There is something of a novel settlement, albeit in a very constrained and pre-determined environment, in the entrance of each newcomer. With some, including Woikat, I have been in the position to witness this (un)doing of presence—that is, both the prequel and the sequel to one's years-long stay. While Woikat may have an unusual dedication to domesticity, his story is a case in point of the ways in which a newcomer enters a bedroom and delimits his space, thereby making himself present, only to leave it behind and "undo" his presence at a later stage. One day, as Woikat enters his new bedroom with me already as a fortunate guest, it doesn't take long for him to carry his stuff along. Carrying it away, a couple of years later, will take remarkably more effort. As a very first thing, he lays out his smartphone and music speakers on the nightstand, with a plastic envelope to protect them, as well as his deodorant and paper towels. As soon as his belongings are in, with the window open wide, Woikat starts making up his bed with the clean linen made available by the staff, laying above it his own blanket with the colorful picture of a Manhattan sunset. As there is nobody else in the room yet, he can afford to choose between two beds. It's better to pick the inner one, close to the corridor wall. This way, "if someone passes by and the door is open, they can't see me—even if they peep in." Protection is a matter of relative invisibility and privacy, as much as of access to a bed.

Meanwhile, Woikat takes up the mattress and turns it on the other side. A rap song in Italian is already keeping us company: "My place is not your place. . . . They tell me I've sold myself for money." In a little while the bed is ready. Now Woikat is spraying deodorant around. Next he opens up a big plastic bag full of dishes, the gift from a couple of old farmers he helped with fruit harvesting. Their place is under the bed. After that it's time to look at the drawer in the nightstand. "Look, they left something for me!" Indeed: a *misbaha*, several coins, a couple of keys. The traces of more people in the same room before. Last, little by little, he'll start to hang his drawings. Now this is his place, until further notice.

Time goes by, even while waiting—it may actually fly, for someone resourceful and lucky enough to fill it with things to do. The eventual ritual of exit, on the agreed-on day, demands a parallel unmaking of one's presence. It's early in the morning, which should make the process less visible to others. Moving elsewhere, with me as a self-interested driver, will require a couple of rounds and as many visits back. The room, Woikat repeats, must be thoroughly empty and the floor perfectly clean. Zero tolerance for the oily stains he has spotted and is looking at with disgust. No more traces from him so that his successor will find "everything clean," as he emphasizes before giving the key back to the staff with an unusually warm goodbye. The traces that matter should rather be those that will hopefully be left back in Senegal over time: money sent and well spent, a new house, maybe a local bride and children.[7] In the meantime, and despite his best efforts, it's unlikely that Woikat will really leave no trace here. If only as a matter of inertia, some distinctive material culture tends to survive. Exploring it, I suggest, is critical to make sense of the interaction between past and present, as much as between presence and absence.[8]

5.2   TRACES OF PRESENCE

Untidy, scruffy, impersonal. That's the impression most bedrooms gave me on my first visits. Anybody—that is, anybody in need of basic accommodation—might be dwelling there. The longer I would stay, however, the more I would nourish an almost opposite perception. Far more is present than the standard, basic and free affordances for social reproduction (i.e., beds, tables, closets, kitchen appliances etc.). That *more* has to do with personal signs and belongings that parallel and often outlast one's bodily presence. Like any inhabited built environment, the center bears traces of its dwellers, present and past. Private and left-behind objects, decorations, writings or signs on the walls are a silent and irrelevant background. They are often related to people or events that are physically absent by now and yet present through the memories they may elicit.[9] They articulate an ambivalent tension between absence as an experiential condition and potential presence, if only one traces the circumstances in which they were left and the life histories behind them. Personal belongings, as much as decorations and writings, collectively make up this silent objectscape.

Belongings

Like most people in ordinary housing, the young male residents have a number of belongings—not necessarily those they would aspire to or would be expected to have. Certain technological goods, such as TV sets, stereos and laptops, are present in a remarkably stratified way. Far more universal are, unsurprisingly, smartphones. Almost as systematic is the absence of books, aside from some old textbooks and, occasionally, a copy of the Koran or the Bible. Certain belongings, like those related to sports, religion, or hygiene and body care, are everywhere, including in the least cluttered rooms or those with most tangible infrastructural deterioration, like Gune's. One shutter is permanently down—it was broken years ago. The door is never fully locked—not a matter of hospitality, as in my naive early understanding, but of dysfunctionality. It also was broken and keeps waiting to be fixed. Anybody could sneak in, if anybody cared. Unrelated to this, and yet in eerie resonance, Gune's roommate has long been staying with no bed linens—

a bare mattress, to host a fortunately not-so-bare life, critical philosophers not-withstanding. Even so, belongings are visible and left items may emerge there, as much as anywhere else.

Importantly, not all belongings have a merely instrumental or pragmatic function. Sneakers are a fascinating case in point.[10] In most bedrooms, what used to be bookshelves have been reconverted into shoe racks. "They leave them there, so they don't need to bend down," a caseworker once casually remarks, before moving on to more important matters. In fact, sneakers in orderly lines are as much an instrumental good as a form of decoration, display and distinction—just what pictures, silverware or paraphernalia would do in the living room of an ordinary domestic space (figure 12). Sneakers on the shelves are utterly implicit and yet meaningful ways of presenting the self within the constraints of refugee life. They are a powerful illustration of the dreams that inspire their owners—young athletic men with the physical ability to literally run into the future. They tacitly show that aesthetics matters, in one's own tastes and terms. Unlike other objects, they symbolize neither absence (the past) nor presence (the present) but *prospect* (the future). Indeed, they are meant to reflect their owners' vitality, masculinity and the goal of the journey: success.[11] On top of this, they are a tangible indicator of income-based stratification, based on their number, quality and brand. In practice, the visible presence of five to a dozen pairs of shoes per resident does not necessarily mean that he did reach the aspired consumer status or that he can afford to send them back home as gifts. The same pairs of sneakers, I realized, may stay put on the same bookshelf for years. Even so, they show that something "better," and/as achieved in Italy, is present and is worth using, displaying and caring for (cf. 6.4).

Writings

Under the apparently blank and peeling face of the inner walls, a number of tiny writings and decorations have survived over time, in a minor and innocuous transgression of the rules. Some are more charged with meaning than others, especially on bedroom walls. They may say little of the person who left them, if not of his contingent mood. Yet, they have revelatory power,[12] as I've realized after informally surveying them under different dwellers. People may scribble something as a message for themselves and hopefully for somebody else. Even a few sparse words make a statement, often with a touch of resistance: I was here, but I'm already gone. You'll only know who I am if you can decipher the code (which only those who know me can).

Some of these minimal messages are tantamount to self-presentation. They state one's identity and even address, as long as the countries of temporary settlement and of origin make for one. "PESCO MALIANO +223 WE ARE MALI AFRICA" reads the text Mamadou left with a black marker on the wall behind his bed, with some annoyance of Daokaate, from Senegal, who will take over the same

FIGURE 12. What was originally a bookcase with five shelves has been converted into a shoe rack, as often happens in the bedrooms. Photo by author.

place. This is like a card that marks one's presence and place and outlasts both. "It's like when you say, 'We're from Italy,' isn't it?" Mamadou casually explains one afternoon while we are chatting. Perhaps it's no coincidence that his room is one of the most decorated I've ever seen, mixing as it does school-like drawings of buildings and mosques with large pictures of soccer players and cars. Even a secondhand sofa ended up there for a while. None of that decoration, however, would talk specifically of Mali. While the use of one's wall as an identity card writ large is uncommon, it is not unique. Cheikh and Khame have done something similar in their room, I realize one day, on the blank wall behind a caseworker who came in to advise them about cheaper internet contracts. In fact, the wall is not blank. There is a concise statement of personal identity, written close to Cheikh's pillow: "[NAME] [SURNAME] ITALIA [TOWN] MALI." Khame has a parallel identity card for his respective corners of the world, stating "[TOWN] AND BISSAU"—here, and there. After all, the room is the only turf on which either has substantive control now. Both wall labels are an unremarkable background to their Black bodies moving around to chat, eat, play, laugh, complain or just stay silent—and then sleep.

Perhaps Cheikh and Khame borrowed the self-presentation idea from another bigger scribble that precedes their entrance in that room. Ullah, an Afghani young man, happened to stay for some months, making the bedroom unique by sticking a small national flag on the external door. He had major health issues, which he apparently expected to sort out in Italy soon. Once he realized this would not be the case, he suddenly left to move farther north. Ullah did not inform anybody and left with his room key. However, he did leave several writings on the door and the wall as a way of stating what there was no point to talk about. In getting in, as a shadow to the caseworker who's taking away his few remains to prepare the room for the next guest, I feel like I'm looking at urban graffiti—one, sadly, with little audience. Big capital letters on the wall, precariously written in a mixed language, seem to read "AFG KING, FUCKOFF ITALIAN, ITALY SHIT, PASHTUN, PASHTUN." Months later, as I happen to be back there with Cheikh and Khame, the bad words are crossed out. Somebody must have thought that they were indecent or that they do not represent the new dwellers. Brunts of punches into the drywall or the door are also visible there and in some other rooms. Each of them is the long-standing "shape" of a "hand"[13] that was probably burdened with exasperation and resentment, just like the body it was a part of. Turned into a fist, the hand left a silent mark to witness that emotional predicament and let it survive across cohorts of residents.

Still other writings are like jots or sketches on a block note that is actually a hard, immobile piece of wall—one that affords their persistent and irrelevant presence. Some articulate deeper meanings, aspirations or frustrations, though. "SUPER MARIO BALOTELLI" reads a large pen writing on a room wall, on top of a half-size drawing of the famous and contentious soccer player—a Black Italian

FIGURE 13. "I'M THINKING OF MY FUTURE / I WANT TO GO BACK TO MY COUNTRY" written in basic Italian on a wall, semi-hidden behind a prayer necklace. Photo by author.

who made it and thereby could be taken as a model, at least by one particular dweller in one particular moment.[14] The drawing will placidly stay there for years, just like another two-line message in capital letters, in another room I often pass by. Partially covered by an old calendar, a post note with a doctor appointment and a prayer necklace, the message, in basic Italian, reads "I'M THINKING OF MY FUTURE / I WANT TO GO BACK TO MY COUNTRY" (figure 13). So many people have been in that room over time. No way of figuring out who left it. Perhaps the same person who wrote "KASAMANCE," another scribble hidden in plain sight, on the shutters. More revealing than the author's identity is his confessional way of articulating something that may resound in the inner dialogue of many more, but is at odds with their dominant self-representation and with the moral register of migration.[15] Never, in years of conversations with my interlocutors, have I heard this explicit message, at least regarding their short-term future.

In sum, some writings are inherently meaningful, including one with the Quran *bismillah* on the inner side of a door. Far more often they are impossible to decipher or include banal (if useful) information such as the client-service number of a phone company. As long as they survive, they do so inertially, out of irrelevance. Even so, they are telling of how the background matters, if only to offer fragments of broader stories that no one will be able or interested to recollect thoroughly.[16] The stories, and the people, were there.

While they no longer are, a scribble could be enough to make them present again, somehow.

5.3   LESS MEANING, MORE INERTIA: ON THE SPECTRAL PRESENCE OF LEFT OBJECTS

"If you work you must leave," a caseworker bluntly remarks one day like any other. You may disagree on how rigid the rule is or on the conditionalities associated with it, but the rule is clearly and predictably there. However, not all that has to do with you does leave. "What I *don't* understand," he adds, shaking his head, is "why they leave so much stuff behind!" Whenever people move, in ordinary life, they carry their stuff along—don't they? However, two large bags with all sorts of objects are still in his office. It often happens when someone is moving out. This may be bothersome in itself, for the staff. It also shows, more uncannily perhaps, that virtually moneyless people accumulate as many petty objects as anybody else. Much of that stuff will be eventually disposed of. For now it looms around as still another absent presence.[17]

Abandoned, broken, useless or irrelevant objects are spread in most rooms and kitchens, as much as in the common regions. Their accumulation is in stark contrast with the substantive lack of objects—other than the body and basic clothes—while crossing the Mediterranean, on the verge between resilient presence and looming absence;[18] and possibly, albeit harder to reconstruct, in everyday life prior to leaving. No way of carrying possessions across the sea, as long as you had any. So tells Cé, in a sudden and ephemeral re-evocation that starts with the sight of people moving around in town with a whole folder of documents in their hands. This is unnecessary, he points out, once you have your temporary residence permit—that is, once you are housed and your presence is not in question. People can, and often have to, travel light. Nevertheless, even Cé will eventually leave with seven suitcases, backpacks and bags. Once you are a resident, clutter mounts and affects the next steps of your housing pathways and even beyond. There are several bags of clothes, mostly blue jeans and T-shirts, at the community lunch prepared by a group of Guineans to commemorate the death of Salim, after the repatriation of his body (see 4.5). That is stuff anyone can pick up for free at the end of the prayer. Unlike him, it is still present and potentially useful. It's unlikely to tell much of Salim by now, though. It would add little to the collective narrative that some friends share on social media, as an attempt of acknowledging his past presence in Italy,[19] and mitigating his ultimate absence— his sooner-than-due irrelevance.

In principle, the resilient presence of unnoticeable objects is telling of personal ways of use and consumption and of their variations along religion, ethnicity or age. However, much of what remains—scribbles on the wall, stuff, garbage in hidden corners—does so by mere inertia. A case in point is the large TV screen in Omokunrin's room. He bought it after some months of apprenticeship, only to

FIGURE 14. A miniature paper flag of Mali (in reverse), drawn with a marker above a headboard. Photo by author.

see it breaking down shortly thereafter (cf. 4.2). Objects fail, objects stay. Just like people in the center, perhaps. "Ruination"[20] may well be a protracted development or a consequence of all that has stayed parked, people and things, after its promise was not fulfilled or waiting for a better use or employment.

What survives the longest is often what goes unnoticed, just like the posters about language classes, volunteering or sports activities in the entrance hall or those about cleaning and waste sorting that are sparse wherever. What would matter the most, instead, is often absent or ephemeral and elusive at best. Physical and spatial hierarchies are out of sync with affective and moral ones. Indeed, physical presence often goes along with social absence. This is tangible in the micro decorations that survive on many walls, ranging from sports stickers to religious calendars, all of them less portable and useful than personal belongings such as crosses, necklaces or rugs. They were there before and hence (over)stay, if they are not too cumbersome. Just like the small paper flag of Mali, in colored markers (albeit, interestingly, with "inverted" colors—see figure 14) that discreetly guarded above Malick's headboard. In practice it has outlived his occupation and the one of his Cameroonian successor. Why bother, if it's not too visible and disturbing—and if one expects to move soon.

A similar message comes from some small wooden boxes, hidden in plain sight on a ground-floor windowsill (see one of them in figure 15). They were specially handcrafted as flowerpots in a participatory workshop of beautification.[21] "WEL-COME WEEK 2017" reads a faded text in black marker. Previous to the 2019 budget and staff retrenchment, they hosted flowers indeed, with the staff taking care of them. Years later, the would-be flowerpots are still in the same spot. Rather than celebrating care for the place, though, they contain remains of arid soil, cigarette butts and long-dried flowers. A pair of socks and work shoes are often there too. Practical utility and possibly irrelevance of external standards of decor are embedded in the windowsill, more than any memory of the refugee week.

FIGURE 15. "Welcome week" flowerpots and a pair of shoes and socks
on a windowsill on the ground floor. One of the flowerpots was built
in a beautification initiative, years ago, and has long been in disuse.
Photo by author.

In short, mundane traces from past residents can pop up anywhere. Even the plastic cover on the bike parking lot is habitually speckled with cumbersome and irrelevant presences—old pillows and clothes, used water bottles or coffee cups, pieces of bicycles. "Once they are outside, they no longer exist," a caseworker bitterly grins. The everyday materiality that exhausted its function must simply get out—of a room, of the building, of the field of perceptive or moral relevance. After all, any way of dealing with waste, or undesired and useless stuff, starts with the need to make it irrelevant. This is achieved through its expulsion, whatever the scale—out of a building, a larger territory or one's body.[22] However, the expulsion may end up with the useless object being *displaced*, rather than "rubbished": something remains, as an ongoing, eerie presence.[23] An uncomfortable parallel emerges again between things and people— objects long left in utter irrelevance and people who risk sharing the same fate.

On a larger scale, the ruination of left objects is paralleled by the surrounding building. No one has much reason to take care of it—neither the staff and the old doormen, nor the young residents who, they say, live very much like the old would do. Whenever the doormen chat together to kill time, they end up joking about their retirement in some years from now—the lure of stopping working, the fear of ending up doing nothing. Which is what they feel they are doing right now, between one cigarette and the next. Meanwhile, the fourth-floor plaster is crumbling down, with some chunks occasionally falling on the ground floor. Whenever it rains, the basement gets flooded, and the CCTV system breaks down. Even the kitchen hotplates stop working. "It's nobody's stuff, nobody cares," the doormen repeat with a mix of disgust and resignation. "The boys" don't care, which is almost taken for granted. The local authority doesn't care either, they add with some resentment. It's just a place for asylum seekers. They'll soon be out anyway, perhaps. Why care about all that is present, including them? After all, what is absent may well attract more attention—whether to connect with it or to keep it at bay.

5.4   PRESENCE AS A WAY OF FLOATING ON THE ABSENT

What is present in the center, from the bodies inhabiting it to the material cultures they produce, is relatively easy to see and describe, if not to understand. Not so much what is absent. Part of this overlaps with what people would call nothing (cf. 1.4)[24]—no things to do, no news on their cases, no better prospects. However, there is more than *nothing* to absence and to its protracted influence.[25] Even its logical counterpart, *presence*, is no self-evident notion. I understand it as the assemblage of what people have with themselves or have tangible access to in the here-and-now: one place to stay in, with its ingrained and frustrating routines; a number of objects and affordances; more or less extended and diverse networks; an already vast and thick field of memories. What is present, for the young male residents, is not only the materiality of a house—"somewhere to go," as Ousmane laconically puts it. The most fundamental unit of presence lies in their own bodies, as the primary site of care and control (see 3.5 and 6.6). Each of them encapsulates and carries along one's sense of self, his habits and lifestyle, his name or nickname—all that he inherited from a background that is now absent. Each of them is exposed to what Italian anthropologist Ernesto De Martino calls a "crisis of presence": the "risk" that, in a "negative existential regime . . ., the individual presence itself gets lost as a center for decision and choice, and drowns in a negation that strikes the very possibility of any cultural action at all."[26] Presence, in this optic, is the possibility to make sense of one's being in a particular timespace, in relation to the history and intelligibility of the context itself (be it a house, a town, or a country—see chapter 3). It is an ever-provisional accomplishment, all the more so under circumstances of displacement and of tentative, conditional re-emplacement.[27]

Under the rubric of *absence*, instead, I understand all that is not tangibly present in the here-and-now and affects it nonetheless, as a reverberation of its past existence (i.e., key biographical events) or of its ongoing existence elsewhere (diasporic, primarily kinship-based ties, obligations and life projects that retain affective and moral power). *Absent* is not simply what does not exist in the center but what is intimately relevant for my interlocutors and out of the scope of sensorial proximity; what shaped their past biographies, including traumatic events that could turn into assets for their right to stay and produce only troublesome thoughts; what lies in some remote place they left and still feeds into opaque and fragmented cross-border relationships. As a way of limiting an already overcrowded field, instead, I do not expand on the *absent* in a more volitional and future-oriented sense—all that has *never* been and that people hope to achieve and become anew.[28] Suffice it to focus on what they have experienced and lost, only to find out that it still matters and looms.

In this optic the center is an institutional dispositif for floating over what is absent and yet haunting—the difficult, often tragic circumstances that came along with displacement. As long as these are not relevant there, institutional accommodation has also a function of caging the absent into the present. It affords asylum seekers to tread over the past without having to reckon with it directly. In practice, the invisibility of residents' previous life does not simply stem from institutional respect for their privacy, or from circumspection toward the Pandora box that would open up otherwise. It is people themselves who implicitly demand silence, to keep the absent at bay.[29]

However, there is nothing surprising or unique in their need and desire to forget the harshest past. Rather, this is an instance among many of "conspiracies of silence,"[30] a pervasive mechanism of coping with the suffering in excess that would be hard to bear otherwise.[31] On a meta-individual scale, the struggle to confine the negative past and the non-visible present into irrelevance reveals the ordinary boundary-making that underpins collective memories and responsibilities.[32] No tragic event that comes to one's knowledge is bound to raise a significant reaction, as long as it occurs out of the field of relevance of a certain group—be that based on shared nationality, religion, class or other categories. The bulk of such events is routinely and effectively invisibilized, for their morally and emotionally disruptive potential to be defused.

Refugees' deaths at sea are a case in point.[33] Nobody is held accountable for them—certainly not migrants' aspired states of destination. At most, responsibility falls on smugglers if not, most cynically, on migrants themselves. Likewise, the institutionalization of remote controls on the undesired mobility of potential refugees is an exemplary societal mechanism whereby their looming presence is maintained sufficiently absent—visually, spatially, even juridically.[34] Importantly, invisibilization occurs in *time* as much as in space, as the "slow violence" of asylum goes through undefined waiting that may well suffocate future life projects.[35] For sure, this spatial and temporal mechanism does not go uncontested, thanks also to powerful and fine-grained accounts of its day-to-day working.[36] However, the allocation of undesired human mobility in a parallel, fictitiously remote timespace is generally taken as obvious, natural and irrelevant—as much as migrant death at sea, as a collective, impersonal and almost inevitable occurrence.[37] Whatever the prospects to subvert this state of things or to renegotiate the underlying moral

FIGURE 16. A depiction of an episode in the apartment Woikat was sharing with other migrants in Libya. One day some militiamen came in while they were watching TV, searched the whole apartment and forced them to give their money and belongings. Artwork by Woikat. Photo by author.

horizon,[38] a fact is clear—the invisibilization of past or remote suffering is not only a psychological resource of coping for young asylum seekers. It is also a form of societal self-protection from the moral wounds that might be acknowledged and the claims for ethical responsibility that might be raised, otherwise.

"People in Italy don't want to see scenes of violence," Woikat ponders while sketching down the key steps of his route from Senegal to Europe, including shootings, kidnappings and makeshift graves. "Perhaps I should delete this," he pragmatically concludes one day, as he looks at a scene with armed Libyan militia threatening him and his friends (figure 16). Erasing death threats from a piece of paper does little to prevent their survival in one's memories or in the collective subconscious and tacit guilt of affluent societies. However, people prefer *not* to see, Woikat believes. Sometimes, perhaps, they just have no clue. Most of them live sufficiently far away from pervasive violence so as not to perceive it as a real thing—for them. Perhaps, instead, Woikat is plainly right. In either case, acknowledging the traces of what is sensorially absent is a precondition for people to take an autonomous stance—whether that means attaching relevance (or even care) to the suffering, threatened, or dead absent or just leave it into irrelevance, hence into nothingness. Against this background, extended and respectful fieldwork opens ways into the absent that matters and creeps into the present, thereby *becoming* present. Certain forms of absence are literally irreversible, as they have to do with death, albeit their aftermath is clearly present. Others, especially in family life, feed into evolving distant relationships and may or may not open up to new forms of literal presence.

5.5 ABSENT, SILENT, EMERGING NONETHELESS

The absence residents cautiously tread on involves both the countries of origin and their loved ones living there, now and in the past. Most of my interlocutors are unsurprisingly reluctant to talk about the place they come from, let alone their past lives. The past becomes present under the guise of silence, as something that is to stay out of ordinary conversation.[39] Absent is any point to reconstruct one's story in-depth once again, unless one spontaneously wishes to do so in particular moments, with particular people. As long as my interlocutors mention their countries of origin, this generally boils down to jokes on local celebrities or lamentations about the incumbent president or the latest coup. In fact, their accounts blend contrasting stances. Fragments of nostalgia and national or ethno-racial pride about Africanness and Blackness as one's essential identity go along with resentment, skepticism and disenchantment. Now and then the narrative zooms on the kin left behind. This is typically to remark that they can't understand what happens here and couldn't do much anyway. The entire responsibility falls on migrants. This interestingly mirrors their own view that white or European people have no clue of everyday life in Africa or of migrants' ways of "betting" on their own lives.

More often than not, the conversation ends before reaching this threshold of disclosure, recollection and suffering. While the country of origin haunts, people have all reasons to keep it away. This is what Larka strives to do whenever we have a coffee together (see 1.5 and 2.3). It is not an issue for him to tell about himself at present, including his major health problems. Not the same with Pakistan, as long as he touches on the topic at all—for instance, when he looks at the pigeons, sometimes challenging the staff's injunction not to feed them, and compares them with those at his homeplace in Gujrat. "Lots of problems there" and "no problem here," he dryly says, his arm waving around as if to dispel something—ideally an entire country, or a past life. *Away*, into the unbounded field of irrelevance. "Everything okay at home?" I occasionally ask. "Yes, yes" is his invariable response, as he shakes his head and grins in irony. "I don't call there—it's not in my mind," he bluntly adds before diving back into the screen of his smartphone. The time to sip his "Pakistani tea," pick up his stuff from the laundry and get back to prepare his everyday share of chapati bread. Away from Pakistan and temporarily stuck and protected, somewhere in Italy. Everything in its desired place, it would seem— Larka here, the rest in Pakistan.

In fact, transnational ties and obligations are there nonetheless. On occasion, Larka mentions a brother who fell severely ill and struggles to maintain his children or a fellow villager who lost his life as a construction worker in Malaysia, before going back to his ordinary silence. The longing for isolation and separation is here to stay. This is precisely what Larka and the others strive to negotiate through their balancing acts between ritual greetings with everybody and friendship or confidence with nobody. Respect is enough as long as one stays in his place and has a place to stay in. What an academic might see as a hopeless expression of methodological nationalism is actually a claim for protection, dignity and respect. No way of being well *here*, as long as you can be well at all, if you keep thinking of *there*.

Importantly, silence about oneself is not at odds with a hospitable attitude to outsiders like me. It rather has to do with marking the narrow field of what should be shared. "Senegal is beautiful," Daokaate tells me, smiling, when we first introduce ourselves, after he has spontaneously mentioned the country he comes from. "But I can't speak about myself," he points out, looking down. "No problem," he replies to my immediate apology. Enough to keep the door of his personal narrative well shut. Telling about the absent, instead, would mean presenting it again, only to tell or show what most people do not want to hear or see, as Woikat says.

All this being said, the absent keeps looming. It does so, most visibly and innocuously, through nostalgia about food, music, people, life rhythms and styles. Absence, here, means that little of that can be meaningfully translated into the present—hence, into a tangible presence. Furthermore, the remote in space or time may come back whenever a banal episode or object elicits a connection with it. Eating together from a bowl of peanuts on a bench, one summer afternoon, is enough to start a conversation on what people cultivate in Italy and in Africa and for Momo to recall the Gambian village where he grew up before moving closer to the capital, with his mother working in the countryside, his father as a teacher, and Momo himself doing "all sorts of jobs." All that has come afterward, instead, will stay out of the narrative. In a similar vein, a T-shirt worn jokingly upside-down to mimic a covid face mask is enough for Olusola to recollect a biographically more disruptive emergency—crossing the desert on the way to Libya. Once in Libya, "they checked us—if we were Muslims or Christians. They didn't want any Christian." Again, just one ephemeral and inchoate fragment of a complex biographical past. One, however, that may emerge any moment after sense- or practice-driven reminiscences.

As mutual familiarity increases, months go by and nothingness seems to stay, silence need not be the end point anyway. At least for some, at least with me, the shared field of narrative gets larger and deeper, while still revealing an inner hierarchy: certain things are more tellable than others. Not much of a problem to talk about Italy, if only to complain about one's predicament. On the other biographical extreme, family life marks the external boundary of silence—what is for oneself and must not or cannot be told. All that lies in between has variable degrees of tellability. In Nigeria "there are fights," hints Paul whenever he invites me into his room, with the very clear desire not to linger on that. Nor does he wish to expand

on the journey—"Of course, it was dangerous. . . . Of course, we were afraid."
Even less on his family, if not for a deeply sad and moving smile. However, Paul is
less hesitant to tell about Libya, as a personal story that resounds across many
others and lies firmly in the past, unlike Nigeria. As the narrative goes, life in Libya
was hard enough to make any alternative more desirable, including sea-crossing
on a hazardous boat. You're already risking your life, repeats Paul, his serious gaze
down to the ground. "They use guns the way you use your smartphone," he adds,
moving his smartphone forward. "They shoot at the Africans, as if they are pointing into the pigeons," recollects Woikat, himself affected by a shooting. However,
this is over by now—for them at least—and can be revisited in a different light: as
a demonstration of resilience, good luck or fate.[40] It also inspires a more nuanced
moral assessment: "Better here," Paul concludes. While biographical suspension
is frustrating and increasingly oppressive, it is still only a segment in larger biographies. "Here," in spite of enforced waiting, some meaningful presence is taking
shape along the way—in his case, with casual jobs as a deejay, with his attendance
of a local choir, with his participation in the "Nigerian" church (cf. 1.5). There is
a relational capital Paul has built, while waiting. No reason to give it up and start
from scratch somewhere else, once again.

5.6   ABSENCE AS WHAT NO LONGER IS

Telling one's story, sometimes, is a way of coping with the most radical and irreversible form of absence—death and its aftermath. The past that should be kept at
bay, lest it suffocates the present, may emerge almost by chance. One afternoon
Sani and I are sitting in his room with a few friends, giving idle looks at the TV
set beside his bed. At some point one seaside scene—a beach, a speedboat, someone is rescuing a woman. "What's there?" I ask, for the sake of chatting. "She's
sinking," whispers Sani. "Do you like the sea? I don't." So starts the story of his
travel across the Mediterranean. "We were 160 and survived in 60." He repeats the
numbers several times to make sure I understand. He saw people dying—presences that turned into absences before him. And that are hauntingly present in
his memory. "When they took me up . . . I couldn't feel my legs. As if I don't have
them." So much to worry and struggle about for Sani, while waiting, now. And so
little, relative to what he has already gone through. Fleeing out of Nigeria, hidden
inside a truck, after an outburst of violence in his village, his mother and brothers
died there. Staying in Libya, first imprisoned, then forced to work in the building
trade to pay for his travel north. And then across the sea with dead people around,
until a ship rescued them after three days adrift. Not all the details of his narrative are necessarily authentic or consistent, as long as any story is. Time, and the
role play in his asylum interview, may have shaped them in different directions.
Whatever the case, his application was rejected. "They couldn't stay in my shoes,"
Sani says. "At my age, with my family, I wouldn't have left if I wasn't forced to."

All that followed his departure is kept in a story that should stay protected inside him and yet sneaks through some emotional or mnemonic interstice. Such a story is by no means unique in showing how death lingers in the memories of someone who was so close to it.[41]

Death is the most radical and irreversible form of absence—and the last threshold of silence.[42] Witnessing the death of a fellow migrant is enough to leave a permanent trace and perhaps share it over time. As of now, those who died on the border might end into nothingness—even more if their corpses are not found or recognized—unless for the individual and collective ways of commemorating them.[43] Individual and informal recollections also emerge from occasional conversations in the center. Even mundane practices such as greetings are revealing, as with Halebugor one afternoon, while we're completing our greeting routine. "I never say *well*," he points out, "not even *that* day." "That" day Halebugor received the long-awaited call from his lawyer—he had "won," as she put it, a five-year subsidiary protection status. His reaction was unusual though. "Instead of cheering up, I burst into crying. I thought of my friends who died . . . and of those who have no papers yet." Enough for a sudden disclosure of the background—the invisible chain of events that ended there. A few ephemeral minutes amid our conversation, his severe gaze down to the ground, before Halebugor stops speaking and moves farther away. A relatively easy task in his case, as the evening shift at the pizzeria will start soon. He can focus on that tangible activity rather than on what has long been absent and still haunts.

Stories of proximity to death are part and parcel of the routes to Europe of every resident. Some revisit them through deeper and paradoxical reflections, which have once again to do with presence and absence—one's presence and the absence of those who lost their lives. This is an intimately nonsensical state of things, unless one rests, perhaps, on some religious explanation or reassurance. The point, reflects Fatou, is not only that the travel was a matter of "life or death" in the first place. A more fundamental ethical question emerges, as his narrative unfolds within the four walls and closed shutter of his room. His story of migration includes crossing the Mali desert, with the truck breaking down and his group of friends walking and walking. Some didn't make it. "I ask myself, why I survived, and my friends not?"[44]

No merit, no sense. Only the vivid memory of death that came about and arbitrarily caught some rather than others. "When I'm alone, I think, think, think . . . why God made *me* survive?" No answer. Just one biographical fragment that turns into a narrative, hopefully to alleviate suffering or at least to make the paradox more visible. And not even the only deadly fragment, as he starts telling of his earlier attempt to "cross the river." That time "the boat capsized . . . three hours hanging, in three, on a plastic tank . . . and then rescued back to Libya," something Fatou has never "told anybody here." Two friends from the Gambia, his fellow travelers, drowning. And Fatou calling their families to say they were dead—and to save their memory.[45] Too much to tell or even remember. "People cannot understand," he believes. Perhaps they cannot even understand how he feels now. "Whenever I think of this"—whenever the absent gets present again—"I've headache," he says, beating on his forehead with a finger. "I wait" for the bad memory to pass over . . . until "I cry it out of my head."

Death, in stories like Fatou's, lies at the very roots of migration. This I gradually understand, thanks to his unremitting hospitality into a world that is as distant from mine as from the center. "It's okay in the Gambia. It's so beautiful. . . . There is no war," he starts telling one day. "But there are people who must flee—including myself." In Fatou's story, fleeing—making oneself absent, with the hope to gain a more dignified presence elsewhere—came after a family loss. Two young stepbrothers, who used to hang out with him, one day disregarded his orders while he's playing soccer with his friends. They suddenly enter the river and drown, before he can even realize it. Loss and bereavement come along with anger and violence against him. Better to flee to Senegal and then Mali, where one relative could help him. No way back, his mother warns on the phone—too dangerous by now. No way to stay either, apparently, as war erupts in Mali, and his host is kidnapped. "I had nowhere to go." No alternative but moving north, making it to Libya with his friends dying or being killed along the way and then to Italy as the last step of "gambling on your life."[46] No return ahead for now. And a constant, looming presence—the faces of his stepbrothers, their drowning, the meaningless of it all. "I would have rather died in their place," murmurs Fatou. However, "this is what God wanted."

Death, in some stories of my interlocutors, creeps from the past into the present along multiple biographical disruptions. It can also take place here and now, *out of place*. "Transnational dying"[47] entails still another form of physical absence—from the passing away of loved ones and from the ritualized collective ways of coping with it; in short, from the ordinary ways of reclaiming the social presence of someone who is by now biologically absent.[48] This is what people like Sani happen to experience here and now, as he tells me one evening in the dark of the staircase. We have casually come across each other on his way back from work. I'm patronizingly worried about his imminent eviction—he's long been told he must leave, as he's above the minimum-income threshold. Any idea about where you can go next? "No," is the plain and disenchanted response. "Nobody gives you a room without papers—and if you're Black." In fact, he'll eventually find his own way out, as most people with good ethnic capital do. However, housing is less of a priority than what *he* wishes to share. "Did you know of my father?"

My negative response already comes with embarrassment and guilt. "He died at the beginning of covid—he was sixty-six." The exact date emerges only from the pictures on his smartphone. One portrays a dead man laying down, with someone caressing his face. One picture as transnational evidence of the fact that he passed away after falling ill. "I've paid for his burial," says Sani, and "I've forbidden myself to forget about him." This is all he can do to turn his absence into a distant presence. There is more to that experience though—or to the need to make sense of it or participate in it. "You know black magic?" he asks with a very serious expression. "I don't believe in that, but I felt in my body that something was about to happen that day." He even missed the bus three times. "That means something," he concludes. Something about looming absence, or at least about the emotional and moral pressure to connect with it from afar. Even death is less a mere absence than a ghostly, immanent, invisible presence.

5.7   ABSENCE AS WHAT COULD STILL BE

Some forms of absence are irreversible, for better or worse. Others are not. While haunting in the here-and-now, they can be brought back to a more literal presence—even too much of it, sometimes. Family life provides many examples in this respect. All that has to do with one's family is as crucial as it is awkward to raise in day-to-day conversations, most of them starting with people gently asking about *my* family. In principle, though, the transnational field of family living holds a potential for restoring physical presence.

Disruptions in family ties and networks, including cases of violent death, are hinted at in the narratives of my interlocutors among the triggers of displacement. This does not necessarily mean that family solidarity, and the underlying moral expectations, get weaker over time. However, far from the topos of the ever-connected migrant, silence matters in family life as much as in the relationships with outsiders in asylum. Transnational communication was apparently limited and elusive along the past migration pathways and so it tends to be now.

How far people keep in touch and what they disclose about themselves are case-specific and private matters. With this premise the bulk of my fieldwork shows that transnational communication tends to be uneven and fraught with a sense of nostalgia and mutual loss but also with tensions and misunderstandings (see 7.4). So is all that has to do with its expected cement—the money to send back. Remittances, as the mainstream society calls "inter vivos transfers"[49] when it comes to migrants, are themselves a way of replacing absence with an indirect and yet effective form of presence.[50] They are the most powerful channel of transnational interaction, instrumentally speaking, albeit not the easiest for migrants themselves. Among the young men in the center, transferring money home sounds like the obvious and necessary thing to do rather than a desirable or inherently good one. In practice, the little money available only exacerbates the tension between sending, and thereby taking care of others with fewer opportunities, and consuming or saving, thereby taking care of oneself and, some would add, of one's future. Talking about remittances is no taboo with my closer interlocutors. However, the difficulty of sending even only a few dozen euros makes the topic emotionally thick and, sometimes, in need of silence too. "We're here, aren't we?"

exclaims Woikat one afternoon, looking at his bedroom. Not much to add. No work, no money, no remittances—perhaps.

Due to the lack of money, and to much more, connecting with home is no easy endeavor for Den. He fled at thirteen, spent years around Africa, and only after arriving in Italy got back in touch with his mother, who believed him dead by then. Even now, as an asylum seeker in institutional accommodation, he seems to communicate in a sketchy and uneven way, while invariably holding a smartphone in his hands. On the days of distribution of the pocket money Den is always ready in advance, in an unusually nervous mood. Some of that money will immediately go to his mother in Mali. The basic allowance for an asylum seeker turns into an indirect aid for someone in even worse economic conditions, in some absent else-where, in an unintended combination of top-down and grassroots transnational social protection.[51] This does not mean that distant family relations are smooth, for Den or anybody else. "Sometimes I don't even want to call her," he says one evening as I'm driving him to the soccer pitch. A few minutes are enough to give him the chance to vent his frustration after three years in waiting, under the rules of institutional hospitality, with no jobs or papers: "This is no life, is it? . . . I'm too tired. . . . Now Den is no longer Den."

Connecting with home is not easy for Fatou, who no longer communicates with his father after the event that pushed him to leave. While being frequently in touch with his mother and sending her money "when possible," he has to constantly navigate uncertainty, (mis)trust, (lack of) control. "Before I die, which might be any moment," he whispers one afternoon after showing me her picture, "I want one thing—see her again" and tell all that has happened. Not just by phone, "it can't contain all this," he adds with a melancholic smile, looking at his smartphone. Last autumn, after the fruit harvest, he sent one hundred euros, only to hear from her: "I don't want to eat your money." If it comes from something "bad," you'd better take it back. "Many think we make money that way," as drug dealers, Fatou explains. "I could never do it. It's against all I've always been taught . . . but I under-stand those who do it because they have no alternative." In the end Fatou had to send his mother a video with him working in the fields. It was *good* money,[52] but that needed to be proved to bridge the absence and make for some morally appro-priate sense of presence again.

Connecting with home is no easy endeavor for the bulk of my interlocutors, including those who wish to tell nothing of their family lives. Even in a very hypo-thetical case of mutually supportive, overt and rewarding transnational family relations, they would pay the price of not living up (yet) to the moral expectations associated with Europe. In fact, such expectations may well exceed their poten-tial, as much as their will to help. "Some send all the time, even if they don't have nothing—I don't," Cé tells me one day. Against the constant pressure of sending, the only thing to do is to "confound them," he adds with an enigmatic expression, while rolling a cigarette by the entrance door. "Sometimes you send, other times you don't . . . or just wait and see." Sometimes you talk with them, sometimes you don't. Better that way than create still higher expectations and obligations.[53] No way of preventing "them" from asking for money all the time otherwise. Also a way of reclaiming agency and autonomy *there*, no less than *here*. For sure, Cé's narrative is only a self-representation—the mask of reflexive detachment he wears with me and, apparently, with many more. Nevertheless, it does show that absence—a degree of distance in space and time—is also a source of self-protection and self-respect. People there are probably needy, Cé admits. However, "they're cunning as well."

In sum, transnational relationships and family life reveal forms of undesired absence that are hard to bridge at present—if not through remittances and video communication—and yet remain potentially convertible in physical presence. This does not mean that all the absent is necessarily negative or undesirable. Migrant transnational relationships are ridden with ambiguities.[54] Certain forms of absence are selectively, even strategically, kept at a distance. Others are a source of suffering or at least nostalgia that may push people to try and replace what is not there through transnational social practices, emplaced forms of homemaking (see 7.3) and, ideally, future shared life projects. Still others oscillate between retention and rejection over time. Different people struggle to leave behind, recover or anticipate the absent through the present—what they can feel and do, even while feeling they are doing nothing. Analytically speaking, absence and presence intermingle into different configurations,[55] none of them being always preferable over the others. Once again, it is a matter of situated ambivalence and of individual struggles to negotiate what is relevant and what is not, accordingly.

6

Dirty, Clean

"We'll have a meeting tomorrow evening at eight," the manager announces, trying to reach out to those who would not reply or say that they're busy or just avoid her. "It's no use staying home," someone says. "Anyway, it must be about cleaning"—that is, the predominant topic of conversation in the center. "Indeed," she replies with a smile. The next evening, twenty residents or so are sitting in the large room where Italian classes and job-search sessions used to take place, as long as there were any. The others may be outside to work or, more likely, just uninterested and good enough at eluding the call. "I'm speaking to you as adult people, because you are," the manager starts. "Look at this   yuck!" Pictures of filthy kitchen corners, with heaps of garbage, start to pop up on her laptop. "As we came here," she says about her organization that took over one year before, "it was all so dirty. . . . *We* made the pest control for you . . . and what about *you*?" Some murmuring but little reaction. Time to shift register—from reciprocity to decency and respectability. "I would feel ashamed" to keep a kitchen like this, adds the manager after a while. In fact, "*you* must feel ashamed!" There's something more puzzling than a moral issue at stake here, though.

"I can't understand. You're so clean—your bodies, I mean—but your rooms are disgusting." *That's the point*, I think within myself, as the murmuring rises. "It's shameful! Whenever someone comes in from outside, they wonder, 'Who on earth lives here?!' and then, don't you complain if you go out and—and they consider you . . . like that." Although she stops before ending the sentence, the message is crystal clear. An awkward, politically incorrect and revealing one. The instant reaction from the audience is less confrontational than I might expect. It has to do less with negation or contestation than with distinction and boundary-making.

"We're not *all* like that," Cé calmly replies. Moreover, "if my roommate doesn't clean up, I can't tell him he must do that. I'd get into trouble." That's up to you, not to us, the counter-message is. Not our problem—as long as we do our job. Each one on his own, even while he has to live with the others, pace all appeals to collaboration and collective responsibility. While this reaction may not come as a surprise, ultimately pointing to indifference, apparent passivity and self-interest as subtle forms of resistance,[1] a major riddle is still there. "How come," the manager repeats, "you take so much care of your own bodies, you're always so clean . . . and *not* the place where you live?" The riddle will outlive the end of the meeting, when another staff member, of Maghrebi background, alone with the manager and me, adds more to it. "The Koran says you must clean up," he points out. "In my place," he proudly adds in a burst of involuntary self-irony, "you will always find everything perfectly clean! It's my wife that takes care of that."

It's dark, coldish, empty and utterly silent outside, as we're about to leave. "They've been here for years, and no way. . . . How come they don't feel that they live better in a clean place? It's always a mess, this cleaning thing. . . . Paolo, please don't write about it in the book!" she concludes, bursting into laughter, before hurrying back home. Not a request I could meet, as the previous paragraph shows. However, not a way of disregarding her confidence either. The point is not to approach, let alone judge the center as a not-so-clean place. This would be uninteresting in itself and unsurprising for an asylum facility.[2] What matters, instead, is the work that the clean/dirty distinction does: the meanings, moral economies and endeavors of boundary-making along the definition of clean, its tentative enactment and the irremediable entanglement between clean and dirt. This is yet another ambivalence within which my interlocutors negotiate the threshold of relevance—what matters and demands care from their side—on distinct and contrasting scales.

Dwelling in a place, if only as temporary guests, means coping with the "matter" that becomes "out of place"[3] one day after another. Cleaning up, as a mandatory task or a spontaneous practice, is an issue of self-evident relevance in the inner economy of the center. It is also a question of analytical leverage. The routines whereby people cope with dirt make for invaluable ethnographic material to revisit questions of decency, visibility, care, control, even aesthetics. There is much to learn from the ways in which my young male interlocutors perceive what is clean or dirty, react to it and position themselves in between. The shifting boundary between dirty and clean has to do with the materiality of place, with the bodily and sensuous experience of it and with a more or less shared moral subtext. Cleaning becomes a performance of distinction and distance between individuals and groups. It tacitly reveals the appropriate reach of care, responsibility and respectability—in short, of relevance—from the viewpoint of each individual. To illustrate this, the chapter starts from the entire building as an expected site of cleaning, zooming then into its inner space, down to the scale of each body—one's primary home, the only one under virtually complete control for the time being.

Overall, cleaning matters for one's intimate way of being, as much as for the management of his temporary house. However, the views and practices about what is (un)clean on different scales are often in friction.

6.1   THE CLEAN, THE DIRTY AND THE CENTER

Questions of (un)clean and (un)cleaning are central to the sensescape of the center and to ordinary interactions inside it. They are equally central to an inter-disciplinary scholarship that is very diverse, holds a potentially enormous field of application in research on home and dwelling and typically starts with the seminal contribution of Mary Douglas. Little chance of making sense of the conflicts, boundaries and scales around the clean/dirty distinction without an excursus into this scholarship.

Why (some) matter is out of place

Dirt, Douglas maintains, is not an autonomous state of things or an objective attribute of space. It is, instead, "the by-product of a systematic order and classification of matter, in so far as ordering involves rejecting inappropriate elements."[4] Rather than being a "fixed quality of particular objects, substances, animals, or human beings," dirt is a radically "contextual phenomenon"[5] that stands in opposition to a given social order(ing). All that is perceived as dirt makes visible the tension between "a set of ordered relations and a contravention of that order";[6] it is the demonstration of a gap between the moral rule or aspiration of ordering a place according to certain standards and its accomplishment. In Douglas's famous phrasing, dirt is "essentially disorder" or "matter out of place."[7]

Without lingering on historically changing views of dirty and clean in public and personal health,[8] it is important to appreciate the deep symbolic, moral and social meaning of this distinction, which invariably results in a continuum, if not a coexistence, between opposites. Coping with dirt encapsulates much more than instrumental questions of hygiene and social reproduction. Making space clean—removing what is perceived or deemed as dirty—is an elementary way of boundary-making, whereby people and groups strive to reproduce a certain social order in their own terms. It is also, on a micro-scale, the outcome of a process of categorization to separate what fits or is in place from whatever is not. To that extent cleaning is a radical version of ordinary, large-scale practices of categorization such as those associated with nationality, gender, race, class and so on.[9] It is, however, a deeply embodied and sensuous form of categorization.[10] Cleaning is as intimately connected with one's self and personal space, as revealing of shared habits and of larger, if contended, moral orders.[11] While it may well fall short of its ideal aim, cleaning as a social process has all to do with the ways of setting, policing, reproducing or contesting the boundary between what is in place and what is not—even when it comes to people who are "out of place" almost by definition.

Within the center, the basic order of institutional hospitality is predominant over the personal order of each resident, and often more demanding than the latter. Moreover, the institutional order of a single building is far more tangible and predictable, and less elusive, than the larger societal order in which migrants would aspire to reposition themselves over time. For now, keeping the place sufficiently clean is what seems to matter the most. Dirt, as a material and sensuous manifestation, becomes the most visible face and the most redeemable aspect of what residents do not do yet, or are not yet, in comparison with proper citizens.

Even so, the meaning of dirt, hence the way of coping with it, is nothing obvious or generalizable. If dirt is matter out of place, the question is still in which (whose) place it lies and where it should be moved, who draws the line between in and out of place and how unequal lines (i.e., different thresholds and scales of relevance) interplay with one another. Coping with dirt is a closed set of repetitive, boring and often evaded chores, as much as an open-ended discursive and moral battlefield. In fact, the dirty/clean relation is not merely symbolic either. It has also to do with materialities, senses and bodies that negotiate their mutual distance under unequal, temporary and procrastinated dwelling conditions.

Clean and dirty in a place for asylum seekers

The metaphorical power of dirt and the practical and moral urge of cleaning illuminate the lived experience of the center in several respects. For one thing, a reception facility per se can be seen as a product of the institutional separation between young male adult newcomers with no means of self-sustenance, called asylum seekers, and the native population. It is designed as a suitable place to overcome the disorder (symbolically speaking, the dirt) caused by undocumented migration, by allocating "an abnormal intrusion of foreign elements"[12] in its proper, separate place. The institutional effort at arranging matter out of place follows a pathway that should lead either to domestication or expulsion, leaving people in a liminal terrain of nothingness for the time being. While the institutional categorization of refugees already follows the pure/impure distinction evoked by Douglas and reflects its practical shortcomings, there is also a more popular, historically rooted and exclusionary understanding of the connection between dirt and migration. Metaphors of dirt and straightforward accusations of *being* dirty are far from rare in xenophobic public discourse against racialized migrants or refugees.[13] A place for refugees per se is not what most people would associate with cleanliness, nor are its dark-skin male residents.[14]

Such a stereotypical and stigmatized resonance with dirt is unlikely to be downright disproved or confirmed as one enters the center. It rather takes up an awkward sensorial weight. Occasional visitors, including inspectors, will likely have a sense of unusual emptiness but also of uncleanliness, with comparison to the city outside (and their own domestic places). This tends to fade, the longer they stay in. Once they become accustomed to the sensescape, they'll probably take on a different, less demanding standard of normality, while still appreciating the unequal levels of care for the inner space. In the meanwhile, this sense of facing matter out of place has also an olfactive dimension.[15] Many different and equally powerful smells compete with one another across rooms and corridors, from one floor to the next. Some—the cologne on the bodies of the residents passing through—are short-lived, if intense, as they move along with them. Others, related to cooking, food and sometimes garbage, are more lingering and possibly unpleasant.

Dirt is "relative," Douglas remarks, as much as relational and positional. Indeed, how (un)clean the center looks, feels or smells varies with spatial position and visibility. Anonymity, rather than clean or dirty, predominates outside, where the little bare lawn siding the entrance lane has a long history of unsuccessful attempts at converting it into a garden. However, while *caring* fails as soon as native volunteers give it up, *cleaning* need not. Little or no litter can be seen near the entrance—the face the center displays to outsiders, as long as the latter are interested in it. The back courtyard instead, where some like having a chat or a drink out of CCTV reach, is often dotted with old tea cups, cigarette butts, used face masks or clothing, meal remains, old bottles or cans. Lack of control in this region comes with lack of care, neither being an issue for the staff, not to mention the residents. The same stratification of care and decor, based on visibility, is reproduced inside. No trace of dirt or objects out of place in the entrance hall. Even less so in the doorman stall, which in pandemic times turned into an anti-covid bulwark to be relentlessly cleaned and protected from intruders. This is not necessarily the case for the caseworker office, where people may get in and out any time, making it far more exposed to contamination. Starting from there, the inner layers tend to be less clean with distance in space (from the ground-floor "stage") and in time (from the latest cleaning shift). Time matters, for the place to be (un)clean, also in a more radical sense. The lesser the public money available for refugee accommodation, the more likely that the staff attends to cleaning and maintenance in a quick *and dirty* way.

The variation in sensescapes is higher in the bedrooms and so is the likelihood of encountering unconventional odors. Whenever the staff are about to visit a room, they hesitate for a couple of seconds with the door ajar. Some fine-tuning is needed with the relatively private space of someone else but also with its sensescape. Dim light and smells are part and parcel of the "mess" they attribute to what would be, otherwise, standardized and repetitive interiors. The ensuing, fragmented conversation starts with exhortations like, "Open the window!" or "Pull up the shutters!" The room needs fresh air. "It smells bad," some add, stressing that they refer to the room and not to the dwellers. Indeed, a thicker smellscape is part of the boundary between a room and the larger environment.

However, the micro-battlefield of (un)cleaning has not to do only with sensorial reactions or with material care. Cleaning is equally salient and contentious as a discursive field—a set of norms, with the moral views and beliefs that inform it. This is remarkably neglected in the literature on dwelling in asylum, and in social research at large.[16] Over the years, cleaning up is an essential activity for the center staff to supervise and for the residents to attend to. It is often their main topic of conversation or even the yardstick for their mutual consideration and respect. In brief, the moralities of cleaning are deep and disputed enough to deserve more elaboration.

6.2   CLEANING AS EVERYDAY PRACTICE AND POLITICS

On the face of it, there is little new or remarkable in cleaning as a highly gendered and racialized set of practices, a quintessential immigrant job or a marker of "proper" and "modern" domestic culture.[17] However, the practice of coping with dirt tells much more, about many more questions. Within the center, in particular, it takes different shapes and gendered subtexts. It is something you have to do, in weekly shifts, as a (minor) price to pay for free hospitality. It is something you may resist, whatever the reason—you can't stand the staff, you want to be autonomous, you don't feel like to. Perhaps you don't see it as a masculine task. It also may be something you do spontaneously, though, up to the reach of the space you see as yours, under control or relevant. Cleaning up may be a matter of habit, of (self-)respect or even only another way of filling time. So many different meanings and pressures coexist in the same sequence of body movements with a broom, a dustpan, a mop and some detergent—all of this "given for free," as the staff occasionally remind the residents.

The weekly allocation of shifts and some surveillance over cleaning in kitchens and bedrooms are part and parcel of the staff job. As a top-down practice, cleaning articulates discipline and control over people, but it could never work by mere imposition. It is rather a situated and negotiated process. Discretion, mutual respect, individual variations in cleaning standards and in the staff workload all result in a variable outcome. "I can't always insist," one caseworker tells me from the beginning. "In my place, I don't clean every single day," he adds with a critical parallel—the center and the home (cf. 7.2). In practice, institutional cleaning often starts from some moral exhortation to take care of a shared dwelling space. It has also to do with the need to (re)establish decor—to set an acceptable hygienic and even aesthetic standard to counter stigmatization of the place as such. Decency matters, no less than order and discipline, although the field of what is decent or not, and to the eyes of whom, is also contentious.

As a resident duty, cleaning up involves primarily the common space (i.e., corridors, terraces, staircases). How far it matters, however, is something one can understand primarily in each bedroom. This is not reducible to the first sensorial impact, as already discussed, or to the view of some Black bodies, sitting or lying on the beds with their smartphones, often engaged in some combination of chatting, watching and listening, or possibly to the encounter with semi-empty and anonymous rooms with beds undone, sparse objects and no decorations. None of these perceptions would do justice to the sensorial thickness and the lived experience of a room, if one can stay in long enough.[18] Against a background of infrastructural deterioration, peeling walls and creeping cockroaches, every bedroom has its own story, just like the dwellers. Likewise, the ways of cleaning—and of ordering, dividing, sometimes personalizing space—are highly variable from one room and bed to the next.

(Un)Cleaning and inner order I

The outsider perception of dirt or disorder is not disjointed from a degree of "factual dirt,"[19] especially in the kitchens. This has to do with a lack of care for waste disposal and basic cleaning that would be disruptive for a shared living environment, if each resident were to replicate it. Gut reactions of disgust[20] may lead to uncomfortably nativist thoughts to circulate between the caseworkers, the doormen and myself—look at the space *we* gave them, look what *they* did out of it. That said, no outsider would have time or interest in acknowledging the routines, material cultures and aesthetics that inform a room and make it familiar, predictable, and more of one's own—in a place you would never call your own.[21]

There is a cumulative order, for instance, in the apparent mess around Omokunrin's bed, which invariably stands out by contrast with his roommate. While his bed is permanently undone, his day-to-day objects are spread around at close reach in a very functional way. The Book of Mormon, a driving-license textbook and his skin lotions are often there on the nightstand. A picture of him with a friend (himself a previous resident), a calendar with a rosary above and a plastic toy cobra are usually stuck on the wall. His caps are hanging on the corners of the broken TV screen that keeps protecting his personal space, as does the constantly high-volume music from the stereo behind. Beside the bed, one chair hosts a heap of everyday clothes, which never includes a winter jacket—"it would cost at least fifty euros," Omokunrin says. Close to the window, with the shutters down, is the customary corner of his suitcase. As he once tells me, this contains his special Sunday clothes—those he uses for religious services or for parties. One year after the other, it always seems ready for departure, as if Omokunrin were about to leave. Which he will do, with some reluctance, only after five years.

In the meantime this inner order of its own, which often goes along with overt mess in the adjacent kitchen, need not be appreciated by his roommates, who periodically complain about their forced co-dwelling—not to mention the staff. One morning I come across the manager, just back from an inspection. She's "nauseated" by the mix of disorder, food remains and garbage in Omokunrin's room. I'm less surprised and more curious, albeit in an awkward position, as I get back in with her. The bedroom, she admits, is now "a bit better." However, that's a relatively private space to be respected as such, as long as one doesn't push it too far. The kitchen, instead, is still "disgusting," she instantaneously exclaims. "You could never live with a girl here!" No woman would ever bear that, although, as it happens, no woman is admitted here in the first place. "Why don't you clean up, instead of playing with the PlayStation all the time?" Some tension in the air, and myself with a tentatively low profile, before she leaves—until the next inspection.

"Help me clean," Omokunrin abruptly tells me. And with the bags overflowing with garbage we carry down and with the detersive he generously spreads around, the conversation takes off. "Ah, this girl," he sneers. Not so easy to receive orders from a young (white, native) woman who's entitled to enter "his" space and rule on its disposition—and have to pretend to obey. "Women talk and talk! . . . Men must let them talk, go out, then get back when they are away!" Men must be out to work, women must clean at home, he adds with a giggle. Right the opposite of what happens here, including the next and last act of this cleaning play. The manager is back to find out that, indeed, he (we?) started to clean. "I know I'm strict, but I'm doing it for your own good, otherwise you'd be lazy—you know, right? I must be like a mommy." "Ok, see you," he sniggers back. And back to cleaning the kitchen, Omokunrin and I, while he exclaims "it has power," with a disgusted face, after smelling the bleach. And while I wonder if there is an alternative to her maternalism—a slippery top-down variant of "kinning,"[22] among the many that circulate in the center. Perhaps there is no real alternative, given the circumstances, and given Omokunrin. One cleaning round after, he eventually opens up a bit. "I do my best. . . . I want only to have work and a house in Italy . . . with God's help." That would already be enough, it seems. Or maybe not. "It's Christmas. . . . My family ask me to send money, but I have no money. I told mum I can't send now." They're in touch "sometimes," Omokunrin explains. "She says okay, no problem, the important thing is that you're happy." And he *is* happy, in his own way, or so he tells me. Then, "little by little," God willing, "my dream will come true."

(Un)Cleaning and inner order II

Omokunrin may be an exceptional case, or so the staff usually see it. However, his bedroom is not simply untidy or dirty. It rather displays a selective combination of (un)clean and (dis)ordered that invites further elaboration. A binary understanding of the relation between dirty and clean would obscure the existence of different ways of taking care of a place, hence of ordering and thresholding it, by distributing and displaying one's possessions and routines. For one thing, all my interlocutors take special care of certain treasured belongings (e.g., technological goods, sneakers, prayer rugs), regardless of the surrounding environment. As important, they have some ways of earmarking their personal space even in the untidiest of rooms.

At the same time, the heuristic potential of the material cultures in each bedroom should not be overstretched. It may have to do with ethno-national background and possibly with taste and personality but not necessarily with one's unique and complex biography. Even a tidy and "wealthy" room such as Koffi's, with carpet on the floor, the shutters up and an air freshener at work, plus a TV set, stereo and PC, says little of him in particular. It is more telling of what he has achieved so far than of his personal history—where he comes from, how he ended up there, what happened along the way, whom he left (and is in touch with) in Togo. As long as this leaves visible traces, it will probably be in the photo archive of one's smartphone. No reason to expect more from a temporary and shared room. Or, if something more can be expected, that regards less individual life stories than the social mechanisms of space thresholding, including their tensions and limitations.

There is an uncanny order, for instance, in the former bed area of Leo's, the most ephemeral of Omokunrin's roommates. Originally from Côte d'Ivoire, he came from a larger reception center, stayed a few weeks and then decided to move north on his own, with no notice. As I enter the room with a caseworker, days after, the scene is weirdly clean. His bed is accurately done, unlike Omokunrin's. No trace of the belongings Leo had carried along, in a number of suitcases. It's all about a silent and material statement of order. This makes no difference to his uncertain future prospects elsewhere, and yet draws a line of self-respect and distinction from this place and its inhabitants.[23]

Some rooms, indeed, have an almost permanent order of their own. So is Halebugor's. He marked the space around his tidy bed by shifting the nightstand, with a little colored tablecloth on it and his laptop above. Right beside lies his suitcase, another marker of micro-territorial sovereignty and of its temporariness (figure 17). And the sequence of his three caps is hung up on the wall behind. Every single item has its special place and retains it for years, including the drawing of a small Senegalese flag above the headboard and a few sticky notes on a corner, visible only from his bed. They're all about kitchen recipes—private and useful at once, for someone who's working as an assistant cook. Meanwhile, the noises from his roommate and the neighbors are enough to shatter any pretension to privacy. Yet the need for order and control is there, as much as in other bedrooms, such as Salim's. This is one of the most welcoming, crowded with guests and richly decorated. It also has its own version of a thresholded space. Not everything needs to be visible, even when you don't have so many things or ways to make them invisible. Both the desk and the bookshelf on his side are covered with old blankets that protect the contents from the eyes of any visitor.

There is nothing "ethnic," likewise, in the room of Kambanoo, in which I'm a privileged and frequent guest. The micro-space around his bed is like an overcrowded island for the self, relative to the surrounding empty, if clean, space. "It's okay, we can't say it is not, right?" murmurs Kambanoo as he's lying on his bed, his smartphone in the hands, a light blanket on his body. He does have a sheltering space, with some approximation of domesticity. The cold and weak

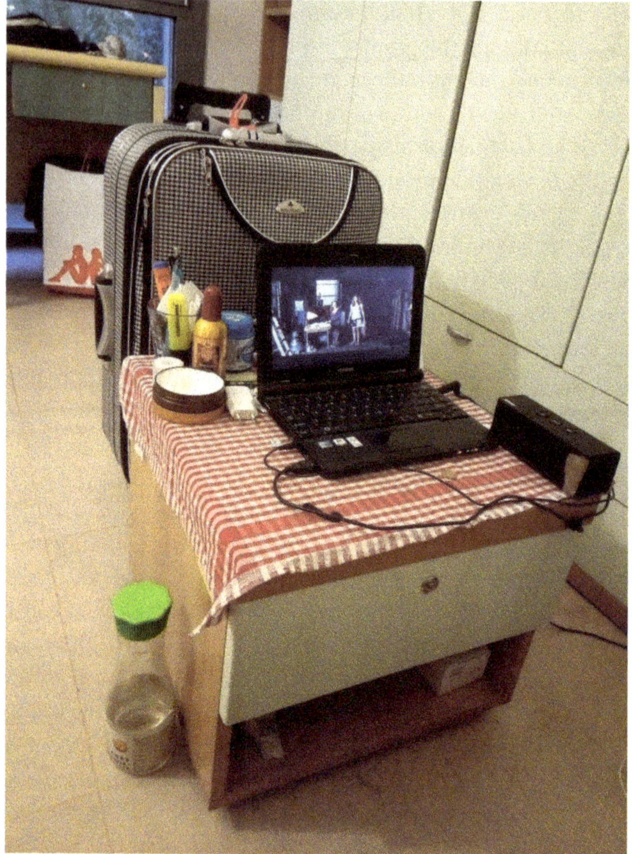

FIGURE 17. The spatial organization of the area just around
Halebugor's bed. Photo by author.

neon light, however, is a constant reminder of the place he's in, if ever one is
needed. Nothing that is not strictly functional is visible, including his prayer
rug on the bookshelf or the old and worn curtain he tangled up to let light
in. No decoration, few visible belongings, an extremely clean environment. As
Kambanoo's domestic routines suggest, there is no necessary overlap between
cleanliness, tidiness, decoration and personalization. Each of these dimensions
has its own course, which may not be in sync with the others. There is still
one social process that cuts across all of them, though: *thresholding*, as a way
of marking the qualitative difference between the personal space and the rest
(see 1.5). This is made manifest in most bedrooms with inner and less material
divides than a doorway. In sum, thresholding is a more fundamental process
than ethnicization, as far as the infrastructure allows. At the same time, the

most intimate and universal form of thresholding has to do with one's body and the ways of taking care of it.

6.3   CLEANING AS A MORAL TERRAIN: PEDAGOGY, DECENCY, WORTH

On the staff side, much talk about clean and dirty ends up in complaints. Corridors, stairs, most bedrooms and kitchens are all too dirty, they habitually say. However, frustration does not make the task any less important. Nor is it at odds with an oft-repeat statement: "it's cleaner, since we've been here." Whenever caseworkers feel like telling the story of the center, they always evoke cleaning as a watershed. *Now* it is relatively decent. *Back then* "you've no idea how filthy and messy it was!" In fact, over a four-year timespan I witnessed a couple of takeovers and did get an idea of the rehearsal of this narrative, with the new managers taking distance from the predecessors' benign tolerance of dirt sedimenting around. After all, to implement "serious" cleaning, or to claim so, is far easier than achieving one's ideal mandate— empowering residents rather than leaving them in passive waiting. Making and displaying a clean place is a reasonable target, unlike making any difference to refugee pathways of social inclusion. More cleaning, better appearance—if not a better outcome.

If there is a watershed at all, this has rather to do with the nationwide cuts on refugee reception from late 2018 onward.[24] The lesser the institutional invest-ment, the greater the need or temptation to focus on in-house decor as a more realistic, externally recognized and perhaps internally rewarding goal. "Check the cleaning!" the staff periodically write in the center diary, which becomes slimmer with the decrease in funding and personnel for individualized support, labor-market orientation, or community-building. After all, nobody could deny that cleaning is a condition for mutual respect in a shared living environment. Even cleanliness, though, is bound to be an elusive and contentious aim. Even in the best case, it is a temporary and precarious state of things that commands constant dedication.[25] And once one goes beyond the surface or the center facade, it is much less than that as a state of things, and far more than that as a moral battlefield.

Cleaning and civic integration

Cleaning is not just a resident duty or a cheap way of demonstrating organizational "success." It is also meant as a pedagogical set of practices that socialize asylum seekers to what they will have to do on their own, wherever they get housed next.[26] Nothing more tangible and effective than cleaning or sorting out waste properly for that purpose. "Here it's like a school," a caseworker explains one afternoon, after staff restructuration, as he starts to feel confident with me. "They get their qualification . . . and then they go!" No point for him, as one operator in charge of more than seventy clients, to wonder *where* they go or *what* qualification they will get. (Of adulthood, symbolically speaking, as in their long-term aspirations? Of integration, in the well-meant discourse of the more progressive, and increasingly less relevant, social and political actors in Italy? Or, in fact, more pragmatically, of cleaning?). Ironically, the national retrenchment of local support services makes it even harder to attend and complete the *real* school. As of now, the center-as-school aims only to teach cleaning of the common space (and ideally of the rooms), waste sorting, and saving on electricity and heating.

Even so, there is more than hygiene at stake. Cleaning is rather constructed as a matter of decor, respect and ultimately as a preliminary exercise in civic integration. "They must understand that we do things this way *[da noi si fa così]*," the doormen repeat. "It's in their best interest," the staff try to rephrase in a less nativist tone. Which may be true but is still easier than reflecting on the social, biographical and psychological reasons whereby some seem to prefer almost suffocating room environments or skipping cleaning tasks altogether.

In practice, much of day-to-day cleaning does not live up to the staff's expectations. In Douglas's terms, this reveals contrasting ways of seeing what "fits" properly and what does not. In staff terms, the question is more pragmatic. "They don't care because they've got all for free" or "because it's not their things." While some rooms and kitchens are filthy indeed, much of the question is around less blatant attitudes and practices. Leaving the lights on at any time is one of them—not a sign of presence or domestic warmth but of disregard for an unnecessary waste. Other mundane details appear equally symptomatic of a lack of responsibility, including very high heating or disregard for the food remains that may attract cockroaches—another "looming presence" that raises shame or irritation among the staff and little or no alarm in their counterparts. No way for people to do this once they're out of the center, caseworkers repeat. And between the lines, many good reasons for native landlords not to trust them. In sum, whether someone sticks to "good" cleaning or not is not a merely instrumental or procedural matter. It is also associated with a strong moral register of reliability, decency, even worth. No better way to congratulate a resident than emphasizing how clean his bedroom is.

The fundamentally moral character of cleaning and, by extension, of those who enact it[27] does not emerge only from staff members. Interestingly, a number of residents replicate the same subtext of moral worth. It is primarily in relation to cleaning that people articulate their (dis)alignment with roommates or neighbors, past, present or future. Whether a roommate does clean up (and perhaps ultimately *is* clean) is a key condition for mutual acceptability. In the abstract this sounds tautological: the more one feels it is important to live in a clean place, the more he will be bothered with those who disregard the task. In fact, it would not have been so obvious, to me, that cleaning dedication would outdo affiliations in language, ethnicity or religion in shaping co-housing sympathies. At the same time, cleaning as a marker of morality rests on strong patterns of collective categorization rather than on the specific character of single individuals.[28] Many of my interlocutors associate the cleaning habits of their roommates with ethno-racial backgrounds, in an ironic variant of statistical discrimination. By way of cognitive and moral simplification, people themselves are portrayed as dirty, particularly if they fall under stigmatized ethno-racial categories.[29]

This racialized understanding of clean(ing) and dirty(ing) turns ethnic differences into a moral boundary of unequal value or deservingness.[30] Dirt as matter out of place, whether stemming from poor cleaning, unusual cooking or eating styles or different complexions and body odors,[31] should then be *re-emplaced* away from one's personal space. "Don't want a Pakistani here; they smell bad," murmurs Mohamed one day, tucked in his threefold bubble—the earphone, the bed and the suffocating, olfactively thick atmosphere of his bedroom—while a caseworker is making space for his next roommate.

Occasionally, the political field of cleaning includes more explicit complaints. "You're looking for my troubles, you know?" Chinedu repeats three times, one afternoon, upon entering the staff office with a gloomy expression, midway between contemptuous neglect and creeping threat. "What troubles?" the manager calmly asks. "I don't want to live in the dirt. And *they* are dirty! They throw everything around in the kitchen. . . . They don't clean nothing." Not even worth mentioning, at first, who "they" are—those who share the same kitchen, one bedroom and one continent away. "The Pakistanis are dirty! We tell them to clean, and it's only worse." As the subtext goes, *we*, West Africans, want to keep things clean. *They* leave filth and mess around; in fact, they're dirty themselves and prevent us from cleaning up. *I*, the resident (guest), have the right not to stay in filth—that is, not so close to them. *You*, the staff (host), have a duty to do something. "How racist you are," blurts out the manager. A technically unquestionable statement, and yet not the best thing to say to a racialized young Nigerian man. On second thought, better to rephrase it, the staff way. "No, I was joking, I mean—okay, we'll do a room inspection" sooner or later. There is always an abundance of time ahead in the center.

For such an ordinary field of micro-conflicts as cleaning, overt stances of micro-racism are relatively uncommon. However, interpersonal tensions that turn into inter-category ones dot everyday life in a dwelling space that is shared only by necessity. Ethno-racial backgrounds may work as an effective catalyst for them. "It was better before," sighs Fatou with some annoyance, referring to his temporarily new neighbors. Due to structural maintenance he had to change his bedroom for a while, ending up close to Den's (and reproducing, in the new room, the precise disposition of his belongings). With "those guys," he says, you can't leave out your eating stuff, not even in the fridge. It disappears! "Thanks God, they've gone," Den will comment some days later, after his temporary neighbors have left. He has no idea of their names or where they come from. What he knows is that they messed up the kitchen and never cleaned—or so he maintains. "It was disgusting," Den finally exclaims, echoing a caseworker who used to urge him to clean up. "I'm not their mummy! We're all adults by now."

Cleaning and self-respect

Yet another moral connotation of cleaning is bound up with one's self—one's values and ultimately one's body—rather than with the place or people around. Cleaning up is not always a top-down imposition. It may also be an ordinary and spontaneous habit that speaks of autonomy and self-worth. "I always clean because I live here," Daokaate clarifies from the first time he invites me in for a cup of tea, while sweeping the kitchen floor. As simple and assertive as a matter of normality, respect, even pride. "If I see filth around, it's like seeing someone who's vomiting," Woikat once tells me, with a grave expression and an eloquent gesture. More often than not, however, no particular explanation is required. You clean up as long as you construct this as the obvious and natural thing to do, at least for the space around you. Fatou's room is a case in point. Sometimes, our parallel chats with the respective smartphones in our hands end up with him standing up to clean his entire room. As a guest, and an older man, I'm not expected to contribute to the task. "Sit back and relax!" he smiles, gently pushing me back to my place (that is, his bed). As he starts wiping dust around, including from the electric fan and the PlayStation set, his patient explanation comes along. "There are people who come here, when my friends come it must be clean. . . . I feel ashamed if it is not." Given this premise, the staff exhortations for cleaning have little relevance. Pride and self-respect do, instead. "My mother," adds Fatou, "used to tell me, 'Clean your room, clean your room!' Now I'm used to it—I always clean."

I find myself in a similar position whenever Kambanoo is hosting me. "It's so clean here!" I end up exclaiming, in sincere astonishment. Besides being unnecessarily patronizing, the statement holds a problematic subtext—his clean room is the real "matter out of place," in a place for asylum seekers. It is precisely this comparative nuance that stands out in Kambanoo's reaction. Shrugging his shoulders, he comments, "It's important to clean my body and the place where I'm living. Don't know what the others do—don't care. I think for myself, not for others. I clean up." Again, cleaning sounds like the most obvious and natural of things. Kambanoo states it with the same tone in which he periodically reminds me that "we must always thank God for what happens to us." Just as for a religious obligation, no point to discuss it further. What does matter is stating his uniqueness and the irrelevance of the others as a term of reference. One feels utterly alone, but he may reclaim this in a positive sense. Living together with seventy people, as young, male, racialized and liminal as you, should not affect your habits and values—if only when it comes to cleaning, if you've no better way to make them real again.

6.4   "THEY'RE WATCHING US: KEEP IT CLEAN!"

Cleaning has also to do with the presentation of the self[32] and of the place where one lives or works. To the eyes of the staff, it is also a matter of normalization. It should de-exceptionalize the place in relation to the native people around, while saving its low profile in the urban fabric. In this perspective, the matter-out-of-place shown or visible outside is as critical as the one that accumulates itself inside. It then happens that certain mundane day-to-day objects take up a symbolic meaning and even a political power of their own.

By all likelihood, the more xenophobic sectors of the public opinion and their political entrepreneurs would construct an asylum center as inherently out-of-place (i.e., dirt in Douglas's sense), regardless of its appearance or location. However, relatively minor details that contrast with the surrounding urbanscape may extend that perception to a larger audience, starting from the neighbors. Incorrect ways of sorting garbage or hanging out the laundry or unnecessarily loud gatherings in the courtyard are typically under scrutiny for this. Even apparently irrelevant things such as shoes or other objects on the windowsills may turn into a source of contention. "You must take away your shoes!" is a refrain in the occasional collective meetings with the staff. Otherwise, the manager explains, neighbors or passersby are bound to wonder, "How come refugees have all these shoes? Maybe they spend all their pocket money this way?!" Some complaints indeed came from the residents of the building on the back side, at a visible distance. Her message is perhaps patronizing and yet protective. Let us prevent people from cultivating prejudices against *us*; it takes little for *you* to move the shoes in. Leaving them out is impolite toward *our* neighbors. "I know it's often old stuff that ex-residents left there, and yet . . . better take it away." As important, "remember—they're watching us!." Surveillance, for an asylum center, can be informally enacted from the outside, even more than from formal surveillants.[33]

That the sneakers are pragmatically removed, after initial reactions of fierce disdain for what "the others think," is not the end of the story. In fact, most of these shoes are not old (see 5.2). They were probably cheap, and yet they are something my interlocutors keep buying, taking good care of, and displaying them orderly. Whether they're visible or not, their bare existence may raise uncanny doubts. How is it that people with virtually no income have a number of sneakers around themselves? More pragmatically, how to reconcile this with the ordinary civil-society narrative on refugees and avoid that nativist political actors appropriate it for their own ends? The latter question speaks to the need for invisibility the center reproduces, one day after another—the less exceptional it appears, the better. The former question links up to the symbolic power of particular objects to display success and

FIGURE 18. Sneakers on the windowsill outside Kambanoo's room, in a position that makes them invisible from the inner room but visible from outside. Photo by author.

futurity but also to the critical interplay between decency and visibility. Irrelevant as they are in relation to the big questions of asylum, the sneakers are revealing of contrasting views and practices of visibility and decor, from inside and outside, from the host and the guest side. Once again what is decent to whom and where the not-so-decent should be situated are not self-evident or universally agreed on.

What appears indecent from the outside may be seen otherwise from the bedroom of Kambanoo, for instance. One day, like many others, Kambanoo, just back from his round of CV-spreading in town, invites me in. He first slowly and methodically places around the few belongings he had in his black backpack. The room includes a special corner for his three caps and another one for his six pairs of shoes. However, that is not the right destination for the sneakers he was wearing outside. Kambanoo places them on the windowsill, out of his second-floor window (figure 18). This way they can get fresh air, rather than leaving an olfactory trace inside. As long as they are out of his smelling reach, they are no issue; if anything, they contribute to a cleaner room. If I were downstairs, close to the entrance, I might frame this as the rude gesture of someone who doesn't care for decor. Watching from outside would only reveal something out-of-place. Watching from inside means appreciating Kambanoo's endeavors to fight against the dirt and set up an order of his own through this minute set of practices. From the vantage point of his hyper-clean room, the sneakers suggest respect for the inner order of things, as much as indifference to the reactions from outside. More than a violation of the rule, it is a statement of its irrelevance. The only order that matters for Kambanoo, right now, is the one of his body and of the ordinary space around it—hence, for now, of his room.

Once he's done with his backpack, Kambanoo cleans the floor back and forth with a broom and a mop, before taking care of his own body with a long shower, leaving me sitting alone in the room, in an unusual demonstration of confidence. The time then comes for the cleaning, or care, of his spirit. Wearing his purple *galabia* with gold-colored shining hems, his rug in one hand, Kambanoo moves into the kitchen to pray. Within these four walls, I like repeating to myself, he's exerting his sovereignty. He can stay in, have showers or prayers as long as he likes. He can let me in (or out) first, in a demonstration of politeness that says something of the perceived ownership of space. He can fix the scansions of his everyday time, at least when it comes to cleaning, washing, eating, praying. And he can afford *not* to be watched, hence judged, whatever he does. However, as he gets back from the kitchen, he murmurs just a few words: "It's ten months" since his appeal hearing, and no news in sight. And no sovereignty, of course, if not of his own self-bubble, as long as he is allowed to nourish it. Final sigh—"What else should I do?"

6.5   BEYOND THE DIVIDE: TRACES OF BEAUTY, FUN, TENDERNESS

In short, a simple clean/dirty binary—with a predominant stress on the *dirty* side—does no justice to the lived experience of the center. Ambivalence reigns between contrasting and coexisting sensorial and aesthetic standards. Moreover, there are practices that do not align with any register of dirty or unclean, literal or symbolic. For one thing, several traces of beauty[34] creep into everyday life and reveal as many ways of caring for space, in one's terms. This is no simple result of top-down beautification—decorations, attempts at gardening, affordances for shared sociability and the like. Beauty has also to do with people's articulation of what they see as beautiful and occasionally with their enchantment for it. "It's style!" Olusola mockingly replies one day, as I ask him why he's wearing, like many others, colorful (and inexpensive) plastic bracelets. "I'm more handsome this way," he adds smiling. As banal as meaningful, I think to myself. Sometimes meaningful *and* banal—not to be overburdened with external meanings besides personal aesthetics and tastes. It's only aesthetics, and yet there is something to it, I think one day after a lively discussion with Fatou. Right in the middle of the kitchen,

FIGURE 19. A colorful nativity and Christmas tree in Shah's room.
This fully occupies the shared table in his bedroom. Photo by author.

he's trying to separate some frozen chicken thighs with a big knife. Around his black wrist, a blue plastic bracelet carries two words in capital letters: "SALVINI PREMIER." A burst of laughter from my side. You know . . . "Of course! I know he hates the Black . . . but what comes from the heart is not the same as what comes from the mouth. Maybe he does so only for those who vote for him." Fatou is fascinatingly more open to the doubt than my presumptions about racialized asylum seekers would admit. More important perhaps, he is open to the possibility of wearing whatever he wishes, with no need to account even for that. "I like to wear it now, and I wear it," he concludes, moving back to his chicken thighs.

Unspoken concerns with beauty do not cover only the personal and intimate space of one's body and self. Rather, a lived field of aesthetics emerges from sparse environmental details that speak (also) a language of beauty. When the

FIGURE 20. Light cords that remind us of Christmas decorations cover shelves full of sneakers in Sani's room. Photo by author.

time comes, Christmas trees and decorations, from tiny handmade wood carvings to larger and flashy infrastructures, emerge in many bedrooms of Christian residents—unlike in the common space, less for a statement of *laïcité* than for decreasing interest in all that is not strictly necessary. The nativity and Christmas tree that Shah patiently assembled in his room, with the help of a few other Pakistanis with a Christian background, is a fascinating case in point. Both the flashing lights among the small statues (with a big white cross towering over them) and the wish cards attached on the tree make it a unique pocket of beauty, dedication and self-identification (figure 19). Shah is eager to show it to me, while a co-national friend exclaims that they collected "300 euros" to set it up. Perhaps less conspicuous but still remarkably creative is a decoration in Sani's room (figure 20). This combines several markers of well-being, beauty and success in the same picture:

lights (to evoke festivity), sneakers (i.e., symbolically powerful possessions), and a soccer bag (for leisure and fun, regardless of anything else).

In a similar vein, some bedrooms host pictures, posters or calendars that are also meant to "make beauty" *(fare bello)*, as Tvel once puts it. There are drawings like Woikat's that, no matter how charged with past memories and untold stories, have an aesthetic depth of their own. And there are spontaneous manifestations of wonder out of beauty, whenever a rosy sunset lies in front of the facade or the maple trees facing it are covered with yellow and red leaves. Such occasional traces of beauty, freely accessible to asylum seekers–in-waiting as much as to anybody else, are also part of the sensorial experience in the center.

As or more important are the intermittent traces of fun that emerge from an apparently undifferentiated gray, boring and dismal environment. Viewing YouTube or TikTok, dancing or singing, may also be a source of leisure and reward— as for many more in their early twenties. "At the end of the day, they're happier than us!" a caseworker comments on the high-volume rap music that welcomes us from a room, as we get back after a long organizational meeting. The statement is far-fetched, and yet it captures the existence of fragments of simple, sheer and generational fun. Staying together for PlayStation games, listening to music or watching all sorts of videos (never, as far as I can see, heavily sexualized ones) plays a similar function. It's a joyful way of filling (some) time, if not of exerting one's right to have "normal" fun, like any young man might wish to do. Joking together and playfully exchanging all sorts of creative bad words in Italian does as much. Just like in a sequence of screams between Suka and Kokou, one afternoon, as they're running to take their bikes out of the center. In a spiraling upward mood of masculine competition, the sequence starts from a plain *fanculo!* to a less obvious *vacacaregrandecosì!* (with a large arm gesture to convey the purported shit size), through a few more creative steps, up to the climax of "Salvini," as an ultimate affront that makes everybody laugh and needs no further reply.

Revealing moments of joking and teasing one another pop up when friends are around—again, interestingly, involving the powerful that are all-too-well known and raise a fascination of their own. "Do you want a job?" Den mockingly asks, one day, to a friend who's complaining about the long time he has spent without much to do. "Come clean my bathroom. . . . I'll pay you 1,000 euros per hour— when I'll be famous like Salvini!" When one is in a good mood, there is nothing bad in playful and imaginary role shifting, displacing on someone else the immigrant-dirty-job identity and taking up the VIP one, ironically embodied by an anti-immigrant figure. "I could kidnap you!" Sani exclaims to me another day, in a burst of laughter, while we are eating together with his friends. "I'll lock you in until you find me a job"—and more laughter, until someone connects the kidnapping idea to what ordinarily happens in Nigeria and stops laughing. As usual, merry moments, sometimes euphoric ones, rest on frail bases. Once these periodically re-emerge, no more shared conviviality. Everybody back to his room—until the next time.

FIGURE 21. A teddy bear on the pillow of someone's bed. Photo by author.

There are also, as importantly, pockets of tenderness. While much of what has to do with sentimental life is relegated elsewhere, several rooms give space to micro-traces of tenderness, if not of childhood, in contrast with the normative self-representation as adult and self-reliant males. A minor and rather frequent detail, which is invisible to the outer world, is the presence of stuffed animals somewhere on one's bed or pillow (figure 21). My interlocutors would smile and joke about them, if they enter our conversation, as Sani's huge tiger or the white teddy bears of Daokaate or Kambanoo periodically do. No reason to be embarrassed. No reason to show or discuss them either, however, out of this relatively intimate and private setting. Indeed, no matching between the assertive self-image one presents outside and the more playful, if not childlike, one that people can afford to nourish inside their rooms.

6.6   FROM THE PLACE TO THE BODY AND THE SELF: REACHES OF CARING AND CLEANING

"Do you clean up in your new flat?" the manager asks Olusola with a smile, one day he has come back to greet people and ask her for some little favor. "I *am* clean," replies Olusola, slightly offended, making no mention of his current status as a couch surfer—no flats in sight. "Of course, I didn't say that. I've asked if you *do* the cleaning!" she rejoins. A succinct yes from Olusola is enough to close the conversation, but not the analytical field that emerges around the tension between doing and being clean. The two variants—taking care of the place where you are and of yourself—need not be as intimately connected as the center staff and common sense would expect.

There is a remarkable scalarity in the ways of cleaning and caring of my interlocutors. For many reasons, the reach of what is relevant, hence to be taken care of, varies from larger portions of space to the most basic and essential one, that is, one's body.[35] Sometimes, when I'm chatting with Paul, we end up in "his" kitchen. The background is always the same: a big case looming above the shelves, cardboard boxes around, a broken chair on the table, a window that has long been broken too. No way of locking it, before. No way of opening it now, as the repairman, a very occasional and oft-evoked visitor, must have fixed it with some nails. "They say they'll arrange it sooner or later," Paul comments with a smile of benign neglect. Meanwhile, the air in the room is stagnant. Dozens of dead flies are lying close to the window frame, and there they will stay upon my subsequent visits. "The heat kills them," notes Paul en passant. As I've asked him for some water, he picks up his personal glass from the bedroom, washes it carefully with dish soap and takes a bottle of water from the fridge. "Is it too cold?" he asks after a while, before starting to juggle between the basin and the hotplate to prepare something to eat "for the whole week—not like you guys in Italy, who cook all the time!"

The cooking space, which is rather clean, is the one that matters, unlike the dead flies' nowhereland, a couple of meters away. Wherever Paul is staying to do something he needs to or wishes to, that's his space of relevance. It is flexible and inclusive if he has guests but unlikely to ever reach to the chair, the window, the dead flies or the lively cockroaches that occasionally get in. At the core of the meaningful space (i.e., the matter-in-place) lies, instead, Paul's own body. Whenever he's about to touch some food, he wipes his hands over and again, thereby protecting himself from dirt as a threat to the "cherished boundary between self and other."[36] And whenever he goes out to work as a DJ, to his church or even only to a supermarket, he wears rather elegant clothes. Each of these settings requires a distinct aesthetic register and more care for the body than anywhere in the center.

In fact, not everybody lacks interest or even care for the place in which he's living. As the previous sections have shown, traces of beautification or personalization emerge here and there, including religion-driven ones. The key point, however, is that both caring and cleaning are selective and stratified practices. There is no necessary overlap between the place in which you are living and the things or objects, not to mention the people, you care the most about. Rather, care and un-care, as much as clean and dirty, are entangled with each other in often unexpected ways.

Omokunrin and his friends help me understand this one autumn afternoon, as they're celebrating the birthday of Ogwu in the backyard. Laughs and a nice atmosphere are facilitated by the music popping up from a mobile speaker and by a suitcase full of alcohol. It is a minor detail, at the moment, that Ogwu is due to leave the center soon, not of his choice. What might ruin the event, instead, is the strong sewage smell from the manhole cover nearby. Sometimes it reaches to the upper floors, producing disgusted faces and complaints to the staff—it is they, ironically, who do not meet their cleaning duties. At some point Omokunrin comes back from the car wash. His secondhand Volkswagen Golf, which was "a bit dirty," is now shining and spotless again—although, he gloomily laments, the cleaning brush left some (tiny) marks on the door. That's what is to be cleaned and taken care of, not his bedroom. However, the car is not alone as a privileged site of cleaning and care. His body obviously matters the most. Witness to this is the wealth of body lotions he uses and of creative haircuts he displays. "Your wife cooks very well!," he once teases me, with a light touch on my ever-expanding belly, in contrast with his (and most residents') perfect physical shape. Care for the body, in multiple forms, is something a visitor can appreciate every single day, if only by opposition to the lack of care for the rest. It often takes an unusually protracted shape and a slow rhythm, in sync with the everyday rhythm inside, when there is "nothing to do."

That the ultimate and basic scale of caring and cleaning has to do with one's body is nothing banal or irrelevant, given the little control one has over any larger space and time. Taking care of one's body—"you're always so clean"—articulates intimate meanings and mirrors societal concerns. It is something more fundamental and bound up with dignity and self-respect than a matter of conspicuous consumption. It is at the reach of anybody and a constant concern for everybody. It is as visible in the barest rooms as anywhere else. Koné, for instance, has very little material belongings around his bed. He has never had a "real" job—he probably wouldn't call that way his activity as bike repairman of the center—and will decide to leave alone, at some point, for the lack of any tangible prospect of improvement. Whenever I'm in to visit his roommate Ninu, in the middle of the afternoon, an extended routine of self-preparation unfolds before our eyes. Washing, deodorizing, combing, trying a couple of shirts. "Are you going out?" I ask Koné at some point. "I'm staying here," he replies with a bitter smile.

For many more, though, going out requires a similar preparation with showers and long sessions of body lotions, deodorant and cologne. "You're a big man of rolls on!" Ogwu once jokingly exclaims to his roommate, Ousmane, who has long been preparing himself before going out, as every afternoon. Cologne on young Black male bodies is a frequent encounter in the center—one that conflates several implicit meanings (see 3.5). Care for oneself and sensorial translation of one's aesthetics, just as for clothes, sneakers, bracelets or watches, are certainly one. Anti-stigmatization, preventing unusual body smells and countering the racist association between poor or Black bodies and bad odors is probably another.[37] "They're watching us," in this case, becomes an equally unsettling "they're sniffing us," which requires proper tactics of self-protection and normalization.

In sum, the ongoing tension between dirty and clean and the search for a balance in between pervade everyday interactions between my interlocutors and their social and material spaces. "It's so annoying," a caseworker once tells me, "when they throw all dirty things on the floor, while they're cooking, so they don't get their hands dirty." There's more than a formulaic complaint about bad cleaning here. The focus has shifted from a normative register to an embodied and affective one—what people do, how they feel, what they bodily feel and construct as their own. "During Ramadan," he continues, "I used to prepare warm milk, biscuits and dates, kind of a special thing" for their evening meal. The next morning "all date seeds were down on the floor." One day after another, he tries it again. No way, he says, in spite of their prayer rugs being right there, near the seeds. "How come you pray close to dirty stuff?!" It is as if the rug and the floor around it were separate worlds. One day the caseworker is fed up enough to shift all the seeds on the rugs. "At that point they cleaned them up!" How can you treat, then, all that lies off the rug and is apparently irrelevant as such, even when it is dirty?

One option is, indeed, to contaminate the rug—dirty and clean all together, which should induce some cleaning as a counter-reaction. Another way ahead, however, is to try and stretch the rug or perhaps replace it with a larger one—that is, try and expand the boundaries of what matters and demands care, if not attachment and belonging. The rug is a fungible and moving object by definition. You can (un)fold it on any single act of prayer. You may replace it with a different one, if needed. And you can make yourself at home again, if only for a fragment of timespace, as you are praying on it (cf. 7.3).[38] However, little by little, you can also rework your rug, for it to cover larger portions of space, and care for them, at least for a while. There's a metaphor but also a potential for more inclusive practice in each rug—and in the ways your body (un)folds it.

7

—

Home, Non-home

"What do you want me to draw?" Woikat asks one day, after my request for a "special drawing." A *casa* (Italian for both "home" and "house"), I say, only to encounter a perplexed and thoughtful gaze that will persist after my translation in French. "Home—you mean, *here?*" The location is as puzzling as the word. What has Italy to do with any image of home, for a young African man in a legal and social liminality? Wherever you wish, Woikat. "Okay, so . . . in Africa!" The artwork he'll prepare has a house against the lush natural background of a river with boats and people fishing, playing or sharing fruits. There is even a dog. "I know Italians like it," he adds with a smile (figure 22). After all, a new and larger house for his family is part of Woikat's silent dreams—and a reasonable target for some of the money he sends back.[1] No point, instead, to portray any place in Italy, including the center. This is obviously a shelter, a camp, a *non*-home. Yet, an ambivalent tension between home and various forms of non-home emerges from its day-to-day inhabitation.

It should not come as a surprise for any house to have something to do with home—and with its opposites. The resonance between *house* and *home* evokes contrasting locations, practices, imaginaries, and aspirations,[2] and as many understandings of *non-home*—something that may be absent, denied, missed but also, in some respects, actively searched for.[3] No one of my interlocutors is homeless, strictly speaking. None of them, though, would accept the center as home proper. Everybody ended up there by chance, as they needed a temporary shelter and luckily got one. It is rather, and *volitionally*, a non-home.

Across its multiple meanings and tensions, the idea of home can nourish a unique reflection on the places that matter, in relation to the accessible ones.[4] Exploring the narratives and practices of the residents in terms of home *and*

143

FIGURE 22. The oil painting Woikat made, on a cardboard sheet, when I asked him to depict "home" (*casa*). Artwork by Woikat. Photo by author.

non-home illuminates the tension between their origin and current position but also between suspended present and aspired future, and between here and there— where they come from and where they could change their lives for good, despite all the suffering and frustrations. The conceptual repertoire of home studies is critical to explore this tension through, and beyond, housing conditions and pathways.[5] For sure, forcibly displaced people are overexposed to protracted housing marginalization, all the more so in Italy.[6] That said, the traditional domain of housing studies may not capture the emotional and moral dilemmas associated with the need to make a home and with the competing pressures to locate it. It is worth asking how far an asylum center can or should reach as a functional equivalent of a domestic space; how residents feel therein, in relation to the places and people most important for them; and what "good" place and destination, if any, they see in the future ahead of them. Indeed, the idea of home invites elaboration on one's perceived and desired position in the world, given their limited room of maneuver.

That my young male interlocutors have in mind their country or local community of origin, as long as they think of home, is nothing surprising for newcomer immigrants.[7] However, it already speaks to the paradox of home and estrangement,[8] since their asylum applications are based on claims of enforced fleeing, whereby homecoming would endanger their lives. In a sociological perspective, moreover, home is also a matter of emplaced practices, or of attempts to negotiate a special relation with particular places, even in a non-home environment. This faceted interplay between narratives and practices, as much as between home and non-home, reveals the last form of ambivalence to be explored in this book.

7.1   NAMING A PLACE

You live in a house, or work in it, with no need to call it a name of its own. It is enough to use the name of the street or perhaps *here* or *there*, depending on your position. No shared designation exists for a place that is of no one in particular. Its institutional mission is all too clear, just as the frustration of its residents. Even so, there is something revealing in the ways you name it. In the everyday basic Italian that flows between staff and residents and among the residents who have no language in common, the center is sometimes pragmatically called *casa*, or *home* among the English speakers. In fact, by their very existence, places like asylum centers disrupt a neat division of the world between separate homes, each with its own prerogatives and inhabitants, in their own place. By definition, a reception facility affords only some of these prerogatives. It is simply the place in which you are staying now. Nothing like the *casa* to which staff members get back after their shift and where, perhaps, somebody is waiting for them. Nothing like the *home* a migrant comes from—a place that was ridden with troubles and contradictions and may no longer exist yet exerts a degree of nostalgia.[9] Relative to it, the center holds much less value, while affording a basic livelihood and sense of safety in a country that promises so much more. And, of course, nothing like the future home people may dream of, wherever they situate it.

Much of the jargon use of *casa* or *home* involves the bedrooms rather than the building as such. That's the place in which you stay, with your own key. This doesn't mean that it can't take up more intimate, even poetic meanings. "My room," Olusola mumbles one day as we venture into a discussion of houses and homes, "is my home. It is where I lay down my head, where I pray, where I do all my secret things. Okay, here I have a shared room but—forget about that! Forget about my roommate. My home is my bed, just the space for me, around my bed [stretching his arms], you know? My room is my friend. My best friend. I must ask it to let people in. Only the people I really trust can come in." I am lucky enough to be one of them, as he repeats while picking up the flour bag for his dinner fufu. "Little by little, I can tell you why I left Africa." So he will do.

It is within the bedrooms that displaced people may enjoy some of the prerogatives of a domestic space.[10] These critically include hospitality, if only of other residents or outsiders like me. Sitting on a bed, possibly with a glass of water or a cup of tea, is a domestic practice that a room selectively affords. It may then be that the scale of what you feel as your own and in charge of—an emic and promising definition of home—is reduced to a room corner, a bed, a smartphone or your own body (see 3.5 and 6.6). As for the larger space around, its only real dwellers are ironically less at home than non-dwellers like the staff members. This is not without *role* ambivalence[11] for the staff themselves: what they'd like the place to be (ideally, the residents' home) and what they are bound to make of it (practically, not their home). "It's as if I'm entering their homes, isn't it?" the new manager remarks one day, after telling me that she visits "each room to greet them" at the beginning of her shifts. Her novel habit will be short-lived. Some, perhaps most, may not look forward to the greeting. As long as they stay in their rooms, they can afford it. More fundamentally, top-down conviviality would be hard to reconcile with the stricter discipline, from cleaning to signing-up rules, imposed by the new service provider (or, the latter would argue, by the new political course). Likewise, as a doorman sighs one afternoon, "I know this is their home, but I must do my job, right?" That is, watch and check who goes in or out—who is allowed to stay in the home and who is not. You do it on behalf of somebody else, a rather invisible and impersonal local authority, but you are the bodily demonstration that this is *not* home. Why feel at home there, after all? And as long as someone does, why should that be desirable, if it means getting used to a life spent mostly indoors with nothing much to do, in the company of others in the same predicament?

The fact remains that, in a practical sense, people say *home* to designate the only dwelling space they have access to. Staying in is a source of protection, if homelessness is the only alternative. It may even feel safer than hanging out. No white people who look down at you. No risk, some would add, to get involved in "bad things" such as drug dealing. And much more risk of ending up in some form of nothingness. If anything, whenever you go out you do have a place to go back to and enjoy some privacy. When I stroll around with Suka or Fatou for some grocery shopping, going back to the house with its lit-up windows at night raises an uncanny sense of domesticity. Inside that place they are less stranger than outside. To the eyes of native or non-resident passersby, instead, the center itself is the ultimate non-home—that is, the place for refugees. There they fit, cognitively and morally. That is the only place where they don't need to account for staying in or getting back. They just enter or exit, as "we" all do in "our" place. With a major proviso—access restricted to economically dependent asylum applicants who comply with the rules—this is indeed the closest approximation to home, as famously evoked by Robert Frost: "The place where, when you have to go there, they have to take you in."[12]

Staying "too much," nonetheless, takes up a negative moral connotation in the jargon of the residents. It is not good, for you are not working—you don't make a livelihood out of your dedication and sacrifice. "No good," just as you would feel "sitting around" with "nothing to do" the whole day in some West African town[13]—and in an even more acute paradox, for now you are in the rich world. Staying home is a diminishment of status compared to what any job would afford. It necessarily means incompleteness, if all your immigrant world is divided between home and work, the lack of the latter forcing you into the former. Staying home, even before covid turns it into a new and uncanny norm, is at odds with masculinity. It clashes with the gendered view of home as the inside and feminized space of domestic care, whereas outside is the man's place for work, hence for autonomy, dignity, respect.[14] It is not just "boring," says Ogwu, while waiting for the new temporary permit that should allow him to resume a precarious job in public park maintenance. It also "hurts," he adds, pointing to his head. "At home, you eat, wash your dishes, sleep"—full stop. Perhaps someone is okay that way, he admits. Not him. Yet this also protects Ogwu from the frequent police checks outside—he's Black and Nigerian enough to be a good candidate for that. "Don't know why, but that's how it is."

All this being said, the moral devaluation of domesticity as something to be avoided, precisely while most do not avoid it, is not the last word. Something, rather than nothing, happens anyway, with a meaning and value of its own. "Staying home is no use!" a resident suddenly exclaims in front of the staff office one afternoon, before running out—and skipping his cleaning shift. However, as I think of it again in Woikat's room, staying home has several uses. It is a timespace in which Woikat draws what he likes, while Joseph, his Cameroonian roommate, occupies in sync the rest of the space to cook for himself, and Larka, in the adjacent room, can listen to some pop radio music at an unusually high volume, for his habits. As little as that may be, it affords a degree of (parallel) normality. Within the same timespace, everyday routines are reproduced, separately or jointly, which need not amount to empty or wasted time.[15] You can do things that you need and that you like or just mind your own business. You can withdraw from the gaze, the sight, the noise and the smell of most others. You can retreat to "rest," even when you have done nothing, precisely because you are tired of waiting with nothing to do.

"I'm always here," Kambanoo invariably repeats when I ask what he's about to do. Still, he does have a place to go back to. This is all too natural and obvious for the well housed like myself. It is not for whoever does not enjoy that privilege, including Olusola on his first months outside. "*This* is bad," he grimaces one day. As a temporary guest of his Yoruba brothers, "it's not like here—I can't stay during the day to eat or rest. . . . I sleep and then I go. That's all." No point, of course, for any romantic or nostalgic account of the quasi-enforced domesticity in the center. The fact remains that this is potentially open to several ways of using time—depending on circumstances, capitals, supports, fates. It need not invariably end up in an oppressive and meaningless timespace—or in nothing.

7.2   AS IF IT WERE HOME: DOMESTICITY AND FEELING AT HOME IN QUESTION

As a prescriptive and emotionally thick construct, *home* is over-ambitious for the housing standards and the living conditions of an asylum facility.[16] Nevertheless, the lived experience of any house has something to do with home, and people therein relate it to their own domestic habits and values. These emerge in ways of thinking, feeling or doing that articulate some form of *as if it were home*. What does the parallel between the center and a domestic space elucidate, and what does it obscure?

Domesticity I: Isomorphic?

If you are managing a reception facility, as much as any house, you'll probably expect its residents to follow certain standards of domestic care. That is what hospitality rules state; that's what you are used to doing at home. The underlying domestic imaginaries and habits are not necessarily obvious or relevant, though, to the eyes of a number of young men from West Africa or Pakistan, in an enforced position of guesthood and waithood. Nor is it obvious what sense they make of this place. How far can you expect them to behave as if it were *theirs?*

The inner atmosphere of non-home stems from infrastructural decay and little cleaning but also from rules such as the night shutdown or the prohibition to have guests. Nevertheless, everyday life is shaped by a certain register of *isomorphic domesticity*: the staff expectation that as *we* do in our place, so *they* should do here. Contrasting standards of domestic order and decor vie with each other, when it comes to cleaning or waste sorting. "Remember, paper towels should go into the organic bin," the manager tells each newcomer, showing him a poster with four waste bins in different colors. The same poster has long been stuck on the kitchen walls, surviving the turnover of its users. "You should just check it," she repeats. "I myself do so, at home. You can't always remember all. . . . Have a look," and the problem will be over.

There are instances, of course, in which the rationale of isomorphic domesticity resonates with the practices of my interlocutors. It does so, however, out of their spontaneous habits rather than for compliance or tactical adaptation to the top-down moral order. The everyday life of Kambanoo is illuminating in this respect (cf. 6.2 and 6.4). "Life is like this," he thoughtfully tells me on his last day in the center, while cleaning up his room like any other day. "When you are . . . you must keep it well as you would do at home." While he prefers omitting who, what or where you are, he does stress housekeeping as an inherent value and form of reciprocity. "They gave it clean. I must leave it clean. It's normal, isn't it?"

In a narrowly statistical sense, it is not. Kambanoo is among the few the staff would never complain about when it comes to cleaning. However, it *is* normal as the thing anybody *should* do. This is the moral texture of Kambanoo's view, as a claim for care and respect, regardless of the circumstances. That day, while picking up his last baggage, he shows no emotional involvement for the place and perhaps the people he's leaving behind. He simply wants to show that his room is as clean as when he arrived or possibly cleaner. That he has spent two years there, from that moment onward, no longer matters.

Generally speaking, though, the implicit domestic terrain is too uneven and unequal for any register of isomorphic domesticity to work out. This is only the place in which one is staying now. That practical concerns such as waste sorting will emerge in any future accommodation and that you'd better be familiar with them, is

FIGURE 23. A makeshift sign in the courtyard stating "PRIVATE PROPERTY / NO ACCESS" in Italian. This is meant to discourage outside drivers from reaching beyond that point, only to dump their garbage, as sometimes happens. Photo by author.

as true as secondary, relative to many more questions and needs. Why should you treat a place *as* home, as long as you have no idea if you'll ever have a place that *is* home.

Domesticity II: Heteronomous

"PRIVATE PROPERTY / NO ACCESS" reads a sign on the driveway to the courtyard (figure 23). As you get closer, you can tell it's rather makeshift—a rectangular piece of board stuck on an old chair back, over the basis of what must have been an electric barrier in one of the previous lives of the building. As the story goes, a doorman set it up one day on his initiative, tired with drivers who occasionally creep in to dump garbage. The message, or at least the claim, is very clear. Like any house, the center has a degree of separation, isolation and protection from outside. This is enhanced by the large and empty courtyard and by the lack of interaction with the neighbors. Indeed, spatial isolation often goes along with relational isolation. This is undesirable for the residents' chances of functional adaptation, if not integration, outside. However, there is more to it than sheer segregation.

If this is the house of the residents, they must have some right to privacy. There is a positive message of protection in this, as the staff members see it, in times with more resources and institutional support. Caseworkers appear reluctant whenever local associations propose shared convivial initiatives—say, a round of visits from university students, the residents' more educated, lucky and gender-mixed peers. *Not in our backyard!* This is no place for orientalist curiosities. Rather, "it's like a condominium," where people have some private space of their own, the manager says. Of course, their need and right to stay away from the spotlight demands respect. For the same reason, though, it is difficult to engage them in any convivial initiative, including those promoted by the staff. On these increasingly rare occasions, such as music or dancing events, the outcome is irremediably ambivalent. Caseworkers and volunteers do their best to invite residents to join a collective meal with rice, pasta or couscous to chat together, or perhaps improvise a rap song or a dance step. In a couple of hours' time it's getting late, loud noises are no longer allowed, and the staff is already in over-time. Time to stop and send people back to their rooms. As long as it lasts, "it helps let the tension out," the staff say. It gives a sense of normality as ephemeral as the party, I think to myself.

After that the bifurcated normality is re-established: the staff, back to their private lives; their counterparts, back to their forcibly shared lives, to be protectively parked there for some more time. "Goodbye," the former say, as they leave the latter's place. "Why is it already over?" the most outspoken protest. "Isn't this our home?" "It is not," the logical response should be. "You should be content with this; it's already a lot for you," the nativist variant would be, one that nobody would ever admit thinking. "It's late, our neighbors complain with the loud music" is instead the pragmatic reply. Enough to close the conversation, while the inner social life goes on in fragments of generally lower volume. Some might carry on like that all night. Perhaps they can't sleep, out of "bad thoughts." Maybe, instead, it's just because there is "nothing to do" the next day. Either way a fact remains: like any house, the center hosts an inner life that is not visible from the public space and may not follow its norms thoroughly. In certain respects, it is a social field in itself,[17] one marked by external discipline and control but also by its own domesticity.

Domesticity III: Feeling at home?

It's not their home, and yet it raises some imaginary, desire or expectation about home. On the staff side, that people should feel at home may sound like a desirable and worthy aim. If we dedicate time to staying with them rather than to "paperwork," they will feel more at home, so some caseworkers initially think. This also leads to a circular explanation of what happens otherwise: "If we don't make them feel at home, they'll leave the place dirty. But it's not because they are dirty! They just don't feel that place as theirs." So ruminates a doorman with an African background, as we engage in a long discussion on the meanings of home during his night shift. "They"—white, European, middle-class caseworkers—don't really understand "the boys" and their "needs", is his afterthought. However, the very expectation that people may feel at home will soon prove naive and patronizing.

Rules, discipline and control do not tell the whole story of the center, and yet they are there. "Let's go away from this fucking place!" someone (just about to leave) exclaims one afternoon, producing a short and improvised rally in the entrance. "This is hell! You can't invite your friends; you can't invite your girl-friend! We're twenty, can't we have sex? Everybody wants to have sex! Even the staff have sex in their homes, don't they?" A few more exclamations and laughter, and the scene fades out by itself. However, once again, "in their homes" is the critical watershed—what the center will never be. What it does afford, instead, is so pragmatic that it may fall even behind the staff's expectations. "We did a workshop on taking care of the domestic space—not just cleaning but, you know, having plants or pictures around. . . . They told us they only want free Wi-Fi!" So a young native intern laments, on one occasion.

Temporality matters, likewise. While institutional accommodation is temporary by definition, adaptation or feeling at home in the larger society, possibly as a synonym with assimilation, will take much longer.[18] What does lie in the remit of institutional hospitality, if properly staffed, is enhancing the *extra*-domestic foundations of migrant homemaking. This matters, I've realized over time, far more than any amelioration of a building in which no current inhabitant, and probably worker, will be in a few years from now. Homemaking has also to do with developing the portable skills needed to navigate a larger societal environment.[19] There is more of a promise, for my young male interlocutors to feel at home at some point, in investing in schooling, labor-market orientation and network building with the local civil society, in spite of the ambiguities that organized civic activities also hold.[20]

"Will they ever feel home?" a caseworker wonders after one of the last moments of conviviality, before budgetary cuts and staff turnover make the gatherings inconceivable. I have no reply, there and then. In hindsight I do have one: the question itself is not the right one—not in the relatively short timespan of life in asylum. The point is rather if and how that timespace is instrumental to enhance homemaking skills outside, for all that will come next. All this being said, home is also *made* through a variety of everyday practices here and now, as long as this contributes to setting the terms of one's being in place, possibly in continuity with life prior to displacement.[21] This is an inherently precarious and contentious endeavor under shared dwelling.[22] It is thus worth exploring how certain micro-forms of homemaking work out in themselves and in relation to others. Food, leisure and religious activities provide several cases in point.

7.3   COUNTER-HOMES: SPACES AND PROSPECTS OF HOMEMAKING FROM BELOW

Importantly, the as-if-it-were home script does not emerge only from the staff. Sometimes my young male interlocutors themselves like or need to do things in ways that reproduce fragments of homes in their memories, emotions or life-styles.[23] Some of their everyday practices reveal implicit claims for domestication over particular timespaces. This may also emerge from their deeper and intimate narratives, where *home* elicits insights into the construction of one's origins, present conditions and aspired or expected futures. Both *doing* home and *talking* home in an unhomely setting demand attention.

Homemaking and music

If one's body is the primary scale of home (cf. 3.5 and 6.6), all ways of taking care of it are minimal, pragmatic and portable forms of homemaking. One of them certainly has to do with music.[24] This is an ordinary companion to much of what one does in the center. Listening to music, with earphones or speakers, means creating a bubble of domesticity around yourself. You can carry the bubble along, in constant negotiation of a context-adequate sonic threshold, until you're fed up or it clashes with other bubbles. Listening to some *kriolo* religious song and humming it is routine practice for Ninu, whether he's preparing something to eat or cleaning up in "his" corridor, under the watchful and surprised gaze of the staff. Some lyrics may stay in people's minds more than the rest. One of them is the "just in case" from a Gambian song that Suka likes humming. It's a love song, like many more, and yet it sounds so consistent with how he is feeling: whatever happens (as he has little clue of what when, or how), just in case, he can listen to his favorite music. Even Foulané, silent and reserved as he usually is, may carve out a timespace of his own to sing the mesmerizing melody he's hearing and reproduce its rhythm with an empty can. As usual, the special atmosphere ends abruptly as soon as he moves elsewhere, while still humming the melody to himself. Bursts of loud music that cover entire corridors, alternated with constant and low-profile flows of sounds, are part and parcel of the sensescape, with contents ranging from rock to rap to religious motifs. While this may be challenging for the relationships between roommates, it does make the place more lively and perhaps livable. In fact, music is conspicuous and saddening by its absence, on the rare occasions in which it is not there.

Homemaking and religion

There is apparently no need to evoke home to describe certain ways of cooking, eating, praying or having fun, possibly with somebody else, in short-lived pockets of conviviality. Much of this takes the register of the normal and natural—what people like doing or have always done. Analytically, though, these are homemaking practices as long as they give back some sense of control over space and time,[25] by "translating"[26] certain aspects of everyday life before displacement.[27] While making no difference to one's structural condition, homemaking from below dots it with some hints of sense—sometimes of pleasure.

Praying, for instance, embodies multiple forms of homemaking: the reproduction of distinctive past habits, the isolation of some timespace from the rest, the re-emplacement of a sense of intimacy and nourishment of the self. My fieldnotes are replete with unexpected encounters with people's ways of praying, including in Fatou's bedroom. One afternoon like many others, his *muezzin* app rings the prayer alarm. It's 5:00 p.m. Fatou immediately takes off his socks and goes to wash himself in the bathroom. "If you want you can stay," is the quiet response to my uncertain gaze. Each prayer I attend tends to reiterate the same performance—one I always find somehow moving, even while I understand no single word. Back in the room, Fatou unfolds his green rug with gold-colored embroidery and the Kaba in the middle. He picks up the *misbaha* from his nightstand. He kneels down and starts reciting a number of sentences in Arabic, with a light and deep voice that seems to stem from his inner body. For almost ten minutes, part of the floor has become sacred, in marked contrast with the sparse objects around, including the small heater close to the point where he's bending down his head. Praying makes for a spiritual bubble that rests on the rug and is nourished by his bodily moves.

You could do the same almost anywhere, with a proper bodily orientation, without particular infrastructures. You can even pray in a bedroom with other people around, in a relation of mutual irrelevance and respect. So does Cé one afternoon, right while the others, myself included, are watching an American Western. The private action he's performing has no visible demarcation from the surrounding sensescape. The screams and punches from the TV set outdo his whispers. "Do you have one million dollars, Yankees?!" comes uncannily along with the last sentence of his prayer, before he picks up the rug and repristinates the status quo—sitting on the bed, the smartphone in his hand, minding his own business. More often than not, however, praying—reproducing one's interiorly felt and externally sanctioned religious home—calls for some space differentiation.[28] So is for Kambanoo, who, after cleaning up his room and himself, moves into the kitchen to pray alone. The room itself is only the interior space where he happens to stay, as long as he can—until, hopefully, something better happens. It is praying that makes it special, for a young man with a deep-rooted religious background like him. The Koranic school in Conakry is central to his self-narrative, on the rare occasions in which he wishes to tell me of his past life. You can pray alone, as much as together. So Mbaye once does, in his room, with a friend who visited him from outside. After laying down two rugs close to each other, the two of them start enacting the same movements in full simultaneity. They lead the litany in turn, in Arabic and Bambara, and shake their hands at the end. "We've prayed for the whole world," they explain. "Also for you."

You can pray in the courtyard, as some visitors do in the post-covid normal, with the support of a rug and a bowl of water from inside. You can pray in a corridor, as Omokunrin's roommate once does to mark his space away from him. It's a five-minute homemaking process that commands respect and invites access only from people with the same religious background. You can pray in a dedicated space, as the middle-aged Pakistani newcomers eventually do in the empty room before the laundry. Not an issue, as long as you don't claim a permanent use of the room and you fold up your rugs (cf. 3.3). The important thing is just to keep praying, Olusola periodically reminds me. Regardless of the location, I think while listening to him, you can reproduce the same ritual with your own body and some minimal affordances. So portable, as a way of infusing meaning, intimacy and selfhood into some timespace. And by the same token, so ephemeral. As soon as the prayer time is over, or so he decides, Fatou folds back the green rug and gently puts it on the upper shelf, protected by Sani's huge soft toy tiger. Everything keeps on as before—except, perhaps, in the interior life of he who has prayed.

Homemaking and food

Eating or drinking, in turn, are basic and unsurprising matters of social reproduction. Nevertheless, they may also embody emotional, mnemonic or ritual connections with life prior to displacement. Certain ways of cooking, eating and sharing food contribute as much as praying to excavate fragments of home within the nonhome. For instance, having tea together is a powerful mode of conviviality, commensality and hospitality.[29] "Would you like tea?" Daokaate asks in one of our first encounters. Of course. While he's picking up his yellow little box, I'm still too fascinated with the exotic and the didascalic to avoid some pedantic questions. Is it the one you used to drink in Senegal? "Yes." Where does it *actually* come from? "No idea," Daokaate smiles back. "Somewhere in Africa! Maybe Morocco or Algeria?" This is irrelevant enough to make my question meaningless, besides unnecessary. What matters is his embodied knowledge of how tea should be prepared—a practical skill and habit from before, and from elsewhere, that resists external changes.[30] There's a ritual to tea preparation. It is an extended sequence of pouring hot tea between a small saucepan and an even smaller glass. Nothing improvised, and quite some skill involved, as no single drop falls out along the way. Once the tea has been shaken enough, each guest will sip it in turn from the glass. The product as much as the process are part of what my interlocutors used to do there and then. While this need not say much of their countries of origin or their individual lives, it does remind them of a sensuous, embodied and selectively good facet of everyday life there—past and, perhaps at some point, future.

Meals do something similar, whenever they are shared in small circles of friends—the variable yet generally limited reach of host-guest relations.[31]

I sometimes happen to find myself in a room with someone who's preparing a meal, in a mid-afternoon that my classed ethno-centrism would not qualify as either lunch or dinner time. This comes with a straightforward invitation: I'm there; thereby I'm a diner.[32] One plastic bowl with food is lying on the kitchen table or floor, with some people around. It won't take more than a few minutes for the bowl to be emptied, the floor or table to be basically clean and impersonal again and people to be back to whatever they were doing. Meanwhile, some commensality has been produced. So is the reminiscence of "how we are used to eating in Africa," as Fatou puts it. It would thoroughly resemble a common prayer, except for the meal bowl in the middle.

Cooking and sharing African food is a positive routine for Suka and his fellow Gambian guests. Suka's way of preparing food is patient and slow, in tune with the rhythm of the center. "I never cooked in the Gambia—I've learnt here," he points out, perhaps in an endeavor of reclaiming masculinity with a native, male and older counterpart. "It's our culture; only women and girls cook. Men must go out to work." If that's culture, no doubt culture changes, if only for necessity. Judging from his expression and jokes at the ethnic market or while he starts cooking, Suka feels better in those moments and better fills a potentially empty time through a practical, creative and often convivial set of practices. While he's busy cooking, his smartphone on the table has something of a TV set in my middle-class imaginary of a dining room (and most likely in Suka's, if he could afford it). It is now broadcasting the trial to a former ally of the Gambian president. "Always the same in Africa" is all Suka wishes to say, mid-way between gloom and resignation. Next comes the Al-Jazeera news channel and then something else. As we gather around the table, the smartphone does as much as the bowl of peppered chicken with rice to create conviviality. If anything similar to a domestic hearth exists in this place, that has all to do with the smartphone—an electronic, portable, private and selectively shared one. During that particular dinner, the smartphone will also be a constant reminder of what is happening in the "real" world. "Hope covid will not make it to Africa, or it kills half of the population," exclaims Fatou. "We must pray and trust in God," Suka replies. "There's no full-time jobs—that's a problem," someone else says, bringing everybody back to the here-and-now. Indeed, from their demographic, biographic and class racialized position, joblessness is worse than the pandemic. Were it not for the fact that the pandemic will worsen their joblessness in turn, for one year or two.

All these grassroots routines follow tacit, deep-rooted and shared scripts that connect what was natural and pleasant there and then with what is doable here and now. Along the way homemaking bubbles articulate a certain sense of normality. Bodily co-presence may well make these routines more "effervescent." Nevertheless, certain lonely activities may also contribute to sort out some timespace from the rest. This is what I see, for instance, in Larka's lengthy preparation of his chapati in a kitchen corner, as he stirs the flour in a plastic bowl above his unauthorized and tolerated microwave. There is something as customary as meaningful in the slow and continuous movements of his hands above the flour mass, as he's telling me that, while his Italian exam was okay, he's moneyless and jobless as ever, aside from a two-day job on call to pick grapes, perhaps. This is what I see in Daokaate's habit of doing gym on the staircase and the terrace, as much as outside. While he has no control of the timing or outcome of his asylum application, he has it for physical activity, in which he shows as much mastery as patience. "Little by little, I keep waiting," he repeats with a large circular movement of both arms, in a pragmatic more than resigned tone. "I always respect the law and behave," he points out before starting again the same sequence of flexions, jumps and short spurts.

Both Larka's chapati preparation and Daokaate's exercise are obviously irrelevant to their social and legal careers. They are also of little help to extend and enhance their social capital. Even so, they make some fractions of everyday life less monotonous, repetitive or anxious than the rest. Moreover, no need for outsider authorization, justification or validation. In these timespace fragments, it is Larka and Daokaate who decide and do not have to account for their doings—precisely the opposite of their ordinary life as dependent asylum claimants.

7.4   WHAT DOES HOME ACTUALLY MEAN? TRACING (DIS)LOCATIONS ACROSS NARRATIVES

Natural home and second home

"It was better before," Ebrima tells me with a grimace, one day, after a rare invitation into his room. I've just asked how he's doing after the staff turnover. Even so, relative to the facilities in which he was housed before, the center is "more peaceful as a place, as home." As *home*? "You know," Ebrima replies with a bitter smile. "After you left, there is no place like home—that's what we say in Mandinka," and in so many languages, I think to myself.[33] If home is where you grew up and where your family was, if your parents are dead and you end up alone, there is no longer home, even before you leave. So it was for Ebrima. More generally, if home means only the place where you were born, then even the most welcoming of places, let alone an asylum center, is bound to be less than home. It's just a fragment of a conversation that went through Ebrima's days in prison in the Gambia and in Libya, the innumerable times he was beaten and the three years he has spent waiting in Italy, with a "good man" who occasionally gives him an informal job. Yet it is in the economy of an episodic self-disclosure that home starts revealing its emic and dilemmatic significance. Does it have to do only with the place one comes from, though?

Yes, and no. "There are two places to call home," Buba ponders, during one of his last days in the center. He has just found a bed elsewhere and a job as a waiter. It's a good moment to chat with me, while looking only ahead. "Don't want to talk of the past," he clarifies with a grave face. In fact, to some extent, he does. Home, says Buba, is "the place where I was born, Africa, the Gambia—that's my real home...."

People who saw me grow up there." However, it is also somehow "here, Italy, one of the biggest experiences I got in my life. I've made friends, also from Italy, and so I can call this my second home." Land and kinship, where you come from, are the primary term of reference. This is not to discard friendship, the relations you build up along the way—potentially in multiple locations or, perhaps, in none. "Home is where you have friends. . . . You can do nothing, or be happy, unless you have friends." To that extent even the center has become a home of sorts for Buba.

Most of my interlocutors, however, might be less positive. If there is no new place, job prospect or legal status in sight, talking about home becomes more complex, painful and revealing.[34] "Where is home?" is a challenging question for Salim, when we happen to chat. "I'm not ready for that yet," he replies with a smile after some hesitation. "Life is too difficult," he sighs, albeit "less here than in my country." "Not ready," that is, not in a condition to see a permanent or at least normal place ahead. "However," adds Salim after a while, as if to encourage himself, "I think it will be here"—somewhere in Italy or anyway in Europe. Hope matters and can make a difference,[35] although it need not suffice. Meanwhile, the center is only a facility "to sleep, eat, read and watch TV" for someone with an extended and diverse network of contacts outside. "I've found it. I was not born here!" Salim concludes, reminding me of the deep entanglement between home and place of origin—all too deep, in his own story. The Guinea village where he was born will turn indeed into his final home, perhaps the only real one, far sooner than anticipated. A few years after leaving the center and several temporary accommodations after, Salim will pass away after a sudden and terminal disease. His body will be repatriated, per his final desire. When death comes too soon, the natural home of the past outdoes the hopeful, potential and chronically precarious home of the future as a migrant (cf. 4.5 and 5.3).

Home is the place where you were born, Salim believes. So do many more, including among the natives. "When he's in a bad mood, you'd better leave him alone," a doorman mildly complains of a young West African he's chatting with out of the entrance. It's early May and I've been coming to the center for only some months. This means more perceived obligation to explain things from his side and less ability to memorize names from mine. "He doesn't even greet me!" adds the doorman with a joking tone. "Yeah," the man replies with a serious and frowning face to mimic the stereotypically cold and grumpy native. "I do like one of you!" Enough to touch a deep chord. "Look, you'll never become one of us, that's for sure," the doorman bluntly replies—"unless you're born here." Our amused interlocutor shrugs and runs out on his bike, flip-flops, shorts and tank top. "Don't run! Be careful, or you'll fall ill!" the doorman exclaims.

Home, objects and portability

Home is where you come from. Home is here. Yet, there is so much more than that in the burgeoning scholarship on home.[36] And so much more emerges from my privileged encounters with young men like Olusola or Fatou. When Olusola and I start talking about *casa*, in Italian (which he speaks better than most), his first thought goes to his uncertain housing prospects. He received papers at last, he must leave and has apparently no idea of where to go next. What he does know is that at some point in the future he'd like to invest his savings in a house of his own: "I mean, if you've got money—even 20,000 euros—people can always steal it. If you got a house, instead, you'll have it for all your life, right?" How to reach that stage is a different matter. Meanwhile, the conversation slowly shifts into English and hence to the distinction between *house* and *home*. This is as obvious for an English speaker as intriguing, even moving, in the words of someone who has neither in a permanent form. "House is the whole place, the building, you understand? Home is where I live. Where I sleep. Where I store my stuff." As long as he can stay in, "my room is my home," the only space in which he has some privacy and control. But if someone asks you, "Where is home?" adds Olusola, "that means 'where I come from.' If that's here, I come from the center. If that's in Africa, I come from Nigeria. Inside Nigeria, home is Ibadan. In Ibadan, home is the place where I live—my family. . . . Home is the strongest thing. . . . The house is not enough."

What lies inside is what really matters. "Can you see my smartphone, Paolo?" It's always in his hands—no way for me to miss it. That day Olusola can't go online, for he has used up its data. This means having to think over and over, with his whole body that "hurts." "Here," in the smartphone, "is all my life . . . all in the SIM card. If it breaks up or I lose it . . . I lose all." As I gain familiarity with Olusola, over the years, I'll learn to decode and contextualize the words he shares with me, invariably creative and insightful as they are.[37] In fact, lost pictures, videos or contacts do not necessarily correspond to lost people, as he seemed to hint as an asylum applicant, before getting a humanitarian permit. Having said that, and while several researchers have approached the smartphone as a small-scale home,[38] there is nothing obvious in the SIM card as a nested and more intimate micro-home, a critical infrastructure that is utterly irrelevant and taken for granted, unless you lose it.

Smartphone and SIM card are only two of the artifacts that can become functional equivalents of home or embody it symbolically, as I learn as a privileged guest of Olusola. However, my obsession with mainstream domesticity is not a good starting point to capture them. Relative to other rooms, Olusola's is rather unremarkable. His bed and the surrounding walls and window could easily be confused with many more. But Olusola's personal space is clearly marked from his Mauritanian roommate. Again, though, this is no prerogative of their room. One day, as Olusola is leaving for good, I try to get back to the point. What about "your" room—was it like all the others? Is there anything that made it yours? Olusola starts smiling, first in nervousness. "I left it in order," he stresses. As empty and

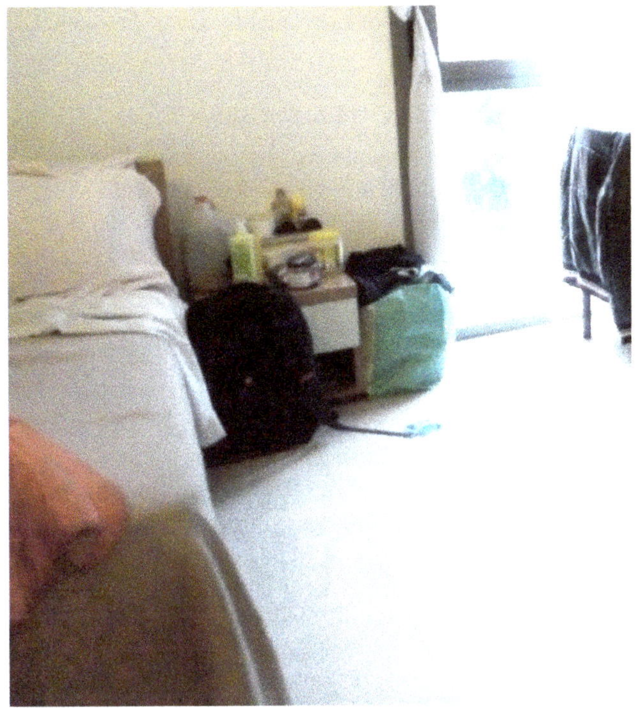

FIGURE 24. Olusola's rucksack, which he habitually leaves next to his
bed. Photo by author.

impersonal "as they gave it to me." Which is a way of reiterating a more fundamental point: "I was welcomed and left with regard, respect, honor. I live a good
life. I'm moving forward," all challenges notwithstanding. As we move beyond this
early defensive stage, though, something important emerges.[39]

"Anything special?" Looking at me in an unusually mocking way, Olusola
replies, "My black rucksack, beside my bed! How come you've never seen it?" The
rucksack, explains Olusola, is "a gift from my girlfriend—I always carry it with
me." What connected that room to some sense of home was not so much the place
or its material decoration. It was, instead, a very portable and mundane object,
routinely carried around and then put back in the same position, close to his body
(figure 24). Enough to question the predominant focus on the ethnic, religious,
identity-based and even aesthetic micro-foundations of home. Home is where the
rucksack is—hopefully in decent-enough housing—at least *as long as* the rucksack
is, before a different affordance, and perhaps a different sentimental relationship
to embody, take over. Nothing necessarily fixed in time or space. The search for

home moves on, albeit with little of the romantic savor that an academic might attach to it.

Home, family and distant connectedness

Following Olusola, home lies in different places, depending on your position and on the sense you make of it. It is not reducible to a building, and yet it is hard to conceive whenever the house is missing.[40] It is portable through micro-affordances, as long as these embody key relationships. It has to do with loved ones far away and thus with the need to fill the distance from them. This is especially striking and elusive in the narrative of Fatou. That home means the Gambia, for him, is no ritual statement. Rather, it logically stems from what he *is, feels* and *does*. This I understand one spring afternoon, at the end of an unusually long WhatsApp call with someone in the Gambia. "It was my sister. . . . She got married yesterday!" Wow, congratulations . . . smiles, hugs and words follow suit.

As an older brother, Fatou recommended the "young and inexperienced" newlyweds to mutually respect and be ready for "the problems that will come—you can't help that." It's important that they "talk and understand each other," since they will have to "love each other for all their life." A number of pictures virtually come to life on the screen of his smartphone—the wedding ceremony and celebrations, the newlyweds' special clothes, the gatherings in the mosque and in their own compound. So normal, so far away. "I'm praying for them," says Fatou, and "I'm praying to see her again." Meanwhile, something more prosaic may be happening. Did they ask you for any help? "No, they didn't ask nothing. . . . I'll give some money to my sister, what I can, in some months"—that is, when he hopefully gets a job. Also when *he* decides to—or so the money recipient must perceive. It should be Fatou that sets the rule. Whether the practice matches the narrative, of course, is a different matter. What is clear is that he's out of money, for the time being.

As for the wedding, "the rule," he explains while we move into the kitchen, is that the future bridegroom's parents should visit their counterparts to ask for the bride's hand. However, "for us it's important that the girl agrees. . . . There are those who enforce her. *We* don't." Now we are standing right beside the sink. "You can't force me to drink this water if I don't want, right? With marriage, it's the same." An unremarkable appliance can help me to make sense of his imaginaries and moralities. "That's how we do in our culture," repeats Fatou, as if he were sitting inside the compound, with the family, right now. *As if it were home.* No doubt, home for Fatou lies there, as the center of affection, morality, identity.[41] However, it does not boil down to mere nostalgia for the lost place and kin. It is rather a matter of active, transnational homemaking, which distance and uncertainty upon his return make only more meaningful and challenging. *Home there* need not be only a matter of ascription, national identification and even historical legacy, as I understand from Fatou's narratives about Kunta Kinte, the (fictitious) hero of anti-slavery Black struggles.[42] As you move beyond the surface, home is something more intimate, narrow and selective—the left-behind family and the dilemmas and struggles that come from distance in space and time. That said, the analytical potential of home, across the narratives of Fatou, Olusola and the others, reaches still beyond.

7.5 EXPANDING THE SCOPE OF HOME: WHERE I'M IN POWER, WHERE I'M HEADING TO

In sum, where you come from and where you're staying are the most obvious, identity-grounded and emically clear meanings of home. However, they are not the whole story. Other deep-rooted meanings cut across the narratives and practices of my young male interlocutors, while being relatively underplayed in the literature. These speak, respectively, the language of control (and power) and that of future (and destination).

Home is the place where I am in power

Whenever my interlocutors wish to have nothing more than a conventional greeting, let alone hosting me in their rooms, a reassuring thought pops up in my mind: this is not a failure from my side but a "home statement" from theirs. Declining any form of participation is not only an obvious right of any potential research subject. It is also a mode of agency that may take the shape of indifference, opacity and silence.[43] Every non-invitation is a reassertion of autonomy and privacy. In substantive terms, though, these reactions prove little of either domesticity or control. "This is their house, not our house," Sani once reflects outside the entrance, as we're looking up at the building. "It is normal that there are rules. We're here for free; we must follow them." It is by no means clear *whose* house it is, but it is very clear that it leaves no space for a fundamental underpinning of home—a gendered, generational and, for once, not so racialized one: the freedom, real or perceived, to do what one wishes, without asking for authorization or accounting for it.

It is commonplace for residents to complain about all that they are not allowed to do. While this is predictable, and perhaps inevitable in refugee accommodations, it also reveals an underlying positive term of reference. "At home," Samuel once exclaims in frustration, "nobody tells me what I have to do!" In practice, it is not so clear what "nobody" would mean in relation to Samuel's left-behind wife and children in Sierra Leone. Home as family life is too intimate, and possibly painful, to demand anything but silence, unless for the few words he wishes to share about the future: "It depends on how life is with me. . . . If there is no work, I must go back. If I work, I want to bring her here." Home is also a matter of access and control over a bounded and private place. This may facilitate the reproduction of gendered, patriarchal, potentially or explicitly oppressive forms of power, as much critical scholarship has shown.[44] Ironically, this gendered background is precisely what is missing from everyday life in the center, which creates disempowerment in relation to traditional scripts of masculinity, without necessarily helping people to deconstruct them or empowering them toward accepting more gender equality.[45] In fact, even someone who lives alone tends to have some expectation of control over one's dwelling circumstances. "You need to have a place you dominate," Paul once rephrases it, thinking of the life he'd like to build in the future, in Italy. One based on a "normal" family to be maintained through his hard work.

Where I am in power—whatever the referents and contents of that power—is the emic understanding of home that has probably the strongest analytical potential, though a relatively neglected one, aside from the literature on domopolitics[46] and hospitality.[47] It articulates a claim for autonomous domesticity but also for recognition, in relation to a house, a city or a whole country. However, the attitudes of my interlocutors also suggest a potential for attachment and belonging, as long as they are allowed a right to stay with some time horizon ahead. "I can't deny that Nigeria is my home, but this is my country too," Ogwu likes repeating, stamping one foot on the ground at the middle of each sentence. Home-here-and-there may sound like wishful thinking. Yet it does reflect the fact that Ogwu is living here, while his mother, kin, and a "special friend" to be hopefully married to and reunified in Italy are in Nigeria. "Thanks God," adds Ogwu, mid-way between gratitude and self-encouragement. "I know somebody. . . . His name is God!"

For the time being, nonetheless, the realm of control does not even reach out to one's bedroom, which is ever subject to external inspections and to internal coexistence between strangers. "He does as if he's at home" is an ordinary complaint about a roommate who does not clean up or transgresses the basic thresholds of sound, light or smell. As long as one is dwelling there, he can afford no *as if it were home*. Whether the complaint is justified or not, in turn, is hard to assess. "I've no clue of what they do when they're home—I'm not there!" a caseworker comments.

Power, or at least control, is indeed something you may be forced to scale down to ever smaller geographies, the minimal one being your own body. You can also negotiate it over particular and short-lived sets of practices, including drawing, as for Woikat. This is an especially telling illustration of a vaguely euphoric, if ephemeral, sense of power. Upon each drawing or painting, Woikat can recreate a world of his own—one that should bear witness to his past, including the violence of displacement, and to his origins—out of a blank paper. "I can add this or delete that," he whispers whenever he's drawing. A pencil and an eraser are enough to change the state of things, following his memories, tastes or moods. What if he could do the same with his life, I wonder—each piece in its place, everything that can be drawn, deleted and redrawn. As it happens, Woikat's creative act, his own demonstration of being in power, does not go much further than the edges of the cardboard. At best, he can stick his drawings on an inner wall as long as the staff allows, with little likelihood that someone sees them. At the same time, his form of homemaking is a highly portable one. Woikat can reproduce it wherever, carrying his drawings along or posting them on Facebook. To that extent he can make himself at home again and again.

Home is the place I must head (back) to

"Without papers they can deport you any moment," Sani once exclaims. "If *you* do something bad and go to prison, you're still Italian. . . . If *we* do something bad and go to prison, they take our documents and send us back." That this is relatively uncommon, in Italy, may not affect one's sense of "deportability" too much.[48] However, there is something more unsettling than precarity to it. Sani knows nobody who was deported, but he does know "a lady" who would like to go back, for she's tired of how she's being treated. "It's normal," he comments, "that someone wants to go home, isn't it?" It's normal that "we want to go back to *our* home . . . and here it's *your* home." Nigeria versus Italy, Africa versus Europe, Black versus white—each term in its place, just like home versus non-home. As natural as a difference, no matter how "groupist" or "sedentarist,"[49] as the mainstream view of migration in the public and political discourse. Full stop for Sani, but not necessarily for me and, more important, for his prospective life experience.

"Cannot Italy become home too?" I rejoin. The question is out of the box, and Sani thinks about it for a while. "It will be home if you can stay here all your life." Home, I mentally rephrase, has to do with the right to stay but also with the future of it—the prospect of a lifelong, permanent place of your own. Perhaps the same where you will be eventually buried.[50] So sneeringly fixed and long-term, for someone who has almost nothing fixed or long-term. No doubt, Italy can hardly ever be home in this sense. But "I swear it on God," adds Sani, "as soon as things go well in Africa, I'll return. For now I'll stay. We owe it to our children, and to their children," although, he enigmatically concludes, "many have been called, few are elected." No apparent reason for him to be among the few.

No one of my interlocutors would be willing to return soon or even only to admit that they thought of this. Almost all, as the conversation goes in depth, would add that at some point in the future they *shall* return, as if to restore the "natural" course of things.[51] As a moral obligation, future homecoming is equally obvious to the West African night doorman, who is in a higher position in the hierarchies of age, length of stay and education. "So, we'll meet back home!" he once says laughing to someone who's about to leave. "That will be," the other responds with a grave face, "because we can't pass all our lives away from our families."

One afternoon in Suka's bedroom, while he's about to prepare dinner, I end up chatting with his roommate Obarima. He actually has one question for me: Is it true that "there is no corona here"? My lukewarm confirmation, along with the more assertive and unconcerned ones from the others around, seem to reassure him. "I feel happy now," he explains. "If I die here, for my children in Africa it's a problem." Obarima, my age, has four children (but "here I declared I've only two," he murmurs with a smile), between eight and twenty-five. Soon their pictures pop up on the screen of his smartphone, along with those of his kin, all of them apparently posing for that. Last comes the scaffolding of the new house he will finish "sooner or later." There is a surreal touch in talking about "remittance houses"[52] from a basically furnished room corner of a refugee center, the perceived antipode of a permanent home. The house will be set up in his village, whereas his wife and children are living in town. "Home is *there*," he points out, but "*here* it's okay . . . for some time."

What if *here* is a bit of home too . . . perhaps? Again, the question is unintendedly baffling. "I don't understand," Obarima replies without losing his smile. "This is a camp." No connection with home, if the latter stands for his wife and children, the place where they are staying and their common place of origin. Even while he's trying to focus on the politics, history and economy of Ghana, some words about his loved ones are enough to shift the narrative toward homecoming. The fact is, Obarima explains, that "I can live here, but I can't die here." He must get back to his village to die and be buried—to stay forever in his real home, as the scholarship on African migration[53] and the lived experience of Salim (see 4.6) have shown. "It's not easy," Obarima repeats, just like most do. Like most, he has no intention to delve any further into his biographical field. What is clear is that he'll return. "Maybe in ten years, but I will."

Whether the moral obligation comes true or not is a different matter. Sometimes, with the friends of the residents who have gained a more stable position (or so they wish to display), talking about home takes a partially different bent— arguably the same of most labor migrants over time.[54] At least for pragmatic and instrumental purposes, home is here by now, they tend to reply. This is not, however, because here you have a roof on your head and no alternative option, as in the residual view of home-as-shelter of the newcomers. It rather comes from awareness of the struggles you have already gone through and from some savvy disenchantment about Africa and family life "back there."

So it is for Ogwu's friend, one afternoon, as we wander between low-cost supermarkets to get beer for his birthday. He's in playful admiration of "the Italian woman—as sweet as a toffee, she makes your head spin like a beer!" He's grateful to Italy "which rescued us" (cf. 3.2). He feels "like Italians—I laugh with them; I cry with them." This does not mean that "Italians" feel like him. "It looks like you've traveled a lot," he says, whereas some of his colleagues have not even been to the next city, one hour away. And on the bus he took to reach us, he was sitting with three free seats around and lots of people standing up. All this being said, by now he goes back to Nigeria "just on holiday." Here he's making his own livelihood with a relatively stable job. "Sending money," he claims, "is not compulsory. . . . My family can make it alone. My parents work. I only send some gifts." Perhaps social class, individual capital or even only good luck do make a difference. Perhaps he's just playing a role—no way to see more into it, with occasional visitors. Whatever the case, "home is here," he repeats, with Ogwu nodding in agreement. "It is the place where you stay . . . not where you come from." Time has gone by, you no longer know what life is like there. "It's good only for visits," Ogwu concludes, while being still legally framed as an (unwanted) visitor in the country he wishes to make home again, and eventually feel home, his own way.

7.6   THE STRUGGLE FOR HOME MUST GO ON: FROM FICTITIOUS DOMESTICITY TO HOMING

"Home is home," my interlocutors exclaim with a painful smile at some point. Not much to add, apparently. Home is (in) Africa—where one was born, where he belongs, where he'll be back. You know all of it, or so you think. Here, instead, is the whites' place. With all its promise for autonomy, adulthood and personhood, it cannot be home. As deep-rooted as this view is, it has a major price—all that comes after fleeing is bound to be non-home. The national flags of Senegal and Italy that Woikat adds into his paintings, revealingly stemming from one and the same root, are a simple and powerful reminder of the "national geographic" mind-set of my young male interlocutors (figure 25).[55]

FIGURE 25. Senegal and Italy, one and the same root: national flags in a detail of a mural of an African landscape. Artwork by Woikat. Photo by author.

However, they also point to their struggle to keep both terms in the same frame. Africa and Africanness, more than local ethnic identities, are a powerful source of continuity, consistency and self-identification. As long as this self-racialized essence is there, as a statement of worth against all vilifications and discriminations, the moral obligation to return follows suit. "We boys all came here to work," Woikat often repeats. No need to stick to the refugee narrative, once we are familiar with each other. "We came," he adds in a more meditative tone, "to improve our houses, little by little." His own house in the village is still to be built up, although he did purchase the terrain and the materials for it. It will have five rooms, enough for his mother and brothers, with a room for him to come back on holiday, "one week or two." Beyond that time horizon, and in fact beyond the here-and-now, "we don't know." A new or better house in the village or in town, for the family or (primarily) for oneself, resounds across many narratives as a future horizon of self-accomplishment. As the scholarship shows, there is a chance that Woikat's house, if it is built indeed, may also turn into a non-home—and that his own home, while overlapping with Africa in terms of self-identification, may have increasingly to do with Italy in all practical respects.

That the present dwelling is non-home, despite the inner bubbles of reluctant homemaking, is only the last word *now*. No place would be better as long as you don't choose it and have no power over it, stuck as you are in your social, legal and biographical predicament. What comes next is not predetermined, though. Nor is one's view or narrative of home, as one navigates his housing, employment and family pathway. If home can no longer be in the country of origin either, unless in an ascriptive sense or as a "yearning to return to a past that never existed but that is hopefully yet to come,"[56] it needs to be somewhere ahead, if at all. It eventually, if reluctantly, turns into a matter of *homing* or of future-oriented mobilities toward a state of things that resembles home and that can only emerge from struggles, relationships and emotional investments—and sufficient opportunities.[57]

Beyond the step of dwelling in asylum, social navigation continues across goals, life positions and human environments that may be changing in turn. This will hopefully come along with better life conditions, a job, a "normal" family. If that is not the case, non-home will keep being the everyday norm, with the distant home as a very poor and ironically demanding equivalent for it. Anything on the way forward can turn into a homing affordance, though. This also holds for dwelling in the center, as an ambivalent entanglement of home and non-home. What people construct as relevant in their everyday social environments, physical and virtual, is the staple of homemaking. However, this will never be enough unless they have resources, rights and opportunities to enlarge their reach of relevance over time—what matters and demands care. Home, as long as it takes a rewarding emplacement at all, can only be in the future. Ahead of you.

Conclusion

I

"*Tutto a posto!*[1] Now this is my city," Ousmane proudly told me some time ago as I came across him, riding on his way back from the repair shop in which he is working. "Nothing" has been effectively undone—at least for him, for now. Reality, sometimes, has a better ending than fiction. Unlike the white main characters of *Waiting for Godot*, who eventually "do not move" after repeating "let's go" once again,[2] the racialized and real protagonists of this book do move at last. They may have not clear ideas of where to go next, and their life pathways will keep being uncertain and open to different outcomes. However, they certainly leave behind the stage of enforced waiting, where many more will soon replace them. As crowded and protracted as it is, this stage cannot be dismissed as a biographical parenthesis or a societally marginal location. Despite its mandate to make asylum seekers invisible and irrelevant to the mainstream, and no matter how context-specific, the center affords to explore and make sense of questions of larger significance on a micro-macro continuum. The ambition of *Undoing Nothing* has precisely been to attend to an "unremarkable" housing and waiting condition, foreground it and produce an original understanding of the everyday life that is caged and protected inside it. This book strives to scale relevance in ways that reach, and are of concern, beyond it.

The idea came from my frequent encounters with *nothing* as a notion in use to describe the void of everyday life in waiting. Building on years of domestic ethnography, I have been in a position to *undo* nothing as a perception and a set of empirical circumstances. Where my interlocutors perceive nothingness, I have learned to see ambivalence. While *nothing* articulates their frustration and disenchantment, their social condition could be analytically described as an overlap between multiple fields of ambivalence. Residents have to (re)position themselves between opposite and equally cogent terms of reference, attraction and pressure. These can be analyzed along lines of spatiality (inside, outside); temporality (still, moving); materiality (present, absent); care (dirty, clean) and domesticity (home, non-home). The encounter with these forms of ambivalence can be equally revealing in many other shared housing arrangements, having in mind how infrastructural conditions and political regimes, as much as gender, class and racial differences and inequalities, shape the room available for people to carve out their own timespace.

In a context of ambivalence, people desire, are emotionally involved in or have to live along with opposite terms of reference. This extended in-betweenness may result in grueling uncertainty. Whatever one's course of action, it need not be the right, let alone the definitive, one. Rather, it may always be reversed, for the time being. Ambivalence is deeply entrenched in the routines and the dwelling space of my interlocutors, in paradoxical contrast with their ordinary categories of sense-making. A faceted predicament of *and-and*, with no given or secure balancing point between the opposites, is harder to bear than the stark *either-or* that underpins their habitual ways of approaching social reality—here or there, us or them, Black or white, Europe or Africa, and so forth. To cope with the nothing that is actually ambivalence and stubbornly resists these binary understandings and hopes, my young male interlocutors seek to threshold their spatial and temporal circumstances by prioritizing limited portions of them over the rest. Their everyday practices reveal an unequal allocation of relevance—a variable interest and commitment to attend to distinct regions of the world around them. The question then becomes how the reach of what deserves and demands care, attention and investment of the self is scaled and diversified, if at all.

Most people in the center tend to earmark their empty timespace in very focused, narrow and self-centered ways. This leaves little interest or energy for whatever exceeds the field of relevance in the here-and-now—a basic accommodation, hopefully a job and papers, some response to family expectations and more freedom than the center can allow. Respect and get respected, as people would phrase it, without necessarily caring for much more—not unlike millions of youth in their early twenties, although with nothing of their societal privilege and family support. In fact, achieving such a focused field of relevance is already more than many residents can afford. In the most restricted version, instead, relevance is scaled down to one's body and self. The place in which the body and self lie need not matter much, as long as there is one. This is the most pragmatic and straightforward way of allocating relevance—as predictable and understandable in the short term as it is problematic and unsustainable in the long term.

In fact, expanding relevance to the mainstream—despite one's racialized marginalization—is critical for young, displaced people to navigate a way ahead and accomplish some social, economic, ultimately existential mobility. This is no mere cosmetic exercise, such as giving proof of "deservingness." It rather means nourishing one's reflexive ability of seeing how the mainstream sees you—fine-tuned with the tacit expectations they may have, not reducible to simply racist stances—and recalibrate the habitual ways of presenting oneself and relating to others accordingly. In a nutshell, moving from the binary register of respect to the multivalent and nuanced register of reputation—one that is most visibly articulated by the unequal ability and success in learning the mainstream language. No way of making oneself at home again, otherwise. For sure, all attempts at fine-tuning and recalibration keep being shaped by legal suspension, structural discrimination, sheer poverty—and the weight of the past.

This leads us back to the larger scenario of the asylum regime, one often portrayed with catch phrases such as *prevention by deterrence, racialized bordering* and *hostile environment* toward those undesired migrants who made it nonetheless. Such a background has a protracted aftermath, even for those who do get a status, in terms of lesser life opportunities. In essence, waiting in asylum articulates an internal temporal border that may harm, albeit not in a physical sense, almost as much as the external spatial border, whenever one struggles to cross it. At the same time, the background does not predetermine one's reach of relevance, nor does it prevent it from changing over time.

Under the joint pressure of institutional constraints, family circumstances, available capital and inner orientations, the horizon of what calls for attention and care shifts over time and space, just like the endeavors to achieve it.[3] No reason to expect former residents not to extend and diversify their field of relevance as soon as they obtain a socio-legal space, some recognition as individuals rather than fungible parts of a collective category (i.e. refugee, black, Muslim etc.) and hence a visible horizon of opportunities ahead of them. Wherever these conditions keep missing, the persistence of self-centered and narrow ways of allocating relevance will be as undesirable as unsurprising. That some "do not really care what is going on" and retain a "deliberate disengagement" from the outer social world, in or out of the center, is a fact. This also invites some skepticism toward any view of agency as necessarily "an act of liberation" for, no doubt, scaling down relevance is also a way of articulating agency.[4] However, similar ways of "doing nothing" or "[not] having a purpose in life"[5]—if situated in real life rather than in art or literature—have all to do with marginalization or lack of choice and very little with demonstrations of freedom, negotiations of alternative lifestyles or new ways of self-realization from the margins.

II

If all social life, and hence all ethnography, has a deeply theatrical side to it, and even neighborhood life can be approached through a theater metaphor,[6] this is all the more obvious and relevant for a single house. The center is the ideal stage for an endless performance of a very specific genre—a theater of the absurd made out of nothingness, invisibility and irrelevance, as much as of surveillance, exceptionality and segregation. Objects, interiors and people on or around the stage seem to share the same minor fate. They ended up there by chance. They are staying on the margins of the city. They have time in excess to spend somehow, until something important will happen elsewhere. They are interdependent, if unequal parts of the same infrastructure for floating over undesired memories and looming absences and for awaiting future developments that are hard to envision. And unlike the fictitious register of theater, they are utterly real.

Within an emotional spectrum that leans toward the tragic and yet has an unwitting tinge of ridiculousness, some of my interlocutors have indeed an eerie resemblance to Estragon and Vladimir, the central figures in *Waiting for Godot*—the latter standing, here, for a personal condition of accomplished masculine adulthood, more than for any unlikely savior from outside. Just as in Samuel Beckett's tragicomedy, the temporality of dwelling in asylum is circular, reiterated, devoid of any forward-looking development. The temporality of every former resident, however, is not. At our occasional meetings, Olusola, Fatou, Woikat and the others have no reason to say more than a few words about that particular timespace in their lives. By now the center stage is irrelevant for them, albeit not for the thousands more who keep dwelling in similar infrastructures. However, not all the ways of societal and existential ambivalence it embodied are over. Some will indeed lose salience over the years, in parallel to people's fine-tuning with the mainstream. No more parallel normality, at least in the labor market, and certainly no more doing nothing. Other forms of ambivalence, such as the intermingling of presence and absence, are only mitigated if immigrant life starts to yield its expected benefits— economic autonomy, wider social networks, a reasonable space to nourish hopes and projects for the future; in short, suitable conditions to fill erstwhile or distant absences with new and tangible presences. However, one form of ambivalence at least—*home, non-home*—seems bound to stay.

Even inside an unhomely place, and probably in any housing infrastructure, fine-grained and patient fieldwork produces fresh food for thought about the analytical, metaphorical and existential power of home and the attendant dilemmas.[7] As an analytical register, the *home, non-home* ambivalence captures an incessant balancing act between different spatial, cultural and moral benchmarks, with their contrasting promises and pressures. Likewise, the residents' ways of thinking or talking about home as a place disclose the ultimate terrain of allegiance and belonging (i.e., "Africa"), as much as the struggle to navigate the cognitive dissonance between this identity marker, the lived experience of violence, oppression and social death associated with it and the elusive potential of mobility, if not existential rebirth, attached to Europe. The deeper one engages with the *home, non-home* ambivalence, the more likely he will find that it can only persist. Once again, though, people are in an unequal position to manage it, whether or not they have a legal status, a job, and sentimental relationships that may feed into new families of their own. Only at that point, with a "normal family," as they would say, the normative transition to adulthood will be accomplished. It is a potentially ever-reversible one, though, depending on the ebbs and flows of their socio-legal, occupational, housing, relational and sentimental lives.

III

Undoing Nothing is a cumulative and emplaced story about ordinary, almost invisible (or invisibilized) people in a very unordinary social, legal and existential position. This calls for a dual exercise of de-exceptionalization, to trace what each of them has in common with others in the same socio-legal category and what "trans-contextual patterns"[8] emerge in relation to many more, under different categories. On one hand, the individual life stories and fragmented mobility routes of my interlocutors are intimate, unique, hard to tell. On the other, they resonate with the rationales, narratives and dilemmas of millions more. This commonality across micro-circumstances of forced mobility and waiting has a potential to nourish the sociological imagination—hence to highlight the connections between disparate individualized predicaments and their aggregate significance. Such potential is yet to be fully exploited, though. The very accumulation of myriad parallel individual stories of forced immobility and protracted irrelevance, as a result of an internal bordering of asylum that is as pervasive as the external one, might be enough for a "transnationalized social question."[9] In practice, forced migration has only been approached along these lines in relation to the necropolitics of border deaths, especially on the Mediterranean "seametery."[10] No point, of course, in comparing death at sea with the social death of asylum seekers trapped in waiting—sometimes even in welfare—while being expected to be grateful for the shelter they are given until further notice. Their irrelevance cannot be equated to persecution, systematic violence or a risk of death, although it does amount to a constant and paradoxical waste of human energies and time. Indeed, its impact on dignity and self-esteem should not go unnoticed. There is something to the systematic reiteration of nothingness, at least as a perception, that calls for more analytical and political attention, beyond the obvious statement that things happen even in apparently empty and meaningless spaces. Being forced into irrelevance is a private predicament that is not without public, societal and political significance, if only for its large-scale diffusion, including under the humanitarian guise of protracted displacement across the Global South.

As important, much of the social experience and position of my interlocutors is not reducible to any refugee or migrant category. It has also, sometimes primarily, to do with age, gender, race and marginalization from the labor and housing market. This means that the insights emerging from my fieldwork speak to different housing and biographical pathways and to broader audiences and debates across disciplinary cages such as refugee, housing, displacement and youth studies. Two conceptual points—the distance between bodily and moral proximity and the inexorable intermingling between presence and absence—are especially worthy of discussion.

For one thing, sociability in the center is marked by a very limited overlap between a sensuous, physical presence and an affective, moral one. This may be as relevant to most forms of shared and somehow enforced living between strangers. The place you are in, the objects around you and the people you come across are not those you would dream of, nor those you would care about. The more irrelevant they appear, the higher the likelihood of tensions around the "proper" way of dwelling therein. Under the cover of emptiness and nothingness, ordinary microconflicts in the center cannot be simply ascribed to its raison d'etre, hence to an enforced and extended sense of suspension. They also stem from something more sensuous, contingent and embodied—everyday forced proximity under contrasting priorities, concerns and ways of emplacing cleanliness, decency and decor.

Contrary to what happens in an ordinary housing environment, in an asylum center, spatiality is not the main determinant of intimacy and privacy. As long as there is a divide between the space for the self and for the rest, this has rather to do with the distinction between online and offline life—that is, between the portable and immaterial space afforded by the smartphone and the tangible, material and unportable space around, where one's body lies and on which one's livelihood relies. In practice people may live together for years in mutual indifference to their affective and existential concerns. "I think for myself, not for the others," my interlocutors constantly remind me. Their respective concerns are decoupled from the center and unevenly distributed in a transnational space of moral economies and obligations that are hard to meet at present and elusive to situate in the time to come.

This also calls for some elaboration on the entanglement between absence and presence. This is critical for any dwelling infrastructure that affords social reproduction but not being at home in a normative sense, and, by extension, wherever the presence of the barely essential is paralleled with the absence of what is affectively and morally relevant. Under fragmented and marginalized biographical and housing pathways, what is present in dwelling spaces is what should materially be protection, but not necessarily what matters the most. One's physical and social presence has to reckon with two forms of absence—that is, two ways in which what would be relevant is not there. On one hand, what happened in the past feeds into significant and possibly unsettling memories or thoughts and haunts everyday life, only to occasionally re-emerge in people's senses and awareness ("like seeing a film again"). On the other hand, what keeps happening at present elsewhere holds a special, if ambiguous value (such as kinship relations), but cannot be brought into tangible and sensuous co-presence.

What is absent, for the temporary inhabitants of places like the center, is more intimate and important than what is present. Whether it overlaps with past events or with significant others elsewhere, it is irremediably elusive and resists control from the here-and-now. Moreover, the absent is often awkward or uncomfortable to deal with. Part of it is to remain in the sphere of the silent, the invisible, the untellable or the untold. This does not make it any less relevant in everyday life.

Last, and as important, questions such as coping with suspended life projects, finding one's way across layered ambivalence and re-scaling the reach of the relevant touch deep chords—and potentially raise interest, empathy or concern—far beyond the boundaries of marginalized and racialized populations. One need not be a young migrant from some perennially crisis-stricken world periphery to be forced, at some point in their lives, to stay afloat in highly unpredictable or oppressive circumstances, walk the fine line between protection and isolation or navigate a way ahead by *homing*[11] out of necessity—searching for a decent place to call home, with limited control on whatever exceeds one's body and self. There is something universal to this predicament, which speaks to the relevance of my proposed analytics.

IV

Doing ethnography in the center has meant learning to shift my own focus of relevance over time, across different steps: from an easy (in retrospect, almost naive) engagement with the place per se as a spatial and material repository of (dis)attachments and material cultures, to the personal histories and shared destinies of the human beings inside it; up to realizing that the bodies in the center, racialized, young, active albeit static as they are, have an ethnographic significance of their own. This has to do with my interlocutors' ways of showing, caring and moving their bodies around and with the discursive, aesthetic and sensuous repertoires whereby they try to articulate respectability, masculinity and a whole range of emotions and affects. This embodied sensoriality holds a promise for further systematic research, in a comparative or at least resonant perspective, in the sociology and anthropology of the body, the senses and affects.

At the end of the day, though, fieldwork in the center has also led me back to the basics of an anthropology of the house.[12] This starts from an ethnographic mode of engagement that should reverse the ordinary host-guest relations that asylum seekers are used to, even while it cannot ultimately question the underlying power inequalities. Being inside as a guest is a precondition to situate the frustration and disenchantment that "staying home" produces, the longer it gets protracted. More fundamentally, it is critical to make sense of the center through the gaze and habits of its ordinary residents. Pivotal to this, especially in the beginning, is an uncanny perception of the center as a world *in inverse*—for its constrained domesticity subverts traditional prerogatives of masculinity, such as autonomy and the priority of public over domestic life or of "going out" over "staying in"—rather than *in reverse*, as in Pierre Bourdieu's[13] famous Kabyle house. The latter is a "microcosm" based on functional and symbolic oppositions that ultimately reproduce, by "inverted reflection,"[14] the power structures of the larger society, including in gender relations. Perhaps this is what the center also does—it reproduces the marginalization of racialized under-dogs from the mainstream. However, it also erodes the model of masculinity and adulthood to which my interlocutors tend—hence their (ideal) world is *inverted*. Put differently, the rationale and organization of the center is disruptive, without being transformative in a normatively positive sense. The isolation and dependency it produces, the longer one stays, is not random—it does articulate the predomi-nant way in which the mainstream society wants to treat its undesired others. To that extent the center as a house is indeed a mirror of society. It is by no means a mirror, though, of the model of masculine adulthood in which the residents iden-tify themselves—one they can still achieve *after* dwelling there, possibly making the most of the opportunities that even dwelling in asylum offered them.

V

Overall, there are as many ways of undoing nothing as the meanings attached to these words in relation to different temporalities. The most tangible and perva-sive one, for the protagonists of this book, is the present, perceived as an empty timespace deprived of meaning and direction. At the same time, evoking noth-ingness reflects one's attempt to take some distance from the past—what already has a major, if not determinant, weight in the economy of a relatively brief life course. However, nothingness cannot really stand for the future unless, perhaps, the long-term one—what occurs (if anything) after death. This is a condition from which the center residents are now distant, age-wise, while having been close to it along the way to Europe.[15] Whether nothing is to be the last word or not, traces and memories remain. Even people that seem bound to lie in societal irrelevance have already left their traces in the rich world, if only by reaching it. To that extent *they've already undone nothing.* In this perspective writing about Olusola, Fatou, Sani and all the others has not only been instrumental to understanding their life experience from inside and to investigate societal questions and dilemmas of a larger reach. It has also been an exercise in public social science. Any ethnogra-phy of everyday life is a claim for relevance of its apparently invisible protago-nists. If its core theme is protracted and racialized waiting and ambivalence, in a blurry terrain between no-longer and not-yet, ethnography is also a lever for *undoing nothing* in two ways: by unpacking what happens there and then (and the sense people make of it) and by foregrounding stories of human beings—most often untold, unheard of and unseen—that claim their own relevance. Gathering together biographical traces of societal relevance and import is what a decent book in an open-access format, hopefully written in not overly academic jargon, should afford.[16] *Nothing* need not be the last word. Better to undo it, only to find out that something relevant lies there and calls for public attention and, hopefully, engage-ment. *Curtain* on the stage of this book. Not, fortunately, on the lives of all those who keep struggling to undo the nothingness that life has forced on them.

INTRODUCTION

1. Hyndman and Giles (2016).

2. Fitzgerald (2019); Grappi and Lucarelli (2022); Vammen et al. (2022).

3. As of February 2025, the Missing Migrants Project reports more than 31,300 deaths in the Mediterranean since 2014.

4. Albahari (2016); Abderrezak (2020).

5. Elaboration on online data from Ministry of Interior and Fondazione ISMU (updated to November 12, 2024).

6. Elaboration on online data (2014–23) from Ministry of Interior (2024), including figures of subsidiary and humanitarian protection.

7. Elaboration on online data from the United Nations High Commissioner for Refugees (UNHCR) and the Istituto Nazionale di Statistica (ISTAT) from January 2024.

8. Within the burgeoning literature on waiting, in refugee studies and well beyond, see, for example, Hage (2009); Jeffrey (2010); Janeja and Bandak (2018); Dobler (2020); and Jacobsen et al. (2021).

9. Zerubavel (2015, p. 28).

10. Goffman (1979, pp. 131–132). On (in)visibility, see also Brighenti (2010) for social theory; Bjarnesen and Turner (2020) for African migration and displacement studies; and Haas (2023) for refugee studies and asylum in the United States.

11. Malkki (1995).

12. Scott (2018); Frederiksen (2018).

13. On relevance as a concept, see Strassheim (2018); and Tamarkin (2022). For an alternative conceptualization, see Rancière's "distribution of the sensible," as "the system of self-evident facts of sense perception that simultaneously discloses the existence of something in common and the delimitations that define the respective parts and positions within it" (2004,

p. 12). This is a societally shared, or at least predominant, perception about "the set horizons and modalities of what is visible and audible as well as what can be said, thought, made or done" (p. 85). In a nutshell, young male asylum seekers, such as the residents in the center, stay at the margins of the naturalized perceptive, cognitive and moral field of the mainstream. However, their very presence, once ethnographically unpacked in terms of *struggling for relevance*, elucidates and questions the preexisting boundaries and blind spots of the *sensible*.

14. This, as far as philosophy is concerned, would require a reference to nihilism—Nietzsche and beyond—and then to the phenomenological work of Sartre on "nothingness" as "non-being," most notably in *Being and nothingness* (1957). See also Richmond (2014) on "nothingness and negation" in Sartre; Mumford (2021) for an exploration of "absence and nothing" across the history of Western philosophy; and Green (2011) for an accessible and provocative introduction to "nothing" across humanities. Overall, the philosophical debate on nothingness—the ontological status of the non-being and its autonomy from individual consciousness—exceeds the scope of this book. For the remit and purpose of social sciences, however, nothing, absence, the missing and other related notions point to very real and significant phenomena, if only for their consequences. Much of what is not there affects what is there in critical ways. It demands attention in its own right, even when this ends up in rather blurred and loose research fields. See, among others, Ehn and Löfgren (2010) and Frederiksen (2018) in anthropology; Zerubavel (2015) and Scott (2019) in sociology; and Kingsbury and Secor (2021) and Roberts (2024) in social geography. All across these examples, and most obviously in *Undoing Nothing*, the focus is on the lived experience of nothingness—an often undesired, perhaps unexpected one—rather than on its conceptualization. In fact, coping with nothingness in everyday life is a source of self-elaboration for those who reluctantly go across it and of insights of larger significance for an ethnographer who stays along with them.

15. Jakobsen (2022).

16. Boccagni (2017); Beeckmans et al. (2022); Grønseth (2023).

17. Jacobsen et al. (2021); Gil Everaert (2021).

18. Van der Horst (2004); Turner (2016); Thorshaug and Brun (2019); Zill et al. (2020).

19. Boccagni and Kivisto (2019).

20. Cf. Lambek (2010).

21. Cf. Lucht (2024).

22. Atkinson (2014).

23. Brekhus (1998); Zerubavel (2015).

24. Zerubavel (2020).

25. Brun and Fabos (2015); Taylor (2015); Hart et al. (2018); Beeckmans et al. (2022); Blunt and Dowling (2022); Boccagni (2023a).

26. Grønseth (2013); cf. De Leon (2015, p. 16).

27. On their housing pathways and stories, see Boccagni (2024).

28. Cabot (2016, p. 648).

1. THE BACKGROUND

1. Gundlach (2020); Zerubavel (2015).

2. Tamarkin (2022).

3. Arar and FitzGerald (2022); Fransen and de Haas (2022).

4. Istituto Studi sulla Multietnicità (ISMU, 2023).

5. Sanchez et al. (2021); Zardo (2022).

6. International Organization for Migration (IOM, 2020).

7. Horsti (2019); Boccagni and Lacroix (2025).

8. Gatrell (2013); FitzGerald and Arar (2018).

9. Zetter (2007, 2015); Jones (2019); Cohen and Van Hear (2019); Tazzioli and De Genova (2023).

10. FitzGerald (2019); Mountz (2020).

11. Arar and FitzGerald (2022, p. 31).

12. Betts (2010a); Arar and FitzGerald (2022); see also Jacobsen and Majidi (2023) for a state of the art in both perspectives.

13. Marchetti (2014); Pitzalis (2018).

14. Sistema di Accoglienza e Integrazione (SAI, 2022).

15. Ambrosini (2022).

16. Fravega et al. (2023).

17. Marchetti (2014).

18. Semprebon (2021); Centri d'Italia (2024); Immigrazione Dossier Statistico (IDOS, 2023).

19. Campomori (2016).

20. Barberis and Boccagni (2014); Sciortino and Finotelli (2015).

21. Squire and Stierl (2020).

22. Cusumano (2018); Cusumano and Gombeer (2020); Esperti (2020).

23. Barnes (2022); Creta and Denaro (2022).

24. Kovras and Robins (2016); Cuttitta and Last (2019); Heller et al. (2023).

25. M'charek and Casartelli (2019); Kobelinsky (2020); Denaro and Boccagni (2023).

26. De Genova (2013).

27. Pallister-Wilkins (2022).

28. Betts (2010b); Linde (2011).

29. Ballatore et al. (2017).

30. Fondazione Moressa (2023).

31. This has to do with the ethnic composition of the center residents in the years of my fieldwork (2018–22), while not necessarily reflecting the composition by national groups of asylum seekers in Italy overall (ISMU, 2023; IDOS, 2023).

32. Arar and FitzGerald (2022).

33. Stasik et al. (2020, p. 1); Cole and Groes (2016).

34. See, for example, Jeffrey (2010) on the "culture of masculine waiting" and the "micro-politics of class power" in northern India. As Jeffrey remarks, the existence of entire "waiting populations," out of the unfulfilled promises of postcolonial development, urbanization, afterwar reconstruction or large-scale migration, can be traced worldwide, as a new form of systemic marginalization. For an overview of the scholarship on waiting as a (failed) transition to adulthood among young men, in Africa and elsewhere, see Dobler (2020).

35. Fioratta (2015).

36. Gaibazzi (2015); Brzezińska (2024).

37. Graw and Schielke (2012); Vigh (2009).

38. Merton (1938).

39. Jackson (2008).

40. Vigh (2009); Freemantle and Landau (2022).

41. Berlant (2011, p. 259).

42. Kleist (2017); Lucht (2016); Kallio et al. (2021).

43. Schapendonk (2020). See also Mazzucato and Ogden (2025) for a comparative account of "transnational youth mobilities" between the Global South and North.

44. Çarpar and Yaylaci (2021).

45. Hyndman and Giles (2011).

46. Çarpar and Yaylaci (2021).

47. Jackson (2008).

48. Jaji (2021, p. 379).

49. Griffiths (2015, p. 471).

50. See Lombardi-Diop (2012); Hawthorne (2022); and Morning and Maneri (2022).

51. Olwig (2023).

52. Schapendonk (2020).

53. Glorius et al. (2016); Kreichauf (2018).

54. Agamben (1998); Diken (2004); Agier (2011); Whyte (2011); Turner (2016); Martin et al. (2020); Bochmann (2021).

55. Rotter (2016).

56. Hage (2009); Griffiths (2014); Jacobsen et al. (2021); Haas (2023).

57. Meier and Donà (2021).

58. Haile and Schapendonk (2024).

59. Khosravi (2019).

60. Tazzioli (2018).

61. Fontanari (2017); Thorshaug and Brun (2019).

62. Fravega et al. (2023).

63. Gil Everaert (2021); Beeckmans et al. (2022); Boccagni (2023a).

64. Hart et al. (2018); Paju et al. (2023); Van der Horst (2004); Steigemann and Misselwitz (2020); Van Liempt and Staring (2021); Hondagneu-Sotelo (2017). See also Scott-Smith (2024) for an empirical exploration of "refugee shelters" across local contexts of settlements in Europe and the Middle East.

65. Taylor (2015); Dossa and Golubovic (2019); Pérez Murcia (2019).

66. Grønseth (2023).

67. Shamma et al. (2023); Dudley (2011); Vandevoordt (2017); Grønseth and Thorshaug (2022).

68. Goffman (1961, pp. 67–68).

69. Bochmann (2019, p. 68).

70. See, respectively, Jefferson et al. (2019); Bauman (2002); Altin and Degli Uberti (2022); and Honwana (2012).

71. Scott (2019).

72. Vigh (2009); Cole and Groes (2016).

73. Rotter (2016).

74. Ehn and Löfgren (2010); Sabetta and Lombardo (2023).

75. Brun (2015).

76. Frederiksen (2018).

77. Cf. Collini (2023).

78. McKinley (1997); Fontanari (2017).

79. Scott (2019).

80. Carsten (2008).

81. Scott (2018).

82. Scott (2019).

83. Schutz (2011); Zerubavel (1993; 2015); Brekhus (1998); Strassheim (2018).

84. Bazurli et al. (2020); Boccagni, Galera, et al. (2020).

85. Massey (2005); Kärrholm et al. (2023); Schmoll (2024).

86. Stavrides (2014); Boccagni and Brighenti (2017).

87. Altman and Werner (1985); Benjamin et al. (1995).

88. Cf. De Backer (2023) for a comparative perspective on multiple urban scales.

89. Diminescu (2008).

90. Lucht (2016); Kallio et al. (2021); Meier and Donà (2021); Olwig (2023); Boccagni (2025).

91. Merton (1976); Smelser (1998); Hillcoat-Nallétamby and Phillips (2011). See also Coates (2023) for an extensive account of ambivalence in action theory and moral psychology.

92. Boccagni and Kivisto (2019).

93. Scott-Smith and Breeze (2020); Van der Veer (2020); Turner and Whyte (2022).

94. Van Maanen (2011b).

95. These are the most striking but not the only forms of ambivalence that emerge from everyday life in the center. Other opposite terms of reference are also relevant and reluctant to a neat binary classification within the spatial and temporal boundaries of institutional hospitality. These include Exceptional and Normal, Children and Adults, Visible and Invisible, as well as Sacred and Lay or, in terms of underlying moral economies, Good and Bad and African and Italian (or European), whatever these sweeping categories are meant for.

2. THE CENTER

1. This picture comes from my fieldwork. So do all the following ones, except figure 11.

2. Zerubavel (2015).

3. Hauge et al. (2017); Zill et al. (2020); Seethaler-Wari et al. (2022); Dreyer (2022); Şenoğuz (2023).

4. Bolzoni et al. (2022); cf. Darling (2022).

5. Achtnich (2022).

6. Mbodj-Pouye (2016); Gargiulo (2023).

7. Fassin (2013); Sorgoni (2019); Giudici and Boccagni (2022).

8. Fontanari (2017); Semprebon (2021); Dotsey and Lumley-Sapanski (2021).

9. Kreichauf (2018); Ghorashi et al. (2018); Thorshaug and Brun (2019); Kivijärvi and Myllylä (2022).

10. Campomori and Ambrosini (2020); Marchetti (2020); Fravega et al. (2023).

11. Berger (1984).

12. Grønseth et al. (2016).

13. Carsten and Hugh-Jones (1995).

14. Gielis (2011).

15. De Certeau (1984).

16. Nayeri (2019); Le Espiritu et al. (2021)

17. Van der Horst (2004).

18. Boccagni (2022a); Neumark (2013); Willems et al. (2020).

19. Mbodj-Pouye (2023).

20. Cf. Mifflin and Wilton (2005).

21. Kärrholm et al. (2023).

22. Cf. Hatuka and Toch (2016).

23. Vandevoordt and Verschraegen (2019).

24. Boccagni (2023b).

25. Neumann (2023).

26. Grønseth (2023).

27. Nasreen (2023).

28. Goffman (1963).

29. Scott (2019).

30. Cole and Groes (2016).

31. Graw and Schielke (2012).

32. I am grateful to Joris Schapendonk for this observation.

33. Lenhard and Samanani (2020); Harney and Boccagni (2023).

34. Murray and Durrheim (2019).

35. Fontanari (2017).

36. Boccagni and Bonfanti (2023).

37. Miller (2001, 2008); Pink et al. (2017); Blunt and Dowling (2022).

38. Desjardins et al. (2015); Weidinger et al. (2021); Ratnam (2023).

39. Thorshaug and Brun (2019); Grønseth (2023); Boccagni (2023b).

40. I have changed all the names of my interlocutors, along with any detail that might facilitate their identification. While this is a mandatory and overall reasonable way to protect their privacy, it is not necessarily the last word in the ever-challenging working balance between moral and ethical obligations to protect people and acknowledge their unique biographies, histories, aspirations and accomplishments.

41. MacKenzie et al. (2007); Van Liempt and Bilger (2012); Grabska and Clark-Kazak (2022); Pérez Murcia (2023).

42. Sbriccoli and Jacoviello (2011); Puumula et al. (2017); Danstrøm and Whyte (2018).

43. Van Maanen (2011a, p. 220).

44. Wagner and Finkielsztein (2021).

45. Marchetti (2020); Campomori and Ambrosini (2020); Semprebon (2021); Degli Uberti (2021).

46. Walters (2023).

47. Boccagni, Galera, et al. (2020).

48. Ehn and Löfgren (2010).

49. Vandevoordt (2017).

50. Harney and Boccagni (2023).

51. Zerubavel (2019).

52. Dragojlovic and Samuels (2021).

53. Cabot (2016).

54. In that regard, a rather obsessive (albeit environment-appropriate) use of the smartphone was part of my learning in fieldwork. So was a short and systematic re-reading and de-briefing session, each time, once back from the center.

55. Hastrup (1990); cf. Fabian (2014).

56. Thorshaug and Brun (2019, p. 240).

3. INSIDE, OUTSIDE

1. Van der Horst (2004); Turner (2016); Hauge et al. (2017).

2. Geschiere and Rowlands (1996); Piot (2010).

3. Cole and Groes (2016).

4. Wyss (2022).

5. Graw and Schielke (2012).

6. Mbodj-Pouye (2023).

7. Nayeri (2019).

8. Jackson (2008).

9. Vigh (2009).

10. Wyss (2022).

11. I am indebted to Aïssatou Mbodj-Pouye for this remark.

12. Kohl (2020); Giudici and Boccagni (2022).

13. Cole and Groes (2016).

14. Schapendonk (2020).

15. Turner (2016); Beeckmans et al. (2022); Kivijärvi and Myllylä (2022).

16. Mbodj-Pouye (2016).

17. Dovey (1985); Douglas (1991).

18. On kinship expectations and dynamics, among the "Argonauts of West Africa" in Europe, see Andrikopoulos (2023).

19. Goffman (1959).

20. Cf. Schapendonk (2020).

21. Thorshaug and Brun (2019); Mbodj-Pouye (2023).

22. Miranda-Nieto (2023).

23. Duyvendak and Kesic (2022).

24. Cf. Harris et al. (2020).

25. Cf. Fontanari (2017).

26. Kule (1997); Donohoe (2011).

27. Fassin (2001).

28. Shilling (2012); Holmes (2019).

29. Simmel (2009); Classen (1992).

30. Cf. Cabot (2016); and Khosravi (2018).

31. Papadopoulos (2021).

32. Goffman (1959).

33. Anderson (2000).

34. Goffman (1959).

35. Harney and Boccagni (2023).

36. Turner and Whyte (2022, p. 2).

37. Hernann (2017); Mbodj-Pouye (2023, p. 137).

38. Garvey (2005); Boccagni (2023b).

4. STILL, MOVING

1. Rotter (2016); Griffiths (2014); Bendixsen and Eriksen (2018).

2. Vigh (2009); Freemantle and Landau (2022).

3. Kleist and Thorsen (2017).

4. Vigh (2009).

5. Lucht (2011); Triulzi and McKenzie (2013); Cole and Groes (2016).

6. FitzGerald (2019).

7. Ghorashi (2005).

8. Meier and Donà (2021).

9. Gil Everaert (2021); Achtnich (2022).

10. Auyero (2011); Janeja and Bandak (2018); Thorshaug and Brun (2019); Jacobsen et al. (2021).

11. Hage (2009).

12. Bathia and Canning (2021); Fravega et al. (2023); Griffiths (2024).

13. Pécoud (2020); Squire (2020).

14. Fontanari (2017).

15. Brekhus (1998).

16. Lems (2018).

17. Mbodj-Pouye (2023).

18. FitzGerald (2019); Boochani (2018).

19. Lucht (2011).

20. Ambrosini and Hajer (2023).

21. Griffiths (2015).

22. Mayblin et al. (2020).

23. See, for example, Harney (2013); Alencar (2020); Leurs and Patterson (2020); Smets et al. (2021); Palmberger (2022); and Moran (2023).

24. Miller et al. (2021).

25. Eriksen (2020).

26. Bauman (2004).

27. I am grateful to Halleh Ghorashi for this remark.

28. Horst and Miller (2020).

29. Mathews (2002).

30. Schapendonk (2020).

31. Giudici and Boccagni (2022); Harbisch (2023).

32. Khosravi (2010); Griffiths (2015).

33. Cole and Groes (2016).

34. Cf. Achtnich (2022).

35. Cf. Fioratta (2015).

36. Grønseth and Thorshaug (2022).

37. Stasik et al. (2020); Kallio et al. (2021).

38. Douglas (1991).

39. Saraiva (2019); Balkan (2023).

40. Cf. Lee and Vaughan (2008); and Moyo et al. (2016).

41. Boccagni (2022b).

5. PRESENT, ABSENT

1. Carsten (2008).
2. Gordon (2008); Blanco and Peeren (2013).
3. Hetherington (2004); Bille et al. (2010).
4. Turner (1979); Bochmann (2021).
5. Mbodj-Pouye (2016).
6. Napolitano (2015).
7. Fioratta (2015).
8. Meyer (2012); Boccagni (2023b).
9. Davidson (2009); Holmes and Ehgartner (2021); Pérez Murcia and Boccagni (2022).
10. Cf. Kawamura (2016).
11. I am indebted to Karsten Paerregaard for these insights.
12. Uzureau et al. (2022).
13. Gordon (2008).
14. Coe (2016).
15. Graw and Schielke (2012).
16. Berger (1984).
17. Neumann (2023).
18. Schneider (2023).
19. Boccagni (2024).
20. Navaro-Yashin (2009).
21. Cf. Neumark (2013); and Boccagni (2022a).
22. Douglas (1966).
23. Hetherington (2004).
24. Scott (2018).
25. Hetherington (2004); Bille et al. (2010); Meyer (2012); Meier et al. (2013).
26. De Martino (2015, p. 87).
27. On this particular point, I'm grateful to Ester Gallo.
28. Bille et al. (2010); Scott (2018).
29. Ghorashi (2008); Dragojlovic and Samuels (2021).
30. Zerubavel (2006).
31. Ginzburg (1994); Smith (2000); Boltanski (2004); Bandura (2011).
32. Zerubavel (2015).
33. Squire (2020); Denaro and Boccagni (2023).
34. FitzGerald (2019); Mountz (2020).
35. Davies (2019); Wyss (2022).
36. See, for example, Boochani (2018) and Hayden (2022).
37. Cuttitta and Last (2019); Kobelinsky (2020).
38. Zerubavel (2015).
39. Kawabata and Gastaldo (2015); Dragojlovic and Samuels (2021).
40. Gaibazzi (2015).
41. McMahon and Sigona (2021); Boccagni (2025).
42. Havik et al. (2018); Walter (2020); Boccagni and Lacroix (2025).
43. Stierl (2017); Banerjee et al. (2024).

44. Cf. Levi (1998).

45. Schindel (2020).

46. Belloni (2019).

47. Havik et al. (2018); Saramo et al. (2019).

48. Maddrell (2016); Hunter (2016).

49. Albertini and Radl (2012).

50. Carling (2014); Paerregaard (2015); Fioratta (2015).

51. Cf. Amelina and Bause (2020).

52. Paerregaard (2021).

53. Schapendonk (2020).

54. Carling et al. (2012); Yeoh and Collins (2022).

55. Bille et al. (2010).

6. DIRTY, CLEAN

1. Kallio et al. (2021); Maculan (2022).

2. Thorshaug and Brun (2019); Kohl (2020).

3. Douglas (1966).

4. Douglas (1966, pp. 43–44).

5. Van der Geest (2014, p. 3).

6. Douglas (1966, pp. 43–44).

7. Douglas (1966, pp. 2, 36).

8. Shove (2003); Pickering and Wiseman (2019).

9. Bredenbröker et al. (2020).

10. Schnall (2016).

11. Shove (2003, p. 80).

12. Douglas and Wildawsky (1982, p. 36).

13. Bauman (2013); Van der Geest (2014); Cisneros (2008); Bonhomme and Alfaro (2022).

14. Shilling (2012).

15. Simmel (2009).

16. Kohl (2020) is an exception; see also Pickering and Wiseman (2019).

17. Kaika (2004).

18. Boccagni (2023b, 2024).

19. Lagerspetz (2018).

20. Speltini and Passini (2016).

21. Grønseth and Thorshaug (2022).

22. Carsten (2020).

23. Neumann (2023).

24. Semprebon (2021); Bolzoni et al. (2022).

25. Bredenbröker et al. (2020).

26. Pickering and Wiseman (2019); Kohl (2020).

27. Duschinsky (2016); Speltini and Passini (2016).

28. Vandevoordt and Verschraegen (2019).

29. Van der Geest (2014).

30. Classen et al. (1994).

31. Classen (1992).

32. Goffman (1959).

33. Cf. Larsen (2011).

34. Acker (2023).

35. Cf. Parrott (2005).

36. Pickering and Wiseman (2019, p. 758).

37. Classen et al. (1994); Shove (2003).

38. Boccagni (2024).

7. HOME, NON-HOME

1. Graw and Schielke (2012); Fioratta (2015).

2. Young (2005).

3. Boccagni and Miranda-Nieto (2022).

4. Boccagni, Pérez Murcia, et al. (2020).

5. Boccagni (2023a); Miranda-Nieto et al. (2020); Blunt and Dowling (2022).

6. Kaur et al. (2021); Beeckmans et al. (2022); Fravega et al. (2023).

7. Boccagni (2017).

8. Ahmed (1999).

9. Dossa and Golubovic (2019).

10. Gil Everaert (2021).

11. Merton (1976).

12. Frost (2001, p. 91).

13. Vigh (2009); Fioratta (2015).

14. Bourdieu (1970); Kaika (2004); Brickell (2012); Blunt and Dowling (2022).

15. Gil Everaert (2021).

16. Van der Horst (2004); Grønseth (2023); see also, in a context of internal displacement, Subasinghe (2019).

17. Bochmann (2019); Kohl (2020).

18. Alba et al. (2018); Boccagni and Vargas-Silva (2021).

19. Lauster and Zhao (2017).

20. Giudici and Boccagni (2022).

21. Hondagneu-Sotelo (2017); Shamma et al. (2023); Back (2023).

22. Easthope et al. (2015); Miranda-Nieto (2023).

23. Thorshaug and Brun (2019); Grønseth (2023).

24. Russell (2011).

25. Douglas (1991).

26. Neumann (2023).

27. Brun (2012); Miranda-Nieto et al. (2020).

28. Mazumdar and Mazumdar (2004); Bertolani and Boccagni (2023).

29. Vandevoordt (2017).

30. Hage (1997); Petridou (2001); Miranda-Nieto and Boccagni (2020); Mata-Codesal (2023).

31. Neumann (2023).

32. Cf. Mbodj-Pouye (2023).

33. Rapport and Dawson (2023); Mathews (2023).

34. Pérez Murcia and Bonfanti (2023).

35. Kleist (2017); Jefferson et al. (2019); Kallio et al. (2021).

36. Boccagni (2023a).

37. Beneduce (2015).

38. Miller (2021); Cabalquinto (2022).

39. Boccagni and Miranda-Nieto (2022).

40. Parsell (2012).

41. Jackson (2008); Gaibazzi (2015).

42. Bellagamba (2009).

43. See, respectively, Fernando (2014); Khosravi (2018); and Murray and Durrheim (2019).

44. Veness (1993); Kaika (2004); Brickell (2012).

45. Çarpar and Yaylaci (2021).

46. Walters (2023).

47. Bulley (2016); Harney and Boccagni (2023).

48. De Genova (2002).

49. Brubaker (2004); Malkki (1995).

50. Balkan (2023).

51. Cf. Markowitz and Stefansson (2004).

52. Boccagni and Bivand-Erdal (2021); Vargas-Silva and Boccagni (2024).

53. Lee and Vaughan (2008); Saraiva (2019).

54. Boccagni and Vargas-Silva (2021).

55. Malkki (1992).

56. Hage (2018, p. 205).

57. Boccagni (2022b); Rapport and Dawson (2023).

CONCLUSION

1. *Tutto a posto* is a way of saying "all right." Literally, and significantly, it means "everything in its place."

2. Cf. Cash (2009); and Frederiksen (2018).

3. Zerubavel (1993); Strassheim (2018).

4. Frederiksen (2018, pp. 106–7).

5. Frederiksen (2018, p. 107).

6. Goffman (1959); Anderson (2000); Nelson et al. (2024).

7. Boccagni (2023a).

8. Zerubavel (2020).

9. Faist (2019).

10. Abderrezak (2020); Stierl (2017).

11. Boccagni (2022b).

12. Bourdieu (1970); Carsten and Hugh-Jones (1995); Birdwell-Pheasant and Lawrence-Züniga (1999); Boccagni and Bonfanti (2023).

13. Bourdieu (1970).

14. Bourdieu (1970, pp. 161, 170).

15. Boccagni (2025).

16. Ghodsee (2016).

REFERENCES

Abderrezak, H. (2020). The Mediterranean sieve, spring and seametery. In E. Cox, S. Durrant, D. Farrier, L. Stonebridge, & A. Woolley (Eds.), *Refugee imaginaries: Research across the humanities* (pp. 372–391). Edinburgh University Press.

Achtnich, M. (2022). Waiting to move on: Migration, borderwork and mobility economies in Libya. *Geopolitics, 27*(5), 1376–1389.

Acker, S. (2023). Beauty and beautification in refugees' lives and their implications for refugee policy. *Refuge, 39*(1), 1–46.

Agamben, G. (1998). *Homo sacer*. Stanford University Press.

Agier, M. (2011). *Managing the undesirables: Refugee camps and humanitarian government*. Polity.

Ahmed, S. (1999). Home and away: Narratives of migration and estrangement. *International Journal of Cultural Studies, 2*(3), 329–347.

Alba, R., Beck, B., & Sahin, D. B. (2018). The US mainstream expands—again. *Journal of Ethnic and Migration Studies, 44*(1), 99–117.

Albahari, M. (2016). After the shipwreck: Mourning and citizenship in the Mediterranean, our sea. *Social Research, 83*(2), 275–294.

Albertini, M., & Radl, J. (2012). Intergenerational transfers and social class. *Acta Sociologica, 55*(2), 107–123.

Alencar, A. (2020). Mobile communication and refugees. *Sociology Compass, 14*, e:12802.

Altin, R., & Degli Uberti, S. (2022). Placed in time. *Journal of Balkan and Near Eastern Studies, 24*(3), 439–459.

Altman I., & Werner, C. (Eds.). (1985). *Home environments*. Plenum.

Ambrosini, M. (2022). Humanitarian help and refugees. *Journal of Immigrant and Refugee Studies, 1*–14.

Ambrosini, M., & Hajer, M. H. (2023). *Irregular migration: IMISCOE short reader*. Springer.

Amelina, A., & Bause, N. (2020). Forced migrant families' assemblages of care and social protection between solidarity and inequality. *Journal of Family Research, 32*(3), 415–434.

Anderson, E. (2000). *Code of the street: Decency, violence, and the moral life of the inner city*. Norton.

Andrikopoulos, A. (2023). *Argonauts of West Africa: Unauthorized Migration and Kinship Dynamics in a Changing Europe*. University of Chicago Press.

Arar, R., & FitzGerald, D. S. (2022). *The refugee system: A sociological approach*. Polity.

Atkinson, P. (2014). *For ethnography*. Sage.

Auyero, J. (2011). Patients of the state: An ethnographic account of poor people's waiting. *Latin American Research Review, 46*(1), 5–29.

Back, L. (2023). The paradox of home. In P. Boccagni (Ed.), *Handbook of home and migration* (pp. 112–120). Elgar.

Balkan, O. (2023). *Dying abroad*. Cambridge University Press.

Ballatore, R. M., Grompone, A., Lucci, L., Passiglia, P., & Sechi, A. (2017). *I rifugiati e i richiedenti asilo in Italia nel Confronto Europeo* (Refugees and asylum seekers in Italy and in the EU). Occasional Papers 377. Banca d'Italia.

Bandura, A. (2011). Moral disengagement. In *The encyclopedia of peace psychology* (pp. 1–5). Wiley.

Banerjee, B., Misrahi-Barak, J., & Lacroix, T. (2024). Thanatic ethics: The circulation of bodies in migratory spaces. *Interventions, 26*(1), 1–20.

Barberis, E., & Boccagni, P. (2014). Blurred rights, local practices: Social work and immigration in Italy. *British Journal of Social Work, 44*(suppl_1), i70–i87.

Barnes, J. (2022). Torturous journeys: Cruelty, international law, and pushbacks and pullbacks over the Mediterranean Sea. *Review of International Studies, 48*(3), 441–460.

Bathia M., & Canning, V. (Eds.). (2021). *Stealing time*. Palgrave.

Bauman, Z. (2002). In the lowly nowherevilles of liquid modernity. *Ethnography, 3*(3), 343–349.

Bauman, Z. (2004). *Work, consumerism and the new poor*. Open University Press.

Bauman, Z. (2013). *Wasted lives: Modernity and its outcasts*. Wiley & Sons.

Bazurli, R., Campomori, F., & Casula, M. (2020). Shelter from the storm. *Social Policies, 7*(2), 201–24.

Beeckmans, L., Gola, A., Singh, A., & Heynen, H. (Eds.). (2022). *Making home(s) in displacement*. Leuven University Press.

Bellagamba, A. (2009). Back to the land of roots: African American tourism and the cultural heritage of the River Gambia. *Cahiers d'études africaines, 1–2*, 453–476.

Belloni, M. (2019). *The big gamble*. University of California Press.

Bendixsen, S., & Eriksen, T. H. (2018). Time and the other. In M. Janeja & A. Bandak (Eds.), *Ethnographies of waiting* (pp. 87–112). Routledge.

Beneduce, R. (2015). The moral economy of lying: Subjectcraft, narrative capital, and uncertainty in the politics of asylum. *Medical Anthropology, 34*(6), 551–571.

Benjamin, D., Stea, D., & Arén, E. (Eds). (1995). *The home: Words, interpretations, meanings and environments*. Avebury.

Berger, J. (1984). *And our faces, my heart, brief as photos*. Vintage.

Berlant, L. (2011). *Cruel optimism*. Duke University Press.

Bertolani, B., & Boccagni, P. (2023). Domestic religion and the migrant home. *Ethnicities, 23*(2), 284–305.

Betts, A. (2010a). The refugee regime complex. *Refugee Survey Quarterly, 29*(1), 12–37.

Betts, A. (2010b). Survival migration: A new protection framework. *Global Governance*, 361–382.

Bille, M., Hastrup, F., & Sorensen, T. F. (2010). Introduction: An anthropology of absence. In M. Bille, F. Hastrup, & T. Sorensen (Eds.), *An anthropology of absence* (pp. 3–22). Springer.

Birdwell-Pheasant, D., & Lawrence-Zúniga, D. (Eds.). (1999). *House life*. Routledge.

Bjarnesen, J., & Turner, S. (Eds.). (2020). *Invisibility in African displacements: From structural marginalization to strategies of avoidance*. Bloomsbury.

Blanco, M., & Peeren, E. (Eds.). (2013). *The spectralities reader: Ghosts and haunting in contemporary cultural theory*. Bloomsbury.

Blunt, A., & Dowling, R. (2022). *Home*. Routledge.

Boccagni, P. (2017). *Migration and the search for home*. Palgrave.

Boccagni, P. (2022a). At home in the center? Spatial appropriation and horizons of home-making in reception facilities for asylum seekers. In L. Beeckmans, A. Gola, A. Singh, & H. Heynen (Eds.), *Making home(s) in displacement* (pp. 139–54). Leuven University Press.

Boccagni, P. (2022b). Homing: A category for research on space appropriation and "home-oriented" mobilities. *Mobilities, 17*(4), 585–601.

Boccagni, P. (Ed.). (2023a). Introduction: Home and migration; Setting the terms of belonging and place-making on the move. In P. Boccagni (Ed.), *Handbook on home and migration* (pp. 1–28). Elgar.

Boccagni, P. (2023b). Rooms with little view: Reluctant homemaking and the renegotiation of space in an asylum center. In P. Boccagni & S. Bonfanti (Eds.), *Migration and domestic space* (pp. 117–136). Springer-IMISCOE.

Boccagni, P. (2024). *Vite ferme: Storie di migranti in attesa*. Il Mulino.

Boccagni, P. (2025) [Forthcoming]. On the (past) verge of death. *Cultural Studies*.

Boccagni, P., & Bivand-Erdal, M. (2021). On the theoretical potential of "remittance houses." *Journal of Ethnic and Migration Studies, 47*(5), 1066–1083.

Boccagni, P., & Bonfanti, S. (2023). Stranger, guest, researcher: A case for domestic ethnography in migration studies. In P. Boccagni & S. Bonfanti (Eds.), *Migration and domestic space* (pp. 1–19). Springer-IMISCOE.

Boccagni, P., & Brighenti, A. M. (2017). Immigrants and home in the making. *Journal of Housing and the Built Environment, 32*, 1–11.

Boccagni, P., Galera, G., Giannetto, L., & Piovesan, S. (2020). *Il tramonto dell'accoglienza*. Tau-Quaderni Migrantes, vol. 15.

Boccagni, P., & Kivisto, P. (2019). Ambivalence and the social process of immigrant inclusion. *International Journal of Comparative Sociology, 60*(1–2), 3–13.

Boccagni, P., & Lacroix, T. (2025) [Forthcoming]. *Death in migration*. Bristol University Press.

Boccagni, P., & Miranda-Nieto, A. (2022). Home in question: Uncovering meanings, desires and dilemmas of non-home. *European Journal of Cultural Studies, 25*(2), 515–532.

Boccagni, P., Pérez Murcia, L. E., & Belloni, M. (2020). *Thinking home on the move*. Emerald.

Boccagni, P., & Vargas-Silva, C. (2021). Feeling at home across time and place. *Population, Space and Place, 27*(6), e2431.

Bochmann, A. (2019). The power of local micro structures in the context of refugee camps. *Journal of Refugee Studies, 32*(1), 63–85.

Bochmann, A. (2021). *Public camp orders and the power of microstructures in the Thai-Burmese borderland.* Lexington.

Boltanski, L. (2004). *Distant suffering. Morality, media and politics.* Cambridge University Press. (Original work published 1999.)

Bolzoni, M., Donatiello, D., & Giannetto, L. (2022). Sailing against the law tides. *Comparative Population Studies, 47.*

Bonhomme, M., & Alfaro, A. (2022). "The filthy people": Racism in digital spaces during Covid-19 in the context of south–south migration. *International Journal of Cultural Studies, 25*(3–4), 404–427.

Boochani, B. (2018). *No friends but the mountains.* Picador.

Bourdieu, P. (1970). The Berber house or the world reversed. *Social Science information, 9*(2), 151–170.

Bredenbröker, I., Hanzen, C., & Kotzur, F. (2020). We have never been clean: Toward an interdisciplinary discourse about cleaning and value. In I. Bredenbröker, C. Hanzen & F. Kotzur (Eds.), *Cleaning and value* (pp. 23–28). Sidestone.

Brekhus, W. (1998). A sociology of the unmarked: Redirecting our focus. *Sociological Theory, 16*(1), 34–51.

Brickell, K. (2012). "Mapping" and "doing" critical geographies of home. *Progress in Human Geography, 36*(2), 225–244.

Brighenti, A.M. (2010). *Visibility in social theory and social research.* Springer.

Brubaker, R. (2004). *Ethnicity without groups.* Harvard University Press.

Brun, C. (2012). Home in temporary dwellings. In S. Smith (Ed.), *International encyclopedia of housing and home* (pp. 424–433). Elsevier.

Brun, C. (2015). Active waiting and changing hopes. *Social Analysis, 59*(1), 19–37.

Brun, C., & Fabos, A. (2015). Making homes in limbo? *Refuge, 31*(1), 5–17.

Brzezińska, M. (2024). "Emigration is luck": Destiny, witchcraft and uncertainty in migratory journeys from the Gambia and Guinea-Bissau. *Ethnos,* 1–14.

Bulley, D. (2016). *Migration, ethics and power: Spaces of hospitality in international politics.* Sage.

Cabalquinto, E.C.B. (2022). *(Im)mobile homes: Family life at a distance in the age of mobile media.* Oxford University Press.

Cabot, H. (2016). "Refugee voices": Tragedy, ghosts, and the anthropology of not knowing. *Journal of Contemporary Ethnography, 45*(6), 645–672.

Campomori, F. (2016). Le politiche per i rifugiati in Italia [Refugee policy in Italy]. Social Cohesion Papers no. 2.

Campomori, F., & Ambrosini, M. (2020). Multi-level governance in trouble. *Comparative Migration Studies, 8*(22), 1–19.

Carling, J. (2014). Scripting remittances. *International Migration Review, 48,* S218–S262.

Carling, J., Menjívar, C., & Schmalzbauer, L. (2012). Central themes in the study of transnational parenthood. *Journal of Ethnic and Migration Studies, 38*(2), 191–217.

Çarpar, M., & Yaylaci, F. (2021). Forced migration as a crisis in masculinity. *Journal of Refugee Studies, 34*(4), 3846–3870.

Carsten, J. (Ed.). (2008). *Ghosts of memory: Essays on remembrance and relatedness.* Wiley.

Carsten, J. (2020). Imagining and living new worlds: The dynamics of kinship in contexts of mobility and migration. *Ethnography, 21*(3), 319–334.

Carsten, J., & Hugh-Jones, S. (1995). Introduction: About the house—Levi-Strauss and beyond. In J. Carsten & S. Hugh-Jones (Eds.), *About the house* (pp. 1–46). Cambridge University Press.

Cash, J. (2009). Waiting for sociality: The (re) birth, astride a grave, of the social. In G. Hage (Ed.), *Waiting* (pp. 27–38). Melbourne University Press.

Centri d'Italia. (2024). *Un fallimento annunciato* [A very predictable failure]. N.p.

Cisneros, J.D. (2008). Contaminated communities. *Rhetoric & Public Affairs, 11*(4), 569–601.

Classen, C. (1992). The odor of the other. *Ethos, 20,* 133–166.

Classen, C., Howes, D., & Synnott, A. (1994). *Aroma: The cultural history of smell.* Routledge.

Coates, D.J. (2023). *In praise of ambivalence.* Oxford University Press.

Coe, C. (2016). Translations in kinscript: Child circulation among Ghanaians abroad. In J. Cole & C. Groes (Eds.), *Affective circuits* (pp. 27–53). Chicago University Press.

Cohen, R., & Van Hear, N. (2019). *Refugia: Radical solutions to mass displacement.* Routledge.

Cole, J., & Groes, C. (2016). Affective circuits and social regeneration in African migration. In J. Cole & C. Groes (Eds.), *Affective circuits* (pp. 1–26). Chicago University Press.

Collini, M. (2023). Italy: The promised land? Journeys of migrants, refugees and asylum seekers towards labour market integration. In *Immigrant and asylum seekers labour market integration upon arrival: NowHereLand* (pp. 129–160). N.p.

Creta, S., & Denaro, C. (2022). Counter-narrating the Mediterranean border regime and reclaiming rights. In *The migration mobile,* 165. N.p.

Cusumano, E. (2019). Migrant rescue as organized hypocrisy: EU maritime missions offshore Libya between humanitarianism and border control. *Cooperation and Conflict, 54*(1), 3–24.

Cusumano, E., & Gombeer, K. (2020). In deep waters: The legal, humanitarian and political implications of closing Italian ports to migrant rescuers. *Mediterranean Politics, 25*(2), 245–253.

Cuttitta, P., & Last, T. (2019). *Border deaths: Causes, dynamics and consequences of migration-related mortality.* Amsterdam University Press.

Danstrøm, M.S., & Whyte, Z. (2018). Narrating asylum in camp and at court. In N. Gill & A. Good (Eds.), *Asylum determination in Europe* (pp. 175–194). Palgrave.

Darling, J. (2022). The politics of discretion. *Political Geography, 94,* 102560.

Davidson, T. (2009). The role of domestic architecture in the structuring of memory. *Space and Culture, 12*(3), 332–342.

Davies, T. (2019). Slow violence and toxic geographies. *Environment and Planning, C40*(2), 409–427.

De Backer, M. (Ed.). (2023). *Refugee youth.* Bristol University Press.

De Certeau, M. (1984). *The practice of everyday life.* University of California Press.

De Genova, N. (2002). Migrant "illegality" and deportability in everyday life. *Annual Review of Anthropology, 31*(1), 419–447.

De Genova, N. (2013). Spectacles of migrant "illegality." *Ethnic and Racial Studies, 36*(7), 1180–1198.

Degli Uberti, S. (2021). Unveiling informality through im/mobility. *Journal of Modern Italian Studies, 26*(5), 528–551.

De Leon, J. (2015). *The land of open graves: Living and dying on the migrant trail.* University of California Press.

De Martino, E. (2015). *Magic. A theory from the South.* HAU Books. (Original work published 1959.)

Denaro, C., & Boccagni, P. (2023). Challenging ungrievability for people missing at sea: Search infrastructures, spaces of public mourning, and claims for justice. *Ethnic and Racial Studies.*

Desjardins, A., Wakkary, R., & Odom, W. (2015). *Investigating genres and perspectives in HCI research on the home* [Conference session]. CHI 2015, Crossings, Seoul, Korea.

Diken, B. (2004). From refugee camps to gated communities. *Citizenship Studies, 8*(1), 83–106.

Diminescu, D. (2008). The connected migrant: An epistemological manifesto. *Social Science Information, 47*(4), 565–579.

Dobler, G. (2020). Waiting: Elements of a conceptual framework. *Critical African Studies, 12*(1), 10–21.

Donohoe, J. (2011). The place of home. *Environmental Philosophy, 8*(1), 25–40.

Dossa, P., & Golubovic, J. (2019). Reimagining home in the wake of displacement. *Studies in Social Justice, 13*(1), 171–86.

Dotsey, S., & Lumley-Sapanski, A. (2021). Temporality, refugees, and housing: The effects of temporary assistance on refugee housing outcomes in Italy. *Cities, 111,* 103100.

Douglas, M. (1966). *Purity and danger.* Ark.

Douglas, M. (1991). The idea of a home: A kind of space. *Social research,* 287–307.

Douglas, M., & Wildawsky, A. (1982). *Risk and culture.* University of California Press.

Dovey, K. (1985). Home and homelessness. In I. Altman & C. Werner (Eds.), *Home environments* (pp. 113–132). Plenum.

Dragojlovic, A., & Samuels, A. (2021). Tracing silences: Towards an anthropology of the unspoken and unspeakable. *History of Anthropology Review 32*(4), 417–425.

Dreyer, M. (2022). Years in the waiting room: A feminist ethnography of the invisible institutional living spaces of forced displacement. In L. Beeckmans, A. Singh, A. Gola, & H. Heynen (Eds.), *Making home(s) in displacement* (pp. 197–218). Leuven University Press.

Dudley, S. (2011). Feeling at home: Producing and consuming things in Karenni refugee camps on the Thai-Burma border. *Population, Space and Place 17*(6), 742–755.

Duschinsky, R. (2016). Introduction. In R. Duschinsky et al. (Eds.), *Purity and danger now* (pp. 1–20). Routledge.

Duyvendak, J. W., & Kesic, J. (2022). *The return of the native.* Oxford University Press.

Easthope, H., Liu, E., Judd, B., & Burnley, I. (2015). Feeling at home in a multigenerational household. *Housing, Theory and Society, 32*(2), 151–170.

Ehn, B., & Löfgren, O. (2010). *The secret world of doing nothing.* University of California Press.

Eriksen, T. H. (2020). Filling the apps: The smartphone, time and the refugee. In C. M. Jacobsen, M. A. Karlsen, & S. Khosravi, S. (Eds.), *Waiting and the temporalities of irregular migration* (pp. 57–72). Routledge.

Esperti, M. (2020). Rescuing migrants in the central Mediterranean. *American Behavioral Scientist, 64*(4), 436–455.

Fabian, J. (2014). *Time and the other: How anthropology makes its object.* Columbia University Press. (Original work published 1983.)

Faist, T. (2019). *The transnationalized social question.* Oxford University Press.

Fassin, D. (2001). The biopolitics of otherness. *Anthropology Today, 17*(1), 3–7.

Fassin, D. (2013). The precarious truth of asylum. *Public Culture, 25*(1), 39–63.

Fernando, M. L. (2014). Ethnography and the politics of silence. *Cultural Dynamics, 26*(2), 235–244.

Fioratta, S. (2015). Beyond remittance: Evading uselessness and seeking personhood in Fouta Djallon, Guinea. *American Ethnologist, 42*(2), 295–308.

FitzGerald, D. (2019). *Refuge beyond reach.* Oxford University Press.

FitzGerald, D., & Arar, R. (2018). The sociology of refugee migration. *Annual Review of Sociology, 44,* 387–406.

Fondazione Moressa. (2023). *Rapporto annuale sull'economia dell'immigrazione* [Annual economic report on immigration]. Il Mulino.

Fontanari, E. (2017). "It's my life": The temporalities of refugees and asylum-seekers within the European border regime. *ERQ, 10*(1), 25–54.

Fransen, S., & de Haas, H. (2022). Trends and patterns of global refugee migration. *Population and Development Review, 48*(1), 97–128.

Fravega, E., Giudici, D., & Boccagni, P. (2023). *La lotta per il tempo: Temporalità contestate nell'esperienza di richiedenti asilo in Italia* [The struggle for time: Contested temporalities in the life experience of asylum seekers in Italy]. Meltemi.

Frederiksen, M. D. (2018). *An anthropology of nothing in particular.* Hunt.

Freemantle, I., & Landau, L. B. (2022). Migration and the African timespace trap: More Europe for the world, less world for Europe. *Geopolitics, 27*(3), 791–810.

Frost, R. (2001). *The death of the hired man.* In R. Frost (Ed.), *Selected poems* (pp. 89–94). Gramercy. (Original work published 1914.)

Gaibazzi, P. (2015). The quest for luck. *Critical African Studies, 7*(3), 227–242.

Gargiulo, E. (2023). Registration as a border. *Geopolitics, 28*(1), 439–463.

Garvey, P. (2005). Domestic boundaries: Privacy, visibility and the Norwegian window. *Journal of Material Culture, 10*(2), 157–176.

Gatrell, P. (2013). *The making of the modern refugee.* Oxford University Press.

Geschiere, P., & Rowlands, M. (1996). The domestication of modernity: Different trajectories. *Africa 66*(4), 552–554.

Ghodsee, K. (2016). *From notes to narrative: Writing ethnographies that everyone can read.* University of Chicago Press.

Ghorashi, H. (2005). Agents of change or passive victims. *Journal of Refugee Studies, 18*(2), 181–198.

Ghorashi, H. (2008). Giving silence a chance: The importance of life stories for research on refugees. *Journal of Refugee Studies, 21*(1), 117–132.

Ghorashi, H., de Boer, M., & Ten Holder, F. (2018). Unexpected agency on the threshold. *Current Sociology, 66*(3), 373–391.

Gielis, R. (2011). The value of single-site ethnography in the global era: Studying transnational experiences in the migrant house. *Area, 43*(3), 257–63.

Gil Everaert, I. (2021). Inhabiting the meanwhile: Rebuilding home and restoring predictability in a space of waiting. *Journal of Ethnic and Migration Studies, 47*(19), 4327–4343.

Ginzburg, C. (1994). Killing a Chinese Mandarin: The moral implications of distance. *Critical Inquiry, 21*(1), 46–60.

Giudici, D., & Boccagni, P. (2022). Exposing the private, engaging in the public. *Environment and Planning D.*

Glorius, B., Doomernik, J., Hinger, S., Schafer, P., & Pott, A. (2016). The local production of asylum. *Journal of Refugee Studies, 29*(4), 440–463.

Goffman, E. (1959). *The presentation of self in everyday life.* Doubleday.

Goffman, E. (1961). *Asylums: Essays on the social situation of mental patients and other inmates.* Aldine Transaction.

Goffman, E. (1963). *Behavior in public places.* Free Press.

Goffman, E. (1979). *Forms of talk.* University of Pennsylvania Press.

Gordon, A. (2008). *Ghostly matters: Haunting and the sociological imagination.* University of Minnesota Press. (Original work published 1997.)

Grabska, K., & Clark-Kazak, C. (Eds.). (2022). *Documenting displacement.* McGill University Press.

Grappi, G., & Lucarelli, S. (2022). Bordering power Europe? The mobility-bordering nexus in and by the European Union. *Journal of Contemporary European Studies, 30*(2), 207–219.

Graw, K., & Schielke, S. (2012). Introduction: Reflections on migratory expectations in Africa and beyond. In K. Graw & S. Schielke (Eds.), *The global horizon* (pp. 7–22). Leuven University Press.

Green, R. (2011). *Nothing matters: A book about nothing.* Hunt.

Griffiths, M. (2014). Out of time: The temporal uncertainties of refused asylum seekers and immigration detainees. *Journal of Ethnic and Migration Studies, 40*(12), 1991–2009.

Griffiths, M. (2015). "Here, man is nothing!" Gender and policy in an asylum context. *Men and Masculinities, 18*(4), 468–488.

Griffiths, M. (2024). Epilogue. *Journal of International Migration and Integration,* 1–17.

Grønseth, A. S. (2013). Introduction. In A. S. Grønseth (Ed.), *Being human, being migrant* (pp. 1–26). Berghahn.

Grønseth, A. S. (2023). Refugee housing and homing: Negotiating self and humanity. In P. Boccagni (Ed.), *Handbook on home and migration* (pp. 350–364). Elgar.

Grønseth, A. S., Stoa, E., Thorshaug, R., & Hauge, A. (2016). *Housing qualities and effects on identity and well-being.* Lillehammer University College Research Report no. 169/2016.

Grønseth, A. S., & Thorshaug, R. (2022). Struggling for home where home is not meant to be. *Focaal, 92,* 15–30.

Gundlach, H. (2020). Gestalt psychology. In *Oxford research encyclopedia of psychology.*

Haas, B. M. (2023). *Suspended lives: Navigating everyday violence in the US asylum system.* University of California Press.

Hage, G. (1997). At home in the entrails of the West: Multiculturalism, ethnic food and migrant home-building. In H. Grace, G. Hage, L. Johnson, J. Langsworth, & M. Symonds (Eds), *Home/world: Space, community and marginality in Sydney's west* (pp. 99–153).

Hage, G. (Ed.). (2009). *Waiting.* Melbourne University Press.

Hage, G. (2018). Afterword. In M. Janeja & A. Bandak (Eds.), *Ethnographies of waiting.* (pp. 203–208). Routledge.

Haile, D. T., & Schapendonk, J. (2024). The "system" as another sea: Contrasting mobility rules and migrant navigations. *Focaal, 99,* 15–27.

Harbisch, A. (2023). Children or productive adults? Infantilization and exploitation of refugees in Germany and Austria. *Journal of Ethnic and Migration Studies*, 1–19.

Harney, N. (2013). Precarity, affect and problem solving with mobile phones by asylum seekers, refugees and migrants in Naples, Italy. *Journal of Refugee Studies, 26*(4), 541–557.

Harney, N., & Boccagni, P. (2023). Calibrating home, hospitality and reciprocity in migration. *Anthropological Theory 23*(3), 313–331.

Harris, E., Brickell, K., & Nowicki, M. (2020). Door locks, wall stickers, fireplaces. *Antipode, 52*(5), 1286–1309.

Hart, J., Paskiewicz, N., & Albadra, D. (2018). Shelter as home? *Human Organization, 77*(4), 371–380.

Hastrup, K. (1990). The ethnographic present: A reinvention. *Cultural Anthropology 5*(1), 45–61.

Hatuka, T., & Toch, E. (2016). The emergence of portable private-personal territory: Smartphones, social conduct and public spaces. *Urban Studies, 53*(10), 2192–2208.

Hauge, A. L., Stoa, E., & Denizou, K. (2017). Framing outsidedness: Aspects of housing quality in decentralized reception centers for asylum seekers in Norway. *Housing, Theory and Society, 34*(1), 1–20.

Havik, P., Mapril, J., & Saraiva, C. (Eds.). (2018). *Death on the move. Managing narratives, silences and constraints in a transnational perspective.* Cambridge Scholars.

Hawthorne, C. (2022). *Contesting race and citizenship: Youth politics in the Black Mediterranean.* Cornell University Press.

Hayden, S. (2022). *My fourth time, we drowned: Seeking refuge on the world's deadliest migration route.* Fourth Estate.

Heller, C., Pezzani, L., & Stierl, M. (2023). Contesting the lethal Mediterranean frontier. In I. van Liempt, J. Schapendonk, & A. Campos-Delgado (Eds.), *Research handbook on irregular migration* (pp. 361–372).

Hernann, A. (2017). Outside Timbuktu's divine cover: The negotiation of privacy among displaced Timbuktians. *American Ethnologist, 44*(2), 275–287.

Hetherington, K. (2004). Secondhandedness: Consumption, disposal, and absent presence. *Environment and Planning D, 22,* 157–73.

Hillcoat-Nallétamby, S., & Phillips, J. E. (2011). Sociological ambivalence revisited. *Sociology 45*(2), 202–217.

Holmes, H. (2019). The body in personal life. In V. May & P. Nordqvist (Eds.), *Sociology of personal life* (pp. 117–129). Bloomsbury.

Holmes, H., & Ehgartner, U. (2021). Loss property and the materiality of absence. *Cultural Sociology, 15*(2), 252–270.

Hondagneu-Sotelo, P. (2017). At home in inner-city immigrant community gardens. *Journal of Housing and the Built Environment, 32,* 13–28.

Honwana, A. M. (2012). *The time of youth: Work, social change, and politics in Africa.* Rienner.

Horst, H. A., & Miller, D. (Eds.). (2020). *Digital anthropology.* Routledge.

Horsti, K. (Ed.). (2019). *The politics of public memories of forced migration and bordering in Europe.* Palgrave.

Hunter, A. (2016). Deathscapes in diaspora. *Social & Cultural Geography, 17*(2), 247–261.

Hyndman, J., & Giles, W. (2011). Waiting for what? The feminization of asylum in protracted situations. *Gender, Place & Culture, 18*(3), 361–379.

Hyndman, J., & Giles, W. (2016). *Refugees in extended exile: Living on the edge.* Routledge.

Immigrazione Dossier Statistico. (2023). *Dossier statistico immigrazione.* Centro Studi e Ricerche Immigrazione.

International Organization for Migration. (2020). *Calculating "death rates" in the context of migration journeys: Focus on the central Mediterranean.* GMDAC Briefing Series.

Istituto Studi sulla Multietnicità. (2023). *Sbarchi e accoglienza di immigrati in Italia negli anni 1997–2002.* Fondazione ISMU.

Jackson, M. (2008). The shock of the new: On migrant imaginaries and critical transitions. *Ethnos, 73,* 57–72.

Jacobsen, C. M., Karlsen, M. A., & Khosravi, S. (Eds.). (2021). *Waiting and the temporalities of irregular migration.* Routledge.

Jacobsen, K., & Majidi, N. (Eds.). (2023). *Handbook on forced migration.* Elgar.

Jaji, R. (2021). "Aberrant" masculinity. In C. Mora & N. Piper (Eds.), *The Palgrave handbook of gender and migration* (pp. 373–386).

Jakobsen, C. O. (2022). "Little prisons": Revisiting trajectories and carcerality in a Danish asylum camp. *Incarceration, 3*(1).

Janeja, M., & Bandak, A. (Eds.). (2018). *Ethnographies of waiting.* Routledge.

Jefferson, A., Turner, S., & Jensen, S. (2019). On stuckness and sites of confinement. *Ethnos, 84*(1), 1–13.

Jeffrey, C. (2010). *Timepass: Youth, class, and the politics of waiting in India.* Stanford University Press.

Jones, R. (Ed.). (2019). *Open borders: In defense of free movement.* University of Georgia Press.

Kaika, M. (2004). Interrogating the geographies of the familiar: Domesticating nature and constructing the autonomy of the modern home. *International Journal of Urban and Regional Research 28*(2), 265–286.

Kallio, K. P., Meier, I., & Häkli, J. (2021). Radical Hope in asylum seeking: Political agency beyond linear temporality. *Journal of Ethnic and Migration Studies, 47*(17), 4006–4022.

Kärrholm, M., Jensen, T. G., Foroughanfar, L., & Söderberg, R. (2023). Migration, place-making and the rescaling of urban space. *European Planning Studies, 31*(2), 270–286.

Kaur, H., Saad A., Magwood O., Alkhateeb Q., Mathew C., Khalaf G., & Pottie K. (2021). Understanding the health and housing experiences of refugees and other migrant populations experiencing homelessness or vulnerable housing. *Canadian Medical Association Open Access Journal, 9*(2), E681–E692.

Kawabata, M., & Gastaldo, D. (2015). The less said, the better: Interpreting silence in qualitative research. *International Journal of Qualitative Methods, 14*(4).

Kawamura, Y. (2016). *Sneakers: Fashion, gender, and subculture.* Bloomsbury.

Khosravi, S. (2010). *"Illegal" traveller. An auto-ethnography of the border.* Palgrave

Khosravi, S. (2018). Afterword: Experiences and stories along the way. *Geoforum, 116,* 292–295.

Khosravi, S. (2019). What do we see if we look at the border from the other side? *Social Anthropology, 27*(3), 409–424.

Kingsbury, P., & Secor, A. J. (Eds.). (2021). *A place more void.* University of Nebraska Press.

Kivijärvi, A., & Myllylä, M. (2022). Layered confinement in reception centers: A study of asylum seekers' experiences in Finland. *Journal of Immigrant & Refugee Studies,* 1–14.

Kleist, N. (2017). Introduction: Studying hope and uncertainty in African migration. In N. Kleist & D. Thorsen (Eds.). *Hope and uncertainty in contemporary African migration.* Routledge.

Kleist, N., & Thorsen, D. (2017). *Hope and uncertainty in contemporary African migration.* Routledge.

Kobelinsky, C. (2020). Border beings. Present absences among migrants in the Spanish enclave of Melilla. *Death Studies, 44*(11), 709–717.

Kohl, K. S. (2020). Ambiguous encounters: Revisiting Foucault and Goffman at an activation programme for asylum-seekers. *Refugee Survey Quarterly, 39*(2), 177–206.

Kovras, I., & Robins, S. (2016). Death as the border: Managing missing migrants and unidentified bodies at the EU's Mediterranean frontier. *Political Geography, 55,* 40–49.

Kreichauf, R. (2018). From forced migration to forced arrival. *Comparative migration studies, 6*(1), 1–22.

Kule, M. (1997). Home: A phenomenological approach. In A. T. Tymieniecka (Ed.), *Passion for place* (pp. 97–112). Kluwer.

Lagerspetz, O. (2018). *A philosophy of dirt.* Chicago University Press.

Lambek, M. (Ed.). (2010). *Ordinary ethics: Anthropology, language, and action.* Fordham University Press.

Larsen, B. R. (2011). Drawing back the curtains: The role of domestic space in the social inclusion and exclusion of refugees in rural Denmark. *Social Analysis, 55*(2), 142–158.

Lauster, N., & Zhao, J. (2017). Labor migration and the missing work of homemaking. *Social Problems, 64*(4), 497–512.

Lee, R., & Vaughan, M. (2008). Death and dying in the history of Africa since 1800. *Journal of African History 49*(3), 341–359.

Le Espiritu, Y., Duong L., Vang, M., Bascara, V., Um, K., Sharif, L., & Hatton, N. (2021). *Departures: An introduction to critical refugee studies.* University of California Press.

Lems, A. (2018). *Being-here: Place-making in a world of movement.* Berghahn.

Lenhard, J., & Samanani, F. (Eds). (2020). *Home: Ethnographic encounters.* Bloomsbury.

Leurs, K., & Patterson, J. (2020). Smartphones: Digital infrastructures of the displaced. In P. Adey et al. (Eds.), *The Handbook of displacement* (pp. 583–597). Palgrave.

Levi, P. (1998). *The drowned and the saved.* Simon and Schuster.

Linde, T. (2011). Mixed migration: A humanitarian counterpoint. *Refugee Survey Quarterly, 30*(1), 89–99.

Lombardi-Diop, C. (2012). *Postcolonial Italy: Challenging national homogeneity.* Springer.

Lucht, H. (2011). *Darkness before daybreak: African migrants living on the margins in southern Italy today.* University of California Press.

Lucht, H. (2016). Death of a gin salesman: Hope and despair among Ghanaian migrants and deportees stranded in Niger. In N. Kleist & D. Thorsen (Eds.), *Hope and uncertainty in contemporary African migration* (pp. 154–172). Routledge.

Lucht, H. (2024). Distressed: Migrant underworlds and travels in hyporeality. *Anthropological Theory.*

MacKenzie, C., McDowell, C., & Pittaway, E. (2007). Beyond "do no harm": The challenge of constructing ethical relationships in refugee research. *Journal of Refugee Studies, 20*(2), 299–319.

Maculan, A. (2022). Asylum seekers, power relations, and everyday resistance practices. *Journal of International Migration and Integration, 23*(2), 431–447.

Maddrell, A. (2016). Mapping grief: A conceptual framework for understanding the spatial dimensions of bereavement, mourning and remembrance. *Social & Cultural Geography, 17*(2), 166–188.

Malkki, L. (1992). National geographic: The rooting of peoples and the territorialization of national identity among scholars and refugees. *Cultural Anthropology, 7*(1), 24–44.

Malkki, L. (1995). Refugees and exile: from "refugee studies" to the national order of things. *Annual Review of Anthropology, 24*, 495–553.

Marchetti, C. (2014). Rifugiati e migranti forzati in Italia. [Refugees and forced migrants in Italy]. *REMHU, 22*(43), 53–70.

Marchetti, C. (2020). Cities of exclusion. In M. Ambrosini, M. Cinalli, & D. Jacobson (Eds.), *Migration, borders and citizenship* (pp. 237–263). Palgrave.

Markowitz, F., & Stefansson, A. H. (Eds.). (2004). *Homecomings: Unsettling paths of return.* Lexington.

Martin, D., Minca, C., & Katz, I. (2020). Rethinking the camp: On spatial technologies of power and resistance. *Progress in Human Geography, 44*(4), 743–768.

Massey, D. (2005). *For space.* Sage.

Mata-Codesal, D. (2023). Feeling at home: Migrant homemaking through the senses. In P. Boccagni (Ed.), *Handbook on home and migration* (pp. 228–238). Elgar.

Mathews, G. (2002). *Global culture/individual identity: Searching for home in the cultural supermarket.* Routledge.

Mathews, G. (2023). Senses of home in the modern world. In P. Boccagni (Ed.), *Handbook on home and migration* (pp. 121–130). Elgar.

Mayblin, L., Wake, M., & Kazemi, M. (2020). Necropolitics and the slow violence of the everyday: Asylum seeker welfare in the postcolonial present. *Sociology, 54*(1), 107–123.

Mazumdar, S., & Mazumdar, S. (2004). Religion and place attachment. *Journal of Environmental Psychology, 24*(3), 385–397.

Mazzucato, V., & Ogden, L. (2025). Transnational youth mobility through trajectories and temporalities. *Journal of Ethnic and Migration Studies*, 1–21.

Mbodj-Pouye, A. (2016). Fixed abodes. *American Ethnologist, 43*, 295–310.

Mbodj-Pouye, A. (2023). *An address in Paris: Emplacement, bureaucracy, and belonging in hostels for West African migrants.* Columbia University Press.

M'charek, A., & Casartelli, S. (2019). Identifying dead migrants: Forensic care work and relational citizenship. *Citizenship Studies, 23*(7), 738–757.

McKinley, M. (1997). Life stories, disclosure and the law. *PoLAR: Political and Legal Anthropology Review, 20*(2), 70–82.

McMahon, S., & Sigona, N. (2021). Death and migration: Migrant journeys and the governance of migration during Europe's "migration crisis." *International Migration Review, 55*(2), 605–628.

Meier, I., & Donà, G. (2021). Micropolitics of time: Asylum regimes, temporalities and everyday forms of power. In M. Bathia & V. Canning (Eds.), *Stealing time* (pp. 39–64). Palgrave.

Meier, L., Frers, L., & Sigvardsdotter, E. (2013). The importance of absence in the present: Practices of remembrance and the contestation of absences. *Cultural Geographies, 20*(4), 423–430.

Merton, R. K. (1938). Social structure and anomie. *American Sociological Review, 3*(5), 672–682.

Merton, R. K. (1976). *Sociological ambivalence and other essays.* Simon and Schuster.

Meyer, M. (2012). Placing and tracing absence: A material culture of the immaterial. *Journal of Material Culture, 17*(1), 103–110.

Mifflin, E., & Wilton, R. (2005). No place like home: Rooming houses in contemporary urban context. *Environment and Planning A, 37*, 403–21.

Miller, D. (Ed.). (2001). *Home possessions: Material culture behind closed doors*. Berg.

Miller, D. (2008). *The comfort of things*. Polity.

Miller, D. (2021). A theory of a theory of the smartphone. *International Journal of Cultural Studies, 24*(5), 860–876.

Miller, D., Abed Rabho, L., Awondo, P., de Vries, M., Duque, M., Garvey, P., Haapio-Kirk, L., Hawkins, C., Otaegui, A., Walton, S., & Wang, X. (2021). *The global smartphone: Beyond a youth technology*. UCL Press.

Miranda-Nieto, A. (2023). Shared flats in Madrid: Accessing and analysing migrants' sense of home. In P. Boccagni & S. Bonfanti (Eds.), *Migration and domestic space* (pp. 85–100). Springer-IMISCOE.

Miranda-Nieto, A., & Boccagni, P. (2020). At home in the restaurant: Familiarity, belonging and material culture in Ecuadorian restaurants in Madrid. *Sociology, 54*(5), 1022–1040.

Miranda-Nieto, A., Massa, A., & Bonfanti, S. (2020). *Ethnographies of home and mobility*. Routledge.

Moran, C. (2023). The "connected migrant": A scoping review. *Convergence, 29*(2), 288–307.

Morning, A., & Maneri, M. (2022). *An ugly word: Rethinking race in Italy and the United States*. Sage Foundation.

Mountz, A. (2020). *The death of asylum: Hidden geographies of the enforcement archipelago*. University of Minnesota Press.

Moyo, K., Núñez, L., & Leuta, T. (2016). (Un)rest in peace: The (local) burial of foreign migrants as a contested process of place making. *Routes and rites to the city*, In M. Wilhelm-Solomon, L. Nunez, P. Kankonde Bukasa, & B. Malcommes (Eds.), *Routes and rites to the city* (pp. 273–305). Palgrave.

Mumford, S. (2021). *Absence and nothing: The philosophy of what there is not*. Oxford University Press.

Murray, A. J., & Durrheim, K. (Eds.). (2019). *Qualitative studies of silence*. Cambridge University Press.

Napolitano, V. (2015). Anthropology and traces. *Anthropological Theory 15*(1), 47–67.

Nasreen, Z. (2023). Migrants' homemaking practices in shared housing. In P. Boccagni (Ed.), *Handbook on home and migration* (pp. 338–349). Elgar.

Navaro-Yashin, Y. (2009). Affective spaces, melancholic objects: Ruination and the production of anthropological knowledge. *Journal of the Royal Anthropological Institute, 15*(1), 1–18.

Nayeri, D. (2019). *The ungrateful refugee*. Canongate.

Nelson, K., Ibarra, P. R., & Kusenbach, M. (2024). Neighborhood as theater: Building a Goffmanian framework for comparative urban ethnography. *Qualitative Sociology*.

Neumann, F. (2023). Home translated: Dispossessions, belongings, and the materiality of lives in asylum reception and exile [Doctoral dissertation, University of Gottingen].

Neumark, D. (2013). Drawn to beauty: The practice of house-beautification as homemaking among the forcibly displaced. *Housing, Theory and Society, 30*(3), 237–261.

Olwig, K. F. (2023). The end and ends of flight: Temporariness, uncertainty and meaning in refugee life. *Ethnos, 88*(1), 52–68.

Paerregaard, K. (2015). *Return to sender: The moral economy of Peru's migrant remittances.* University of California Press.

Paerregaard, K. (2021). Remittances and belonging. In J. H. Cohen & I. Sirkeci (Eds.), *Handbook of culture and migration* (pp. 301–312).

Paju, E., Lena, N., & Merikoski, P. (2023). Home and homemaking during refugee journeys. In P. Boccagni (Ed.), *Handbook on home and migration* (pp. 265–278). Elgar.

Pallister-Wilkins, P. (2022). *Humanitarian borders: Unequal mobility and saving lives.* Verso Books.

Palmberger, M. (2022). Refugees enacting (digital) citizenship through placemaking and care practices near and far. *Citizenship Studies, 26*(6), 781–798.

Papadopoulos, R. K. (2021). *Involuntary dislocation: Home, trauma, resilience, and adversity-activated development.* Routledge.

Parrott, F. R. (2005). "It's not forever": The material culture of hope. *Journal of Material Culture, 10*(3), 245–262.

Parsell, C. (2012). Home is where the house is: The meaning of home for people sleeping rough. *Housing Studies, 27*(2), 159–173.

Pécoud, A (2020). Death at the border: Revisiting the debate in light of the Euro-Mediterranean migration crisis. *American Behavioral Scientist, 64*(4), 379–388.

Pérez Murcia, L. E. (2019). The sweet memories of home have gone. *Journal of Ethnic and Migration Studies, 45*(9), 1515–1531.

Pérez Murcia, L. E. (2023). Researching home through the narratives of displaced people. In P. Boccagni (Ed.), *Handbook on home and migration* (pp. 554–566). Elgar.

Pérez Murcia, L. E., & Boccagni, P. (2022). Do objects (re)produce home among international migrants? *Journal of Intercultural Studies, 43*(5), 589–605.

Pérez Murcia, L. E., & Bonfanti, S. (Eds.). (2023). *Finding home in Europe.* Berghahn.

Petridou, E. (2001). The taste of home. In D. Miller (Ed.), *Home possessions: Material culture behind closed doors* (pp. 87–104). Berg.

Pickering, L., & Wiseman, P. (2019). Dirty scholarship and dirty lives: Explorations in bodies and belonging. *Sociological Review, 67*(4), 746–765.

Pink, S., Mackley, K., Morosanu, R., Mitchell, V., & Bhamra, T. (2017). *Making homes: Ethnography and design.* Taylor & Francis.

Piot, C. (2010). *Nostalgia for the future: West Africa after the Cold War.* University of Chicago Press.

Pitzalis, S. (2018). La costruzione dell'emergenza: Aiuto, assistenza e controllo tra disastri e migrazioni forzate in Italia. [The construction of emergency: Aid, assistance, and control in the middle of disasters and forced migration in Italy]. *Argomenti, 10*, 103–132.

Puumula, E., Ylikomi, R., & Ristimaki, H. (2017). Giving an account of persecution: The dynamic formation of asylum narratives. *Journal of Refugee Studies, 31*(2), 197–215.

Rancière, J. (2004). *The politics of aesthetics: The distribution of the sensible.* Continuum.

Rapport, N., & Dawson, A. (2023). Migrants of identity. In P. Boccagni (Ed.), *Handbook on home and migration* (pp. 30–41). Elgar.

Ratnam, C. (2023). Visual research and participatory research methods. In P. Boccagni (Ed.), *Handbook on home and migration* (pp. 543–553). Elgar.

Richmond, S. (2014). Nothingness and negation. In S. Churchill & J. Reynolds (Eds.), *Jean-Paul Sartre* (pp. 105–117). Routledge.

Roberts, L. (2024). Minding the emptiness of nothing: Methodological nothingness and the spatial anthropology of futility. *Social & Cultural Geography*, 1–20.

Rotter, R. (2016). Waiting in the asylum determination process. *Time & Society, 25*(1), 80–101.

Russell, A. (2011). Home, music and memory for the Congolese in Kampala. *Journal of Eastern African Studies, 5*(2), 294–312.

Sabetta, L., & Lombardo, C. (2023). What is done when nothing special is being done. In C. Lombardo & L. Sabetta (Eds.), *Against the background of social reality* (pp. 1–18). Routledge.

Sanchez, G., Arrouche, K., & Capasso, M. (2021). *Beyond networks, militias and tribes: Rethinking EU counter-smuggling policy and response. Euromesco*, Policy Study no. 19.

Saraiva, C. (2019). Ancestors and death. In H. Selin & R. Rakoff (Eds.), *Death across cultures* (pp. 151–165). Springer.

Saramo, S., Koivisto, E., & Snellnam, H. (Eds). (2019). *Transnational death*. Studia Fennica.

Sartre, J.P. (1957). *Being and nothingness: An essay on phenomenological ontology.* Methuen.

Sbriccoli, T., & Jacoviello, S. (2011). The case of S: Elaborating the "right" narrative to fit normal/political expectations in asylum procedure in Italy. In L. Holden (Ed.). *Cultural expertise and litigation* (pp. 172–194). Routledge.

Schapendonk, J. (2020). *Finding ways through Eurospace: West-African movers re-viewing Europe from the inside.* Berghahn.

Schindel, E. (2020). Deaths and disappearances in migration to Europe. *American Behavioral Scientist 64*(4), 389–407.

Schmoll, C. (2024). *Women and borders in the Mediterranean.* Springer.

Schnall, S. (2016). The mind beyond the boundaries. In R. Duschinsky, S. Schnall, & D. Weiss (Eds.), *Purity and danger now.* Routledge.

Schneider, C. (2023). Making a home in the world. *Journal of Material Culture 28*(2): 287–301.

Schutz, A. (2011). Reflections on the problem of relevance. In A. Schutz (Ed.), *Collected papers 5* (pp. 93–199). Springer. (Original work published 1951.)

Sciortino, G., & Finotelli, C. (2015). Closed memberships in a mobile world? In L. S. Talani & S. McMahon (Eds.), *Handbook of the international political economy of migration* (pp. 185–208). Elgar.

Scott, S. (2018). A sociology of nothing: Understanding the unmarked. *Sociology, 52*(1), 3–19.

Scott, S. (2019). *The social life of nothing: Silence, invisibility and emptiness.* Routledge.

Scott-Smith, T. (2024). *Fragments of home: Refugee housing and the politics of shelter.* Stanford University Press.

Scott-Smith, T., & Breeze, M. E. (Eds.). (2020). *Structures of protection? Rethinking refugee shelter.* Berghahn.

Seethaler-Wari, S., Chitchian, S., & Momic, M. (Eds.). (2022). *Inhabiting displacement: Architecture and authorship.* Birkhauser.

Semprebon, M. (2021). Towards a parallel exceptional welfare system. *Urban Geography 42*(7): 915–36.

Şenoğuz, H. P. (2023). Seeking normalcy in impossible homes. In N. Akdemir, J. Ullmann, J. Elle, E. Grittmann, S. Hess, U. Koopmann, D. Müller, H. Schwenken, & H. P. Senoguz (Eds.), *Gender, Flucht, Aufnahmepolitiken* (pp. 225–251). Springer.

Shamma, Y., Ilcan, S., Squire, V., & Underhill, H. (Eds.). (2023). *Migration, culture and identity: Making home away*. Springer.

Shilling, C. (2012). *The body and social theory*. Sage.

Shove, E. (2003). *Comfort, cleanliness and convenience*. Berg.

Simmel, G. (2009). *Sociology: Inquiries into the construction of social forms*. Brill. (Original work published 1908.)

Sistema di Accoglienza e Integrazione. (2022). *Rapporto annuale SAI—Sistema di Accoglienza e Integrazione*. Anci-Ministero dell'Interno.

Smelser, N. J. (1998). The rational and the ambivalent in the social sciences. *American Sociological Review, 63*(1), 1–16.

Smets, P., Younes, Y., Dohmen, M., Boersma, K., & Brouwer, L. (2021). Social media in and around a temporary large-scale refugee shelter in the Netherlands. *Social Media + Society, 7*(2).

Smith, D. M. (2000). *Moral geographies: Ethics in a world of difference*. Edinburgh University Press.

Sorgoni, B. (2019). The location of truth: Bodies and voices in the Italian asylum procedure. *PoLAR: Political and Legal Anthropology Review, 42*(1), 161–176.

Speltini, G., & Passini, S. (2016). Cleanliness issues: From individual practices to collective visions. In R. Duschinsky, S. Schnall, & D. Weiss (Eds.), *Purity and danger now* (pp. 162–178). Routledge.

Squire, V. (2020). *Europe's migration crisis: Border deaths and human dignity*. Cambridge University Press.

Squire, V., & Stierl, M. (2020). Precarious migrations and maritime displacement. In P. Adey et al. (Eds.), *The Handbook of Displacement* (pp. 345–361).

Stasik, M., Hänsch, V., & Mains, D. (2020). Temporalities of waiting in Africa. *Critical African Studies, 12*(1), 1–9.

Stavrides, S. (2014). Emerging common spaces as a challenge to the city of crisis. *City, 18*(4–5), 546–550.

Steigemann, A. M., & Misselwitz, P. (2020). Architectures of asylum: Making home in a state of permanent temporariness. *Current Sociology, 68*(5), 628–650.

Stierl, M. (2017). Contestations in death: The role of grief in migration struggles. In J. B. Turner (Ed.), *(En) gendering the political* (pp. 33–51). Routledge.

Strassheim, J. (2018). Relevance and irrelevance. In J. Strassheim & H. Nasu (Eds.), *Relevance and irrelevance: Theories, factors and challenges* (pp. 1–18).

Subasinghe, C. (2019). Is my house my home? An analysis of "nowhereness" among "noknowers" in transitional settings. *Space and Culture, 22*(4), 509–521.

Tamarkin, E. (2022). *Apropos of something: A history of irrelevance and relevance*. Chicago University Press.

Taylor, H. (2015). *Refugees and the meaning of home*. Palgrave.

Tazzioli, M. (2018). The temporal borders of asylum. *Political Geography, 64*, 13–22.

Tazzioli, M., & De Genova, N. (2023). Border abolitionism. *Social Text, 41*(3), 1–34.

Thorshaug, R. Ø., & Brun, C. (2019). Temporal injustice and re-orientations in asylum reception centers in Norway: Towards critical geographies of architecture in the institution. *Fennia, 197*(2), 232–248.

Triulzi, A., & McKenzie, R. (2013). *Long journeys: African migrants on the road*. Brill.

Turner, S. (2016). What is a refugee camp? *Journal of Refugee Studies, 29*, 139–48.

Turner, S., & Whyte, Z. (2022). Introduction: Refugee camps as carceral junctions. *Incarceration, 3*(1), 1–9.

Turner, V. (1979). Frame, flow and reflection: Ritual and drama as public liminality. *Japanese Journal of Religious Studies, 6*(4), 465–499.

Uzureau, O., Rota, M., Lietaert, I., & Derluyn, I. (2022). Transient lives and lasting messages: Graffiti analysis as a methodological tool to capture migrants' experiences while on the move. In K. Grabska & C. Clark-Kazak (Ed.), *Documenting displacement* (pp. 173–200). McGill-Queen's University Press.

Vammen, I. M., Cold-Ravnkilde, S., & Lucht, H. (2022). Borderwork in the expanded EU-African borderlands. *Geopolitics, 27*(5), 1317–1330.

Van der Geest, S. (2014). Pollution and purity. In W. C. Cockerham, R. Dingwall, & S. Quah (Eds.), *The Wiley Blackwell encyclopedia of health, illness, behavior, and society* (pp. 1–4). Wiley.

Van der Horst, H. (2004). Living in a reception center: The search for home in an institutional setting. *Housing, Theory and Society, 21*, 36–46.

Van der Veer, L. (2020). Residents' responses to refugee reception: The cracks and continuities between care and control. *Ethnic and Racial Studies, 43*(16), 368–387.

Vandevoordt, R. (2017). The politics of food and hospitality. *Journal of Refugee Studies, 30*(4), 605–621.

Vandevoordt, R., & Verschraegen, G. (2019). Demonstrating deservingness and dignity: Symbolic boundary work among Syrian refugees. *Poetics, 76*, 101343.

Van Liempt, I., & Bilger, V. (2012). Ethical challenges in research with vulnerable migrants. In C. Vargas-Silva (Ed.), *Handbook of research methods in migration* (pp. 451–466). Elgar.

Van Liempt, I., & Staring, R. (2021). Homemaking and places of restoration: Belonging within and beyond places assigned to Syrian refugees in the Netherlands. *Geographical Review, 111*(2), 308–326.

Van Maanen J. (2011a). Ethnography as work: Some rules of engagement. *Journal of Management Studies, 48*(1), 218–234.

Van Maanen, J. (2011b). *Tales of the field: On writing ethnography.* University of Chicago Press.

Vargas-Silva, C., & Boccagni, P. (2024). Dreaming of a remittance house: Understanding transnational housing aspirations. *International Migration Review 58*(3), 1226–1249.

Veness, A. (1993). Neither homed nor homeless. *Political Geography, 12*, 319–40.

Vigh, H. (2009). Wayward migration: On imagined futures and technological voids. *Ethnos, 74*(1), 91–109.

Wagner, I., & Finkielsztein, M. (2021). Strategic boredom: The experience and dynamics of boredom in a refugee camp. *Journal of Contemporary Ethnography, 50*(5), 649–682.

Walter, T. (2020). *Death in the modern world.* Sage.

Walters, W. (2023). Governing the state as a home: Domopolitics and migration. In P. Boccagni (Ed.), *Handbook on home and migration* (pp. 154–157). Elgar.

Weidinger, T., Kordel, S., & Kieslinger, J. (2021). Unraveling the meaning of place and spatial mobility. *Journal of Refugee Studies, 34*(1), 374–396.

Whyte, Z. (2011). Enter the myopticon: Uncertain surveillance in the Danish asylum system. *Anthropology Today, 27*(3), 18–21.

Willems, S., De Smet, S., & Heylighen, A. (2020). Seeking a balance between privacy and connectedness in housing for refugees. *Journal of Housing and the Built Environment, 35,* 45–46.

Wyss, A. (2022). *Navigating the European migration regime.* Bristol University Press.

Yeoh, B. S., & Collins, F. L. (Eds.). (2022). *Handbook on transnationalism.* Elgar.

Young, I. M. (2005). House and home: Feminist variations on a theme. In S. Hardy & C. Wiedmer (Eds.), *Motherhood and space* (pp. 115–147). Palgrave.

Zardo, F. (2022). The EU trust fund for Africa: Geopolitical space making through migration policy instruments. *Geopolitics, 27*(2), 584–603.

Zerubavel, E. (1993). Horizons: On the sociomental foundations of relevance. *Social Research, 60*(2), 397–413.

Zerubavel, E. (2006). *The elephant in the room: Silence and denial in everyday life.* Oxford University Press.

Zerubavel, E. (2015). *Hidden in plain sight: The social structure of irrelevance.* Oxford University Press.

Zerubavel, E. (2019). Listening to the sound of silence: Methodological reflections on studying the unsaid. In A. J. Murray & K. Durrheim (Eds.), *Qualitative studies of silence* (pp. 59–70). Cambridge University Press.

Zerubavel, E. (2020). *Generally speaking: An invitation to concept-driven sociology.* Oxford University Press.

Zetter, R. (2007). More labels, fewer refugees. *Journal of Refugee Studies, 20*(2), 172–192.

Zetter, R. (2015). Protection in crisis. *Forced migration and protection in a global era.* Research Report.

Zill M., van Liempt, I., Spierings, B., & Hooimeijer, P. (2020). Uneven geographies of asylum accommodation. *Migration Studies, 8*(4), 491–509.

Founded in 1893,

UNIVERSITY OF CALIFORNIA PRESS
publishes bold, progressive books and journals
on topics in the arts, humanities, social sciences,
and natural sciences—with a focus on social
justice issues—that inspire thought and action
among readers worldwide.

The UC PRESS FOUNDATION
raises funds to uphold the press's vital role
as an independent, nonprofit publisher, and
receives philanthropic support from a wide
range of individuals and institutions—and from
committed readers like you. To learn more, visit
ucpress.edu/supportus.

www.ingramcontent.com/pod-product-compliance
Ingram Content Group UK Ltd.
Pitfield, Milton Keynes, MK11 3LW, UK
UKHW020104230425
457764UK00002B/4